Peterson's

MASTER THE AIR TRAFFIC SELECTION AND TRAINING TEST (AT-SAT)

Peterson's

Master the Air Traffic Selection and Training Test (AT-SAT)

Michael S. Nolan

PETERSON'S

A **nelnet** COMPANY

An ARCO Book

ARCO is a registered trademark of Peterson's, and is used herein under license by Peterson's.

About Peterson's, a Nelnet company
Peterson's (www.petersons.com) is a leading provider of education information and advice, with books and online resources focusing on education search, test preparation, and financial aid. Its Web site offers searchable databases and interactive tools for contacting educational institutions, online practice tests and instruction, and planning tools for securing financial aid. Peterson's serves 110 million education consumers annually.

For more information, contact Peterson's, 2000 Lenox Drive, Lawrenceville, NJ 08648; 800-338-3282; or find us on the World Wide Web at: www.petersons.com/about.

Editor: Therese DeAngelis; Production Editor: Mark D. Snider; Manufacturing Manager: Ray Golaszewski; Composition Manager: Gary Rozmierski

ISBN-13: 978-0-7689-2475-6
ISBN-10: 0-7689-2475-8

Printed in the United States of America

10 9 8 7 6 5 4 3 2 1   09 08 07

First Edition

Petersons.com/publishing

Check out our Web site at www.petersons.com/publishing to see if there is any new information regarding the tests and any revisions or corrections to the content of this book. We've made sure the information in this book is accurate and up-to-date; however, the test format or content may have changed since the time of publication.

OTHER RECOMMENDED TITLES

Contents

PART III: THE AIR TRAFFIC SELECTION AND TRAINING TEST (AT-SAT)

PART IV: SEVEN PRACTICE TESTS

APPENDIXES

Before You Begin

HOW THIS BOOK IS ORGANIZED

Taking the Air Traffic Selection and Training Test (AT-SAT) is a skill. It shares some aspects with other skills, such as competing in athletics, singing opera, or calculating mathematical formulas. Such skills can be improved through coaching, but ultimately, improvement also requires practice and discipline. This book gives you both.

- **Part I** provides essential information about air traffic control. You'll learn about what types of jobs are available, the flight rules air traffic controllers must follow, and the three types of workplaces where air traffic controllers operate. You'll also find out about salaries and benefits, the employment process, and what you need to qualify as an air traffic controller.

- **Part II** is an in-depth review of the U.S. air traffic control system, with comprehensive information on airspace, communications, navigation systems, aircraft identification, and runways and taxiways. This section also provides a complete review of weather forecasting and observations, and explains how weather affects air travel and air traffic control. You'll also learn how controllers map airspace, what navigation and charting methods they use, and how they operate airport terminal instrumentation.

- **Part III** provides an overview of what you need to know if you're planning on taking the AT-SAT, with information on scoring, availability, and registration.

- **Part IV** contains seven practice tests followed by answer keys. These tests simulate the actual AT-SAT. The answer keys are very important because they'll help you learn from your mistakes.

- **The Appendixes** contain a detailed glossary of air traffic controller and pilot terms, a list of frequently used acronyms, information about U.S. and other airports and aircraft, and a list of printed and online resources for studying air traffic control.

SPECIAL STUDY FEATURES

Peterson's Master the Air Traffic Selection and Training Test (AT-SAT) is designed to be as user-friendly as it is complete. To this end, it includes the following features to make your preparation more efficient.

Overview

Each chapter begins with a bulleted overview listing the topics covered in the chapter. This will allow you to quickly target the areas in which you are most interested.

Summing It Up

Each chapter ends with a point-by-point summary that reviews the most important items in the chapter. The summaries offer a convenient way to review key points.

HOW TO USE THE PRACTICE TESTS

At some point in your initial training at the Federal Aviation Administration (FAA) Academy, you will be given a test to determine your basic aviation and air traffic control knowledge. This test will cover areas such as the air traffic control (ATC) systems, airports, separation, Notices to Airmen (NOTAMs), fundamentals of radar, FAA orders and manuals, Letters Of Agreement (LOAs), standard operating procedures (SOPs), airspace, Federal Aviation Regulations (with particular emphasis on FAR 91), principles of flight, wake turbulence, aircraft characteristics, special operations, basic and radio navigation, Visual Flight Rules (VFR) and Instrument Flight Rules (IFR) charts, emergencies, search and rescue, fundamentals of weather including weather reports and forecasts, basic communications, stripmarking, and clearances.

The seven practice tests in this book provide examples of the types of questions you will encounter on the FAA Academy's test to determine your knowledge of aviation and aeronautics. Each test is followed by an answer key.

To make the best use of this book, study the material presented in Chapters 1 through 6 and in other reference books mentioned in Appendix B. Then take the first practice test. Check your answers against the correct responses in the answer key. This will help you determine your strengths and where you may need to improve. Once you've worked on your areas of improvement, try taking Practice Test 2, and continue the process. As you do so, you should find that your overall performance improves with each new test.

YOU'RE WELL ON YOUR WAY TO SUCCESS

You've made the decision to take the AT-SAT and have taken a very important step in that process. *Peterson's Master the Air Traffic Selection and Training Test (AT-SAT)* will help you score high on the exam and prepare you for everything you'll need to know on the day of your exam. Good luck!

GIVE US YOUR FEEDBACK

Peterson's publications can be found at your local bookstore and library, and you can access us online at www.petersons.com.

We welcome any comments or suggestions you may have about this publication and invite you to complete our online survey at www.petersons.com/booksurvey. Or you can fill out the survey at the back of this book, tear it out, and mail it to us at:

Publishing Department
Peterson's, a Nelnet company
2000 Lenox Drive
Lawrenceville, NJ 08648

Your feedback will help us make your educational dreams possible.

PART I

BECOMING AN AIR TRAFFIC CONTROLLER

Air Traffic Control: The Basics

OVERVIEW

- **Types of air traffic control jobs**

- **Flight rules**

- **How tower controllers direct flights**

- **TRACON facilities**

- **En route control: ARTCC**

- **Summing it up**

The air traffic control system provides a safe, organized, and efficient means for private, commercial, and military flights to operate throughout the United States. The system employs air traffic controllers working for the Federal Aviation Administration (FAA), as well as military controllers and private contractors. All are responsible for directing the flow of air traffic and maintaining the safe separation of aircraft from one another.

TYPES OF AIR TRAFFIC CONTROL JOBS

Controllers operate in any of three types of workplaces:

1. A control tower

2. A Terminal Radar Approach Control (TRACON)

3. An Air Route Traffic Control Center (ARTCC)

As you probably know, a control tower—more properly known as an air traffic control tower, or ATCT—is the tall, windowed structure prominently located at every airport. From this vantage point, controllers who work in ATCTs can easily observe all aircraft operating on the ground or within the immediate vicinity of the airport.

Controllers who work at radar-equipped approach and departure controls—more formally known as Terminal Radar Approach Controls or TRACONs—are responsible for all aircraft operating within a radius of about 50 nautical miles of the airport and up to an altitude of about 10,000 feet. Approach and departure controllers usually operate from a small building located at the base of a control tower. In large metropolitan areas, such as New York City, Chicago, and Los Angeles, more expansive TRACONs are sometimes located away from the airport.

A third type of air traffic controller workplace is located in about twenty large Air Route Traffic Control Centers (ARTCCs) throughout the United States. These centers monitor aircraft as they travel between airports. ARTCCs are located outside of large metropolitan areas; each one typically employs 300 to 500 controllers.

FLIGHT RULES

Contrary to popular belief, not all aircraft in the United States are required to contact air traffic control (ATC) while flying. In general, there are two types of aircraft flight operations, each with very different rules and procedures. These sets of rules are known as Visual Flight Rules (VFR) and Instrument Flight Rules (IFR). Depending on the weather and the type of aircraft involved, pilots may elect to operate under either set of flight rules.

Visual Flight Rules

Pilots flying under Visual Flight Rules (VFR) assume responsibility for the separation of their aircraft from all other aircraft; they are not normally assigned routes or altitudes by ATC. Unless they are near busy airports, pilots flying under VFR are normally not required to contact ATC. However, they must either avoid busy airports or obtain ATC permission (clearance) to operate in those areas.

Instrument Flight Rules

If the weather conditions are such that pilots cannot maintain their own separation, or if they wish to operate in busy airspace, pilots are required to fly under Instrument Flight Rules (IFR). Virtually all business aircraft and airliners, as well as many smaller private aircraft, operate under IFR, regardless of weather conditions. Pilots flying under IFR must file a flight plan before takeoff, and they cannot depart until they receive a clearance from ATC. Once a pilot receives clearance, it is the ATC system's responsibility to ensure that the aircraft is safely separated from other aircraft during its entire flight.

U.S. DEPARTMENT OF TRANSPORTATION FEDERAL AVIATION ADMINISTRATION **FLIGHT PLAN**	(FAA USE ONLY) ☐ PILOT BRIEFING ☐ VNR ☐ STOPOVER		TIME STARTED	SPECIALIST INITIALS

1. TYPE	2. AIRCRAFT IDENTIFICATION	3. AIRCRAFT TYPE/ SPECIAL EQUIPMENT	4. TRUE AIRSPEED	5. DEPARTURE POINT	6. DEPARTURE TIME		7. CRUISING ALTITUDE
☐ VFR ☒ IFR ☐ DVFR	N252MN	C182/G	140 KTS	LAF	PROPOSED (Z) 1300	ACTUAL (Z)	70

8. ROUTE OF FLIGHT

LAF IND V50 DQN V12 MELAN OSH

9. DESTINATION (Name of airport and city)	10. EST. TIME ENROUTE		11. REMARKS
OSH	HOURS 1	MINUTES 15	

12. FUEL ON BOARD		13. ALTERNATE AIRPORT(S)	14. PILOT'S NAME, ADDRESS & TELEPHONE NUMBER & AIRCRAFT HOME BASE	15. NUMBER ABOARD
HOURS 4	MINUTES 30	CMH	MICHAEL NOLAN, LAF	3
			17. DESTINATION CONTACT/TELEPHONE (OPTIONAL)	

16. COLOR OF AIRCRAFT	CIVIL AIRCRAFT PILOTS, FAR 91 requires you file an IFR flight plan to operate under instrument flight rules in controlled airspace. Failure to file could result in a civil penalty not to exceed $1,000 for each violation (Section 901 of the Federal Aviation Act of 1958, as amended). Filing of a VFR flight plan is recommended as a good operating practice. See also Part 99 for requirements concerning DVFR flight plans.
BLACK/GOLD	

FAA Form 7233-1 (8-82)   CLOSE VFR FLIGHT PLAN WITH _____ FSS ON ARRIVAL

Pilots flying under Instrument Flight Rules (IFR) must file a flight plan before takeoff.

HOW TOWER CONTROLLERS DIRECT FLIGHTS

At the beginning of each flight, a pilot contacts controllers working in the ATCT. Tower controllers are responsible for ensuring the safety of aircraft as they land and take off and as they operate on the airport's taxiways. These controllers generally monitor these flights visually, but busier towers are equipped with special radar systems that assist the controllers in identifying aircraft.

The duties in a typical control tower are assigned to a team of controllers. The specific control positions in a tower are clearance delivery, ground control, and local control. Let's take a look at what each position entails.

Clearance Delivery

The clearance delivery controller uses both computers and telephone equipment to coordinate all departing flights with the Air Traffic Control System Command Center (ATCSCC) located in Leesburg, VA. The ATCSCC's responsibility is to reduce excessive airborne delays and air space congestion. It accomplishes this either by rerouting aircraft or delaying aircraft takeoff or landing.

If weather conditions either en route or at the destination airport are expected to cause traffic disruptions, the clearance delivery controller must hold aircraft on the ground until each one's assigned departure time arrives. The clearance delivery controller is responsible for issuing each aircraft its first clearance to operate within the air traffic control system.

Ground Control

Once a pilot receives a clearance, he or she contacts the ground controller for permission to taxi to the departure runway. Ground control is responsible for all traffic operating in airport "movement" areas. These include taxiways and inactive runways (those not in use for takeoffs and landings). A pilot radios the ground controller for permission to taxi when the ground controller decides which runway the aircraft should use and assigns a safe taxi route.

Ground controllers monitor the progress of all taxiing aircraft and ensure that each pilot is taking the proper route. They are also responsible for monitoring any vehicular traffic operating on runways and taxiways and for obtaining permission from the tower controller if vehicles need to cross any active runway.

Ground controllers observe aircraft as they taxi; in poor weather conditions, they request position reports from pilots as they taxi aircraft within the airport. Busier airports have a ground radar system to assist the ground controller. This radar system is known as Airport Surface Detection Equipment (ASDE).

Local Control

Once an aircraft arrives at a runway, the pilot switches radio frequencies to speak with the local controller. Local control (often referred as the tower controller) is responsible for maintaining safety on and near all active runways. The local controller ensures that the runway is clear of all traffic before authorizing an aircraft to take off or land. Departing aircraft are advised to remain clear of the runway until a safe condition exists for departure. Arriving aircraft are placed in what is called a traffic pattern; the local controller adjusts the pattern as needed to ensure safe arrivals or to make room on the runway for departing aircraft when needed.

TRACON FACILITIES

The TRACON is usually located near the control tower, although in some major metropolitan areas it is a stand-alone facility located miles off the airport grounds. A typical TRACON is responsible for the airspace 50 miles outside the airport and up to 10,000 feet in altitude. Within the TRACONs are multiple radar displays and associated equipment. The controller at each of these workstations is responsible for a "block" of airspace known as a sector. Most TRACON controllers are assigned either to a departure or an approach sector.

Departure Control

Each departure controller in a TRACON is responsible for the safety of each aircraft within his or her sector while the aircraft departs and moves to its en route airway. Once an aircraft is safely separated and routed correctly, departure control informs the adjacent ARTCC of the aircraft's identity and altitude. When the departure controller receives permission from the ARTCC controller, he or she advises the aircraft's pilot to change radio frequencies and contact the ARTCC controller directly. This process is called a hand-off.

Approach Control

The approach controllers merge streams of inbound aircraft and assign headings and altitudes to line up the aircraft for landing on the appropriate runway. During good weather conditions, pilots who can see the airport will be issued a "visual approach." This means that the pilot simply flies to the airport and lands, while the controller monitors the airspace around the aircraft to guard against traffic conflicts. During poor weather conditions, the controller will "vector" the aircraft onto an instrument approach. This means that the pilot will be guided to a point about one-half mile from the end of the appropriate runway. Once the pilot has the runway in sight, he or she takes over and lands the aircraft.

ATCT RESPONSIBILITIES

Once the approach controller has established that an aircraft is on the proper approach path, the controller advises the pilot to contact the control tower. The local controller then monitors the flight so that no other aircraft operates on or near the runway as the aircraft lands. After the aircraft lands and turns off the runway, the ground controller in the ATCT monitors the aircraft to be sure that it safely reaches the terminal gate.

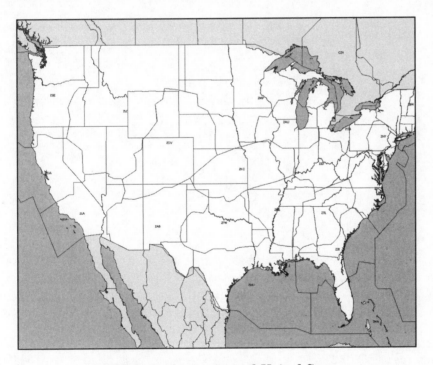

ARTCCs in the continental United States

EN ROUTE CONTROL: ARTCC

En route ATC services are handled by multiple teams of controllers working in one of about twenty ARTCCs across the country. Center controllers, as they are known, operate in small teams, each of which is responsible for one sector of the ARTCC's assigned airspace. A sector normally covers about 200 square miles; it is either a low-altitude (from ground to 24,000 feet) or a high-altitude (24,000 feet and higher) sector. Center controller teams monitor aircraft as they transit the sector, then perform a hand-off to an adjacent sector. On a long flight—say from New York City to Los Angeles—an aircraft might contact controllers in twenty to forty individual sectors, repeating this process for each sector.

Once an aircraft nears its destination, the en route controllers begin issuing instructions for the pilot to descend, and they organize the airport arrivals into streams of traffic. Specific routes and altitudes are assigned based on the type of aircraft and its destination. When an aircraft is within 50 miles of an airport, it will be handed off to the approach control operating out of the appropriate TRACON.

SUMMING IT UP

- Air traffic controllers work in three types of positions: in a control tower, in a Terminal Radar Approach Control (TRACON), or in an Air Route Traffic Control Center (ARTCC). All controllers are responsible for directing air traffic and ensuring that aircraft are safely separated from one another.

- Depending on weather and type of aircraft, a pilot may operate either under Visual Flight Rules (VFR) or Instrument Flight Rules (IFR). If under IFR, pilots are required to file a flight plan and cannot depart until they receive a clearance from air traffic control.

- Tower controllers are responsible for ensuring the safety of aircraft as they land and take off and as they operate on the airport's taxiways. Tower control teams consist of clearance delivery, ground control, and local control.

- Each TRACON is responsible for 50 miles of airspace surrounding an airport and up to 10,000 feet in altitude. TRACON controllers are each responsible for a "block" of airspace known as a sector.

- En route air traffic controllers work in one of twenty ARTCCs across the country and are each responsible for one sector of ARTCC's assigned airspace. Controller teams monitor aircraft as they transit a sector, then perform a hand-off to an adjacent sector.

Working for the
Federal Aviation
Administration

OVERVIEW

- **How do I qualify as an air traffic controller?**

- **What kind of salary and benefits can I expect?**

- **How do I apply for a position as an air traffic controller?**

- **Summing it up**

Approximately 15,000 air traffic controllers are currently employed in the United States. Some are military controllers working for the Department of Defense; others work in control towers operated by private or contract operators. Most privately operated control towers hire only controllers who have previous related experience. The majority of control towers, and virtually all TRACONs and ARTCCs, are operated by the FAA using federal employees.

If you're interested in becoming an air traffic controller, there may be no better time than the present. In 2006, the FAA announced plans to hire nearly 12,000 new air traffic controllers to address the current shortage and to replace thousands of air traffic controllers due for retirement within the next ten years.

The agency also has plans to improve its training program for new controllers. In 2005, it established a new high-altitude training lab and installed four new high-fidelity tower simulators at the FAA Academy in Oklahoma City, OK, to provide a more realistic tower environment. It also installed new tower cab simulations at Chicago O'Hare; Ontario, California; and Miami facilities. These simulators are expected to reduce training time and improve safety.

chapter 2

HOW DO I QUALIFY AS AN AIR TRAFFIC CONTROLLER?

To become an air traffic controller with the FAA, an applicant must:

- be a citizen of the United States.

- be at least 18 years old but not more than 30.

- possess a high school diploma or GED equivalent.

- have three years of full-time work experience, a full four years of college, or a combination of both.

- pass medical, psychological, and aptitude tests.

- pass a security and suitability screening.

- complete the training program at an FAA training academy (if hired) and successfully complete a one- to three-year on-the-job training program.

The FAA is currently hiring from three specific pools of applicants:

1 Ex-military air traffic controllers

2 Graduates of approved college programs

3 Applicants from the general public

For the foreseeable future, the FAA plans to hire roughly equal numbers of controllers from each of these three groups.

Ex-Military Air Traffic Controllers

Applicants who have previous military experience in ATC must be able to prove that they worked for at least fifty-two consecutive weeks either in a military or civilian air traffic control facility. The work must have been directly related to the separation of air traffic—similar to the job they would perform as an FAA employee. The experience must have provided a comprehensive knowledge of the laws, rules, regulations, and procedures governing the movement of air traffic and knowledge of aircraft separation standards and control techniques. A background review is conducted for each applicant to confirm that he or she has the appropriate experience and can demonstrate the knowledge, skills, and abilities required to perform the work of an air traffic controller.

Graduates of Approved College Programs

Graduates of FAA-approved college programs may apply directly to the FAA upon completion of the program. The programs, known as collegiate training initiatives or CTI programs, provide an additional source for air traffic control employees. A student must receive an approved degree from a CTI school, complete the required ATC courses, and receive a recommendation from the school before applying to the FAA. Here is a list of schools that currently offer FAA-approved CTI study programs.

FAA-Approved CTI Schools

ALASKA
Department of Aviation Technology
University of Alaska-Anchorage
2811 Merrill Field Drive
Anchorage, AK 99501
(907) 264-7406
http://www.uaa.alaska.edu/ctc/programs/
   aviation/

CALIFORNIA
Aeronautics & Transportation
Mt. San Antonio College
1100 North Grand Avenue
Walnut, CA 91789
(909) 594-5611, ext. 3098
http://aeronautics.mtsac.edu

FLORIDA
Aeronautical Science
Embry-Riddle Aeronautical University
600 South Clyde Morris Blvd.
Daytona Beach, FL 32114-3900
(904) 226-6445
http://www.erau.edu/

Aviation Department
Miami-Dade College
500 College Terrace
Homestead, FL 33030
(305) 237-5130
http://www.mdc.edu

INDIANA
Department of Aviation Technology
Purdue University
1 Purdue Airport
West Lafayette, IN 47906-3398
(765) 494-9962
http://www.tech.purdue.edu/

MINNESOTA
Air Traffic Control Training Program
Minneapolis Community &
   Technical College
1501 Hennepin Avenue
Minneapolis, MN 55403
(612) 659-6000
(800) 247-0911
http://www.minneapolis.edu/

NEW HAMPSHIRE
Aviation Division
Daniel Webster College
Twenty University Drive
Nashua, NH 03063-1699
(800) 325-6876
http://www.dwc.edu/

NEW YORK
School of Aviation
Dowling College
Shirley, NY 11967
(631) 244-1381
http://www.dowling.edu/

Vaughn College
(formerly College of Aeronautics)
LaGuardia Airport
Flushing, NY 11371
http://www.vaughn.edu/

NORTH DAKOTA
University of North Dakota
4201 University Ave
Grand Forks, ND 58202-9023
(800) 258-1525, ext. 4744
http://www.ndus.edu/

PENNSYLVANIA
Community College of Beaver County
Aviation Science Center
125 Cessna Drive
Beaver Falls, PA 15010-1060
(800) 335-0222, ext. 101
http://www.ccbc.edu/

PUERTO RICO
School of Aeronautics, Bayamon Campus
InterAmerican University of Puerto Rico
Carr. 830 Num 500
Cerro Gordo
Bayamon, PR 00957
(787) 725-1912, ext. 2004
http://bc.inter.edu/

TENNESSEE
Aerospace Department
Middle Tennessee State University
Box 67, MTSU
Murfreesboro, TN 37132
(615) 898-2788
http://www.mtsu.edu/

VIRGINIA
Department of Aviation
Hampton University
Hampton, VA 23668
(757) 727-5418
http://www.hamptonu.edu/

Applicants from the General Public

At various times and in various locations, the FAA may advertise that it is taking applications from the general public. Applicants must apply in person during the limited time that the advertised position is available. This process of application can and does change regularly, so be sure to check the FAA's Web site (http://www.faa.gov) to obtain more current information. After reviewing the applications received, the FAA will select applicants to continue the employment process.

WHAT KIND OF SALARY AND BENEFITS CAN I EXPECT?

Air traffic controllers' salaries are based on length of time they have worked for the FAA and the complexity of traffic at the FAA facility where they work. Each FAA facility is assigned a pay grade based on the type of traffic it controls. This pay grade assignment determines the base salary for controllers working at that facility.

Within each pay grade is a pay band and a locality adjustment. A pay band is the range of pay available at each facility based upon a controller's time with the FAA. New controllers tend to be paid at the lower end of the band; those with more experience are paid at higher band levels. The locality adjustment is a cost-of-living adjustment for all the controllers at a particular facility. This helps to even out the differences in cost-of-living rates throughout the country.

In addition to base pay and locality adjustments, controllers also earn additional pay for working weekend, evening, and holiday shifts. In general, these add-ons can add 10 to 20 percent to a controller's annual income above actual pay bands.

Air Traffic Control Facility Pay Levels (As of 2005)

Facility Name	ATC Level	Locality Adjustment (percentages)
ABILENE DYESS RAPCON	7	11.72
ADDISON ATCT	7	15.07
AKRON CANTON REGIONAL ATCT	8	14.24
ALBANY COUNTY ATCT	8	11.72
ALBUQUERQUE ARTCC	10	11.72
ALBUQUERQUE ATCT	9	11.72
ALLEGHENY COUNTY ATCT	6	12.86
ALLENTOWN ATCT	8	11.72
AMARILLO ATCT	7	11.72
ANCHORAGE	10	—

Air Traffic Control Facility Pay Levels (As of 2005) *(continued)*

Facility Name	ATC Level	Locality Adjustment (percentages)
ANCHORAGE INTL ATCT	8	—
ANCHORAGE TRACON	9	—
ANDREWS AFB ATCT	6	15.98
ANN ARBOR MUNICIPAL ATCT	6	19.67
ASHEVILLE REGIONAL ATCT	6	11.72
ASPEN PITKIN COUNTY ATCT	5	11.72
ATLANTA ARTCC	12	13.87
ATLANTA HARTSFIELD ATCT	12	13.87
ATLANTA LARGE TRACON	12	13.87
ATLANTIC CITY ATCT	8	16.67
AUGUSTA ATCT	6	11.72
AURORA MUNICIPAL ATCT	6	19.70
AUSTIN ATCT	9	11.72
BAKERSFIELD ATCT	8	11.72
BALTIMORE INTL ATCT	9	15.98
BANGOR INTL ATCT	7	11.72
BATON ROUGE METRO ATCT	7	11.72
BEDFORD ATCT	7	18.49
BILLINGS INTL ATCT	7	11.72
BIRMINGHAM MUNICIPAL ATCT	8	11.72
BISMARCK TRACAB	5	11.72
BOEING FIELD ATCT	8	16.53
BOISE ATCT	8	11.72
BOSTON ARTCC	11	18.49
BOSTON CONSOLIDATED TRACON	11	18.49
BOSTON LOGAN ATCT	11	18.49
BOSTON TRACON	11	18.49
BRADLEY INTL ATCT	7	19.52
BURBANK ATCT	7	21.65

Air Traffic Control Facility Pay Levels (As of 2005) *(continued)*

Facility Name	ATC Level	Locality Adjustment (percentages)
BURLINGTON INTL ATCT	7	11.72
CALDWELL ATCT	7	20.99
CAMARILLO ATCT	7	21.65
CAPE TRACON	8	18.49
CARLSBAD ATCT	7	17.68
CASPER ATCT	5	11.72
CEDAR RAPIDS MUNI ATCT	6	11.72
CENTENNIAL ATCT	9	18.06
CENTRAL FLORIDA REGIONAL ATCT	8	11.75
CHAMPAIGN ATCT	7	11.72
CHARLESTON ATCT	7	11.72
CHARLESTON INTL ATCT	8	11.72
CHARLOTTE ATCT	11	11.72
CHATTANOOGA ATCT	7	11.72
CHICAGO ARTCC	12	19.70
CHICAGO MIDWAY ATCT	8	19.70
CHICAGO O'HARE INTL ATCT	12	19.70
CHICAGO TRACON	12	19.70
CHINO ATCT	7	21.65
CLARKSBURG ATCT	6	11.72
CLEVELAND ARTCC	12	14.24
CLEVELAND HOPKINS ATCT	10	14.24
COLORADO SPRINGS ATCT	8	11.72
COLUMBIA METRO ATCT	7	11.72
CONCORD ATCT	6	26.39
CORPUS CHRISTI ATCT	9	11.72
DALLAS LOVE FIELD ATCT	9	15.07
DALLAS/FORT WORTH ATCT	12	15.07
DALLAS/FORT WORTH TRACON	12	15.07

Air Traffic Control Facility Pay Levels (As of 2005) *(continued)*

Facility Name	ATC Level	Locality Adjustment (percentages)
DAYTON INTL ATCT	9	12.86
DAYTONA BEACH ATCT	10	11.72
DE KALB PEACHTREE ATCT	7	13.87
DENVER ARTCC	10	18.06
DENVER INTL ATCT	11	18.06
DENVER TRACON	11	18.06
DES MOINES MUNI ATCT	8	11.72
DETROIT METRO ATCT	11	19.67
DETROIT TRACON	11	19.67
DULLES INTL ATCT	11	15.98
DULUTH INTL ATCT	6	11.72
DUPAGE ATCT	7	19.70
EAST ST. LOUIS ATCT	6	12.09
EDWIN A. LINK ATCT	6	11.72
EL MONTE ATCT	6	21.65
EL PASO INTL ATCT	8	11.72
ELMIRA ATCT	6	11.72
ERIE INTL TRACAB	6	11.72
EUGENE ATCT	7	11.72
EVANSVILLE DRESS REG ATCT	7	11.72
EVERETT ATCT	6	16.53
FAIRBANKS INTL ATCT	7	—
FARGO ATCT	6	11.72
FAYETTEVILLE MUNI ATCT	7	11.72
FLINT ATCT	8	19.67
FLORENCE CITY CNTY ATCT	6	11.72
FLYING CLOUD ATCT	7	15.99
FORT LAUDERDALE ATCT	8	16.77
FORT MYERS ATCT	8	11.72

Air Traffic Control Facility Pay Levels (As of 2005) *(continued)*

Facility Name	ATC Level	Locality Adjustment (percentages)
FORT PIERCE ATCT	6	11.72
FORT SMITH TRACAB	8	11.72
FORT WAYNE MUNI ATCT	7	11.72
FORT WORTH ALLIANCE ATCT	6	15.07
FORT WORTH ARTCC	12	15.07
FORT WORTH MEACHAM ATCT	9	15.07
FRESNO ATCT	8	11.72
FT. LAUDERDALE EXEC ATCT	7	16.77
GILLESPIE FIELD ATCT	7	17.68
GRAND CANYON ATCT	5	11.72
GRAND FORKS ATCT	7	11.72
GRAND RAPIDS ATCT	8	11.72
GRANT COUNTY ATCT	7	11.72
GREAT FALLS INTL ATCT	6	11.72
GREATER BUFFALO INTL ATCT	8	11.72
GREATER CINCINNATI INTL ATCT	11	16.04
GREATER PEORIA ATCT	7	11.72
GREATER WILMINGTON ATCT	6	16.67
GREEN BAY ATCT	7	11.72
GREENSBORO ATCT	8	11.72
GREER ATCT	7	11.72
GREGG COUNTY TRACAB	7	11.72
GRIFFISS AFB ATCT	6	11.72
GUAM	8	—
GULFPORT BILOXI REG ATCT	7	11.72
HARRISBURG INTL ARPT ATCT	8	11.72
HAYWARD ATCT	6	26.39
HELENA REGIONAL ATCT	6	11.72
HIGH DESERT TRACON	8	21.65

Air Traffic Control Facility Pay Levels (As of 2005) *(continued)*

Facility Name	ATC Level	Locality Adjustment (percentages)
HILO ATCT	7	—
HONOLULU CONSOLIDATED FACILITY	11	—
HONOLULU INTL ATCT	11	—
HOUSTON ARTCC	11	24.77
HOUSTON HOOKS ATCT	7	24.77
HOUSTON INT'L ATCT	11	24.77
HOUSTON TRACON/ATCT	11	24.77
HUNTINGTON ATCT	6	11.72
HUNTSVILLE ATCT	7	12.42
INDIANAPOLIS ARTCC	12	12.01
INDIANAPOLIS INTL ATCT	9	12.01
JACKSON INTL ATCT	7	11.72
JACKSONVILLE ARTCC	11	11.72
JACKSONVILLE INTL ATCT	9	11.72
JEFFERSON CNTY ARPT ATCT	6	18.06
JEFFERSON COUNTY ATCT	6	11.72
JOHN F KENNEDY INTL ATCT	10	20.99
JUNEAU INTL ATCT	5	—
KAHULUI ATCT	7	—
KALAMAZOO COUNTY ATCT	7	11.72
KANSAS CITY ARTCC	11	12.36
KANSAS CITY DOWNTOWN ATCT	5	12.36
KANSAS CITY INTL ATCT	10	12.36
KNOXVILLE ATCT	8	11.72
KWAJALEIN	6	—
LA GUARDIA ATCT	10	20.99
LA VERNE BRACKETT ATCT	7	21.65
LAFAYETTE REGIONAL ATCT	7	11.72
LAKE CHARLES TRACAB	6	11.72

Air Traffic Control Facility Pay Levels (As of 2005) *(continued)*

Facility Name	ATC Level	Locality Adjustment (percentages)
LAKEFRONT ATCT	6	11.72
LANSING ATCT	8	11.72
LAS VEGAS INTL ATCT	10	11.72
LAS VEGAS TRACON	10	11.72
LEXINGTON ATCT	7	11.72
LINCOLN MUNICIPAL ATCT	7	11.72
LITTLE ROCK ATCT	9	11.72
LIVERMORE ATCT	6	26.39
LONG BEACH ATCT	9	21.65
LONG ISLAND MACARTHUR ATCT	7	20.99
LOS ANGELES ARTCC	11	21.65
LOS ANGELES INTL ATCT	12	21.65
LOUISVILLE BOWMAN ATCT	6	11.72
LOUISVILLE STANDIFORD ATCT	9	11.72
LUBBOCK ATCT	7	11.72
MADISON ATCT	8	11.72
MANASSAS ATCT	5	15.98
MANCHESTER ATCT	8	18.49
MANCHESTER ATCT	5	18.49
MANSFIELD MUNICIPAL ATCT	6	11.72
MEMPHIS ARTCC	12	11.72
MEMPHIS INTL ATCT	10	11.72
MERIDIAN NAS RATCF	7	11.72
MERRILL FIELD ATCT	7	—
MESA ATCT	7	11.72
MIAMI ARTCC	11	16.77
MIAMI INTL ATCT	12	16.77
MIDLAND REGIONAL ATCT	8	11.72
MILWAUKEE MITCHELL ATCT	9	13.62

Air Traffic Control Facility Pay Levels (As of 2005) *(continued)*

Facility Name	ATC Level	Locality Adjustment (percentages)
MINNEAPOLIS ARTCC	11	15.99
MINNEAPOLIS CRYSTAL ATCT	7	15.99
MINNEAPOLIS ST. PAUL ATCT	11	15.99
MINNEAPOLIS TRACON	11	15.99
MOBILE ATCT	8	11.72
MOLINE QUAD CITY ATCT	6	11.72
MONROE REGIONAL TRACAB	6	11.72
MONTEREY PENINSULA ATCT	5	26.39
MONTGOMERY RAPCON	7	11.72
MORRISTOWN MUNICIPAL ATCT	7	20.99
MUSKEGON CNTY ATCT	7	11.72
MYRTLE BEACH ATCT	7	11.72
N.E. PHILADELPHIA ATCT	6	16.67
NANTUCKET ATCT	7	11.72
NAPA COUNTY ATCT	5	26.39
NASHVILLE METRO ATCT	9	11.72
NEW ORLEANS MOISANT ATCT	9	11.72
NEW YORK ARTCC	12	20.99
NEW YORK TRACON	12	20.99
NEWARK INTL ATCT	10	20.99
NORFOLK INTL ATCT	9	11.72
NORTH LAS VEGAS ATCT	7	11.72
NORTHERN CALIFORNIA TRACON	12	16.51
OAKLAND ARTCC	11	26.39
OAKLAND ATCT	10	26.39
OKLAHOMA CITY ATCT	9	11.72
OMAHA ATCT	7	11.72
OMAHA TRACON	8	11.72
ONTARIO INTL ATCT	6	21.65

Air Traffic Control Facility Pay Levels (As of 2005) *(continued)*

Facility Name	ATC Level	Locality Adjustment (percentages)
ORANGE COUNTY ATCT	9	21.65
ORLANDO EXECUTIVE ATCT	7	11.75
ORLANDO INTL ATCT	11	11.75
PAGO PAGO	6	—
PALM BEACH INTL ATCT	9	11.72
PALM SPRINGS ATCT	7	21.65
PALO ALTO ATCT	7	26.39
PALWAUKEE ATCT	7	19.70
PATRICK HENRY INTL ATCT	7	11.72
PENSACOLA REGIONAL ATCT	6	11.72
PENSACOLA TRACON	9	11.72
PHILADELPHIA INTL ATCT	11	16.67
PHOENIX DEER VALLEY ATCT	8	11.72
PHOENIX INTL ATCT	11	11.72
PHOENIX TRACON	11	11.72
PITTSBURGH INTL ATCT	11	12.86
PONTIAC ATCT	8	19.67
PORT COLUMBUS INTL ATCT	9	13.98
PORTLAND HILLSBORO ATCT	6	15.93
PORTLAND INTL ATCT	7	11.72
PORTLAND INTL ATCT	9	15.93
PORTLAND TRACON	9	15.93
POTOMAC LARGE TRACON	12	15.98
POUGHKEEPSIE ATCT	6	20.99
PRESCOTT ATCT	7	11.72
PROVIDENCE ATCT	9	18.49
PUEBLO MEMORIAL TRACAB	7	11.72
RALEIGH DURHAM ATCT	9	11.72
READING MUNI ATCT	7	11.72

Air Traffic Control Facility Pay Levels (As of 2005) *(continued)*

Facility Name	ATC Level	Locality Adjustment (percentages)
REID HILLVIEW ATCT	7	26.39
RENO ATCT	8	11.72
REPUBLIC ATCT	7	20.99
RICHMOND INTL ATCT	6	13.15
ROANOKE REGIONAL ATCT	7	11.72
ROCHESTER MONROE CNTY ATCT	8	11.72
ROCHESTER MUNICIPAL TRACAB	6	11.72
ROCKFORD ATCT	7	11.72
ROSWELL ATCT	7	11.72
SACRAMENTO METRO ATCT	6	16.51
SAGINAW ATCT	7	11.72
SALT LAKE ARTCC	10	11.72
SALT LAKE CITY INTL ATCT	10	11.72
SALT LAKE CITY TRACON	10	11.72
SAN ANTONIO ATCT	10	11.72
SAN DIEGO ATCT	8	17.68
SAN DIEGO MONTGOMERY ATCT	7	17.68
SAN FRANCISCO INTL ATCT	10	26.39
SAN JOSE INTL ATCT	8	26.39
SAN JUAN	9	—
SAN JUAN INTL ATCT	7	—
SANTA BARBARA MUNI ATCT	8	21.65
SANTA MONICA MUNI ATCT	7	21.65
SARASOTA ATCT	7	11.72
SAVANNAH INTL ATCT	8	11.72
SCOTTSDALE ATCT	7	11.72
SEATTLE ARTCC	10	16.53
SEATTLE TACOMA INTL ATCT	10	16.53
SEATTLE TACOMA TRACON	11	16.53

Air Traffic Control Facility Pay Levels (As of 2005) *(continued)*

Facility Name	ATC Level	Locality Adjustment (percentages)
SHREVEPORT ATCT	7	11.72
SIOUX CITY ATCT	5	11.72
SIOUX FALLS ATCT	6	11.72
SO. CALIFORNIA TRACON	12	17.68
SONOMA COUNTY ATCT	5	26.39
SOUTH BEND ATCT	7	11.72
SPIRIT OF ST. LOUIS ATCT	6	12.09
SPOKANE INTL ATCT	8	11.72
SPRINGFIELD ATCT	7	11.72
SPRINGFIELD REGIONAL ATCT	8	11.72
ST. THOMAS ATCT	5	—
ST. LOUIS TRACON	11	12.09
ST. LOUIS/LAMBERT INTL ATCT	11	12.09
ST. PAUL DOWNTOWN ATCT	6	15.99
ST. PETERSBURG ATCT	7	11.72
STOCKTON ATCT	5	11.72
SYRACUSE INTL ATCT	8	11.72
TALLAHASSEE ATCT	7	11.72
TAMIAMI ATCT	7	16.77
TAMPA INTL ATCT	11	11.72
TERRE HAUTE ATCT	6	11.72
TETERBORO ATCT	7	20.99
TOLEDO EXPRESS ATCT	8	11.72
TORRANCE MUNICIPAL ATCT	7	21.65
TRAVERSE CITY ATCT	5	11.72
TRI-CITIES ATCT	7	11.72
TRI-CITY REGIONAL ATCT	7	11.72
TUCSON INTL ATCT	8	11.72
TUCSON TRACON	9	11.72

Air Traffic Control Facility Pay Levels (As of 2005) *(continued)*

Facility Name	ATC Level	Locality Adjustment (percentages)
TULSA INTL ATCT	9	11.72
TULSA JONES ATCT	8	11.72
TWIN FALLS ATCT	5	11.72
VAN NUYS ATCT	9	21.65
VERO BEACH MUNICIPAL ATCT	6	11.72
WACO ATCT	7	11.72
WASHINGTON ARTCC	12	15.98
WASHINGTON NATIONAL ATCT	10	15.98
WATERLOO MUNICIPAL ATCT	5	11.72
WEST LAFAYETTE ATCT	5	11.72
WESTCHESTER CNTY ATCT	7	20.99
WICHITA MIDCONTINENT ATCT	9	11.72
WILKES-BARRE ATCT	8	11.72
WILLIAM P. HOBBY ATCT	8	24.77
WILLOW RUN ATCT	6	19.67
WILMINGTON ATCT	7	11.72
YANKEE TRACON	9	19.52
YOUNGSTOWN MUNICIPAL ATCT	7	11.72

Air Traffic Controller Pay Bands (As of 2005)

Facility ATC Level	Minimum Annual Base Salary	Maximum Annual Base Salary
1A	$26,276	—
1B	$32,845	—
2	$37,224	$52,114
3	$43,793	$61,310
4	$46,747	$65,446
5	$53,058	$74,281
6	$58,630	$82,082

Air Traffic Controller Pay Bands (As of 2005) *(continued)*

Facility ATC Level	Minimum Annual Base Salary	Maximum Annual Base Salary
7	$ 64,787	$ 90,702
8	$ 71,589	$100,225
9	$ 79,106	$110,748
10	$ 90,971	$127,359
11	$ 95,745	$134,043
12	$100,534	$140,748
13	$105,561	$147,785
14	$110,839	$155,175

In the Air Traffic Controller Pay Bands chart above, Levels 1 through 4 are reserved for controllers in the FAA's training program. Levels 5 through 14 include air traffic controllers, facility managers, and support personnel.

Additional Benefits

Air traffic controllers receive standard life insurance and health benefits as part of their jobs. This includes thirteen days of paid sick leave per year and between thirteen and twenty-six days of paid vacation every year, depending on length of employment. Air traffic controllers may retire after a shorter period of service and at an earlier age than most other federal workers: Controllers aged 50 and older qualify for retirement if they have completed twenty years of active service, and all controllers may retire after twenty-five years of active service, regardless of age.

HOW DO I APPLY FOR A POSITION AS AN AIR TRAFFIC CONTROLLER?

Regardless of how you apply to the FAA for an air traffic control position, if you are selected, you must complete an interview, pass medical and psychological screenings, and pass a security/suitability background investigation before you will be offered a position.

General Medical Requirements

The medical requirements for controller applicants are very specific. You should contact the FAA if you have specific questions about medical conditions or problems, but in general you must have:

- distance and near vision of 20/20 or better in each eye separately without correction, or corrective lenses for distance and near vision to 20/20 in each eye separately.

- normal color vision.

- no hearing loss in either ear of more than 25 db at 500, 1,000, and 2,000 Hz.

- no more than a 20-db loss in the better ear.

- no medical history of any form of heart disease (a history of high blood pressure requiring medication might be acceptable, but it requires special review).

Applicants for air traffic control positions must take and pass a psychological exam. All other medical conditions are evaluated on an individual basis. Your medical history and any current medical examinations are carefully reviewed by the FAA, including past medical records and any military medical records. A history or diagnosis of diabetes is not automatically disqualifying, but it requires special review. In addition, any substance abuse or history of substance abuse and/or dependency, including alcohol, narcotic, non-narcotic drugs, and other substances, is extensively investigated. Additional requirements include:

- no medical history or clinical diagnosis of a convulsive disorder or disturbance of consciousness without satisfactory medical explanation of the cause.

- no treatment, including preventive, for any condition of the nervous system.

- no medical history or clinical diagnosis of a psychosis or other severe mental disorder (this would disqualify you).

Security and Suitability Check

Every applicant for FAA employment must pass a rigorous background security investigation before being offered a job as an air traffic controller. Although the FAA has no specific qualification requirements, many security issues are routinely investigated as part of this background check. Problems such as the following will likely result in your being disqualified:

- General or dishonorable military discharge

- Actions or convictions for which there is statutory debarment from federal employment

- Government loyalty issues

- Evidence of dishonesty in an application or examination process (e.g., falsification of application)

- Drug-related offenses

- Felony offenses

- Firearms or explosives offenses

- Alcohol-related incidents

- Willful disregard of financial obligations

- Derogatory employment terminations

- Patterns and/or combinations of incidents that lead to questions about behavior and intent

The security/suitability investigation is a meticulous background check into your work history, management of finances, and personal behavior. As part of this check, you will be asked to truthfully provide a substantial amount of personal information to the FAA. During the course of the investigation, the FAA will check the accuracy of your information and look into any omissions or gaps in information.

To prepare yourself for such intense scrutiny, take a close look at the sample federal government security form that follows. The questions here are very similar to those you'll encounter when applying for a position with the FAA. Your previous employers and any personal references you provide will also be contacted during your background check. You may want to "practice" for your security check by copying these forms and trying to fill them out completely—and as truthfully as possible. When your actual FAA background investigation begins, you'll have all the information readily available.

Keep in mind that the medical, psychological, and security checks the FAA performs for prospective air traffic controllers are also conducted throughout your employment. Drug tests can be administered at any time during your career with the FAA. A working air traffic controller who fails to continue meeting any of these employment requirements can be immediately terminated.

Standard Form 85P
Revised September 1995
U.S. Office of Personnel Management
5 CFR Parts 731, 732, and 736

Form approved:
OMB No. 3206-0191
NSN 7540-01-317-7372
85-1602

Questionnaire for Public Trust Positions

Follow instructions fully or we cannot process your form. Be sure to sign and date the certification statement on Page 7 and the release on Page 8. *If you have any questions,* call the office that gave you the form.

Purpose of this Form

The U.S. Government conducts background investigations and reinvestigations to establish that applicants or incumbents either employed by the Government or working for the Government under contract, are suitable for the job and/or eligible for a public trust or sensitive position. Information from this form is used primarily as the basis for this investigation. Complete this form only after a conditional offer of employment has been made.

Giving us the information we ask for is voluntary. However, we may not be able to complete your investigation, or complete it in a timely manner, if you don't give us each item of information we request. This may affect your placement or employment prospects.

Authority to Request this Information

The U.S. Government is authorized to ask for this information under Executive Orders 10450 and 10577, sections 3301 and 3302 of title 5, U.S. Code; and parts 5, 731, 732, and 736 of Title 5, Code of Federal Regulations.

Your Social Security number is needed to keep records accurate, because other people may have the same name and birth date. Executive Order 9397 also asks Federal agencies to use this number to help identify individuals in agency records.

The Investigative Process

Background investigations are conducted using your responses on this form and on your Declaration for Federal Employment (OF 306) to develop information to show whether you are reliable, trustworthy, of good conduct and character, and loyal to the United States. The information that you provide on this form is confirmed during the investigation. Your current employer must be contacted as part of the investigation, even if you have previously indicated on applications or other forms that you do not want this.

In addition to the questions on this form, inquiry also is made about a person's adherence to security requirements, honesty and integrity, vulnerability to exploitation or coercion, falsification, misrepresentation, and any other behavior, activities, or associations that tend to show the person is not reliable, trustworthy, or loyal.

Your Personal Interview

Some investigations will include an interview with you as a normal part of the investigative process. This provides you the opportunity to update, clarify, and explain information on your form more completely, which often helps to complete your investigation faster. It is important that the interview be conducted as soon as possible after you are contacted. Postponements will delay the processing of your investigation, and declining to be interviewed may result in your investigation being delayed or canceled.

You will be asked to bring identification with your picture on it, such as a valid State driver's license, to the interview. There are other documents you may be asked to bring to verify your identity as well.

These include documentation of any legal name change, Social Security card, and/or birth certificate.

You may also be asked to bring documents about information you provided on the form or other matters requiring specific attention. These matters include alien registration, delinquent loans or taxes, bankruptcy, judgments, liens, or other financial obligations, agreements involving child custody or support, alimony or property settlements, arrests, convictions, probation, and/or parole.

Instructions for Completing this Form

1. Follow the instructions given to you by the person who gave you the form and any other clarifying instructions furnished by that person to assist you in completion of the form. Find out how many copies of the form you are to turn in. You must sign and date, in black ink, the original and each copy you submit.

2. Type or legibly print your answers in black ink (if your form is not legible, it will not be accepted). You may also be asked to submit your form in an approved electronic format.

3. All questions on this form must be answered. If no response is necessary or applicable, indicate this on the form (for example, enter "None" or "N/A"). If you find that you cannot report an exact date, approximate or estimate the date to the best of your ability and indicate this by marking "APPROX." or "EST."

4. Any changes that you make to this form after you sign it must be initialed and dated by you. Under certain limited circumstances, agencies may modify the form consistent with your intent.

5. You must use the State codes (abbreviations) listed on the back of this page when you fill out this form. Do not abbreviate the names of cities or foreign countries.

6. The 5-digit postal ZIP codes are needed to speed the processing of your investigation. The office that provided the form will assist you in completing the ZIP codes.

7. All telephone numbers must include area codes.

8. All dates provided on this form must be in Month/Day/Year or Month/Year format. Use numbers (1-12) to indicate months. For example, June 10, 1978, should be shown as 6/10/78.

9. Whenever "City (Country)" is shown in an address block, also provide in that block the name of the country when the address is outside the United States.

10. If you need additional space to list your residences or employments/self-employments/unemployments or education, you should use a continuation sheet, SF 86A. If additional space is needed to answer other items, use a blank piece of paper. Each blank piece of paper you use must contain **your name and Social Security Number at the top of the page.**

Final Determination on Your Eligibility

Final determination on your eligibility for a public trust or sensitive position and your being granted a security clearance is the responsibility of the Office of Personnel Management or the Federal agency that requested your investigation. You may be provided the opportunity personally to explain, refute, or clarify any information before a final decision is made.

Penalties for Inaccurate or False Statements

The U.S. Criminal Code (title 18, section 1001) provides that knowingly falsifying or concealing a material fact is a felony which may result in fines of up to $10,000, and/or 5 years imprisonment, or both. In addition, Federal agencies generally fire, do not grant a security clearance, or disqualify individuals who have materially and deliberately falsified these forms, and this remains a part of the permanent record for future placements. Because the position for which you are being considered is one of public trust or is sensitive, your trustworthiness is a very important consideration in deciding your suitability for placement or retention in the position.

Your prospects of placement are better if you answer all questions truthfully and completely. You will have adequate opportunity to explain any information you give us on the form and to make your comments part of the record.

Disclosure of Information

The information you give us is for the purpose of investigating you for a position; we will protect it from unauthorized disclosure. The collection, maintenance, and disclosure of background investigative information is governed by the Privacy Act. The agency which requested the investigation and the agency which conducted the investigation have published notices in the Federal Register describing the system of records in which your records will be maintained. You may obtain copies of the relevant notices from the person who gave you this form. The information on this form, and information we collect during an investigation may be disclosed without your consent as permitted by the Privacy Act (5 USC 552a(b)) and as follows:

PRIVACY ACT ROUTINE USES

1. To the Department of Justice when: (a) the agency or any component thereof; or (b) any employee of the agency in his or her official capacity; or (c) any employee of the agency in his or her individual capacity where the Department of Justice has agreed to represent the employee; or (d) the United States Government, is a party to litigation or has interest in such litigation, and by careful review, the agency determines that the records are both relevant and necessary to the litigation and the use of such records by the Department of Justice is therefore deemed by the agency to be for a purpose that is compatible with the purpose for which the agency collected the records.

2. To a court or adjudicative body in a proceeding when: (a) the agency or any component thereof; or (b) any employee of the agency in his or her official capacity; or (c) any employee of the agency in his or her individual capacity where the Department of Justice has agreed to represent the employee; or (d) the United States Government is a party to litigation or has interest in such litigation, and by careful review, the agency determines that the records are both relevant and necessary to the litigation and the use of such records is therefore deemed by the agency to be for a purpose that is compatible with the purpose for which the agency collected the records.

3. Except as noted in Question 21, when a record on its face, or in conjunction with other records, indicates a violation or potential violation of law, whether civil, criminal, or regulatory in nature, and whether arising by general statute, particular program statute, regulation, rule, or order issued pursuant thereto, the relevant records may be disclosed to the appropriate Federal, foreign, State, local, tribal, or other public authority responsible for enforcing, investigating or prosecuting such violation or charged with enforcing or implementing the statute, rule, regulation, or order.

4. To any source or potential source from which information is requested in the course of an investigation concerning the hiring or retention of an employee or other personnel action, or the issuing or retention of a security clearance, contract, grant, license, or other benefit, to the extent necessary to identify the individual, inform the source of the nature and purpose of the investigation, and to identify the type of information requested.

5. To a Federal, State, local, foreign, tribal, or other public authority the fact that this system of records contains information relevant to the retention of an employee, or the retention of a security clearance, contract, license, grant, or other benefit. The other agency or licensing organization may then make a request supported by written consent of the individual for the entire record if it so chooses. No disclosure will be made unless the information has been determined to be sufficiently reliable to support a referral to another office within the agency or to another Federal agency for criminal, civil, administrative, personnel, or regulatory action.

6. To contractors, grantees, experts, consultants, or volunteers when necessary to perform a function or service related to this record for which they have been engaged. Such recipients shall be required to comply with the Privacy Act of 1974, as amended.

7. To the news media or the general public, factual information the disclosure of which would be in the public interest and which would not constitute an unwarranted invasion of personal privacy.

8. To a Federal, State, or local agency, or other appropriate entities or individuals, or through established liaison channels to selected foreign governments, in order to enable an intelligence agency to carry out its responsibilities under the National Security Act of 1947 as amended, the CIA Act of 1949 as amended, Executive Order 12333 or any successor order, applicable national security directives, or classified implementing procedures approved by the Attorney General and promulgated pursuant to such statutes, orders or directives.

9. To a Member of Congress or to a Congressional staff member in response to an inquiry of the Congressional office made at the written request of the constituent about whom the record is maintained.

10. To the National Archives and Records Administration for records management inspections conducted under 44 USC 2904 and 2906.

11. To the Office of Management and Budget when necessary to the review of private relief legislation.

STATE CODES (ABBREVIATIONS)

Alabama	AL	Hawaii	HI	Massachusetts	MA	New Mexico	NM	South Dakota	SD
Alaska	AK	Idaho	ID	Michigan	MI	New York	NY	Tennessee	TN
Arizona	AZ	Illinois	IL	Minnesota	MN	North Carolina	NC	Texas	TX
Arkansas	AR	Indiana	IN	Mississippi	MS	North Dakota	ND	Utah	UT
California	CA	Iowa	IA	Missouri	MO	Ohio	OH	Vermont	VT
Colorado	CO	Kansas	KS	Montana	MT	Oklahoma	OK	Virginia	VA
Connecticut	CT	Kentucky	KY	Nebraska	NE	Oregon	OR	Washington	WA
Delaware	DE	Louisiana	LA	Nevada	NV	Pennsylvania	PA	West Virginia	WV
Florida	FL	Maine	ME	New Hampshire	NH	Rhode Island	RI	Wisconsin	WI
Georgia	GA	Maryland	MD	New Jersey	NJ	South Carolina	SC	Wyoming	WY
American Samoa	AS	District of Columbia	DC	Guam	GU	Northern Marianas	CM	Puerto Rico	PR
Trust Territory	TT	Virgin Islands	VI				

PUBLIC BURDEN INFORMATION

Public burden reporting for this collection of information is estimated to average 60 minutes per response, including time for reviewing instructions, searching existing data sources, gathering and maintaining the data needed, and completing and reviewing the collection of information. Send comments regarding the burden estimate or any other aspect of this collection of information, including suggestions for reducing this burden to Reports and Forms Management Officer, U.S. Office of Personnel Management, 1900 E Street, N.W., Room CHP-500, Washington, D.C. 20415. Do not send your completed form to this address.

Standard Form 85P (EG)
Revised September 1995
U.S. Office of Personnel Management
5 CFR Parts 731, 732, and 736

**QUESTIONNAIRE FOR
PUBLIC TRUST POSITIONS**

Form approved:
OMB No. 3206-0191
NSN 7540-01-317-7372
85-1602

OPM USE ONLY	Codes	Case Number

Agency Use Only *(Complete items A through P using instructions provided by USOPM)*

A Type of Investigation	B Extra Coverage		C Sensitivity/ Risk Level	D Compu/ ADP	E Nature of Action Code	F Date of Action	Month	Day	Year

G Geographic Location		H Position Code	I Position Title						

J SON	K Location of Official Personnel Folder	None / NPRC / At SON	Other Address					ZIP Code	

L SOI	M Location of Security Folder	None / At SOI / NPI	Other Address					ZIP Code	

N OPAC-ALC Number	O Accounting Data and/or Agency Case Number		

P Requesting Official	Name and Title	Signature	Telephone Number ( )	Date

Persons completing this form should begin with the questions below.

① FULL NAME
- If you have only initials in your name, use them and state (IO).
- If you have no middle name, enter "NMN".
- If you are a "Jr.," "Sr.," "II," etc., enter this in the box after your middle name.

② DATE OF BIRTH

Last Name	First Name	Middle Name	Jr., II, etc.	Month	Day	Year

③ PLACE OF BIRTH - Use the two letter code for the State.

City	County	State	Country *(if not in the United States)*

④ SOCIAL SECURITY NUMBER

⑤ OTHER NAMES USED

Name #1	Month/Year Month/Year To	Name #3	Month/Year Month/Year To
Name #2	Month/Year Month/Year To	Name #4	Month/Year Month/Year To

⑥ OTHER IDENTIFYING INFORMATION

Height *(feet and inches)*	Weight *(pounds)*	Hair Color	Eye Color	Sex *(Mark one box)* Female / Male

⑦ TELEPHONE NUMBERS

Work *(include Area Code and extension)* Day / Night ( )	Home *(include Area Code)* Day / Night ( )

⑧ CITIZENSHIP

ⓐ Mark the box at the right that reflects your current citizenship status, and follow its instructions.

- I am a U.S. citizen or national by birth in the U.S. or U.S. territory/possession. *Answer items b and d.*
- I am a U.S. citizen, but I was NOT born in the U.S. *Answer items b, c and d.*
- I am not a U.S. citizen. *Answer items b and e.*

ⓑ Your Mother's Maiden Name

ⓒ UNITED STATES CITIZENSHIP If you are a U.S. Citizen, but were not born in the U.S., provide information about one or more of the following proofs of your citizenship.

Naturalization Certificate *(Where were you naturalized?)*

Court	City	State	Certificate Number	Month/Day/Year Issued

Citizenship Certificate *(Where was the certificate issued?)*

City	State	Certificate Number	Month/Day/Year Issued

State Department Form 240 - Report of Birth Abroad of a Citizen of the United States

Give the date the form was prepared and give an explanation if needed.	Month/Day/Year	Explanation

U.S. Passport

This may be either a current or previous U.S. Passport	Passport Number	Month/Day/Year Issued

ⓓ DUAL CITIZENSHIP If you are *(or were)* a dual citizen of the United States and another country, provide the name of that country in the space to the right.

Country

ⓔ ALIEN If you are an alien, provide the following information:

Place You Entered the United States:	City	State	Date You Entered U.S. Month	Day	Year	Alien Registration Number	Country(ies) of Citizenship

Exception to SF65, SF85P, SF85P-S, SF86, and SF86A approved by GSA September, 1995.
Designed using Perform Pro, WHS/DIOR, Sep 95

Page 1

⑨ WHERE YOU HAVE LIVED

List the places where you have lived, beginning with the most recent (#1) and working back 7 years. All periods must be accounted for in your list. Be sure to indicate the actual physical location of your residence: do not use a post office box as an address, do not list a permanent address when you were actually living at a school address, etc. Be sure to specify your location as closely as possible: for example, do not list only your base or ship, list your barracks number or home port. You may omit temporary military duty locations under 90 days (list your permanent address instead), and you should use your APO/FPO address if you lived overseas.

For any address in the last 5 years, list a person who knew you at that address, and who preferably still lives in that area (do not list people for residences completely outside this 5-year period, and do not list your spouse, former spouse, or other relatives). Also for addresses in the last 5 years, if the address is "General Delivery," a Rural or Star Route, or may be difficult to locate, provide directions for locating the residence on an attached continuation sheet.

Month/Year Month/Year	Street Address		Apt. #	City (Country)			State	ZIP Code
#1 To Present								
Name of Person Who Knows You	Street Address	Apt. #	City (Country)		State	ZIP Code	Telephone Number ( )	
Month/Year Month/Year	Street Address		Apt. #	City (Country)			State	ZIP Code
#2 To								
Name of Person Who Knew You	Street Address	Apt. #	City (Country)		State	ZIP Code	Telephone Number ( )	
Month/Year Month/Year	Street Address		Apt. #	City (Country)			State	ZIP Code
#3 To								
Name of Person Who Knew You	Street Address	Apt. #	City (Country)		State	ZIP Code	Telephone Number ( )	
Month/Year Month/Year	Street Address		Apt. #	City (Country)			State	ZIP Code
#4 To								
Name of Person Who Knew You	Street Address	Apt. #	City (Country)		State	ZIP Code	Telephone Number ( )	
Month/Year Month/Year	Street Address		Apt. #	City (Country)			State	ZIP Code
#5 To								
Name of Person Who Knew You	Street Address	Apt. #	City (Country)		State	ZIP Code	Telephone Number ( )	

⑩ WHERE YOU WENT TO SCHOOL

List the schools you have attended, beyond Junior High School, **beginning with the most recent (#1) and working back 7 years.** List all College or University degrees and the dates they were received. If all of your education occurred more than 7 years ago, list your most recent education beyond high school, no matter when that education occurred.

•Use one of the following codes in the "Code" block:

   1 - High School   **2** - College/University/Military College   **3** - Vocational/Technical/Trade School

•For schools you attended in the past 3 years, list a person who knew you at school (an instructor, student, etc.). Do not list people for education completely outside this 3-year period.

•For correspondence schools and extension classes, provide the address where the records are maintained.

Month/Year Month/Year	Code	Name of School		Degree/Diploma/Other		Month/Year Awarded
#1 To						
Street Address and City (Country) of School					State ZIP Code	
Name of Person Who Knew You	Street Address	Apt. #	City (Country)	State ZIP Code	Telephone Number ( )	
Month/Year Month/Year	Code	Name of School		Degree/Diploma/Other		Month/Year Awarded
#2 To						
Street Address and City (Country) of School					State ZIP Code	
Name of Person Who Knew You	Street Address	Apt. #	City (Country)	State ZIP Code	Telephone Number ( )	
Month/Year Month/Year	Code	Name of School		Degree/Diploma/Other		Month/Year Awarded
#3 To						
Street Address and City (Country) of School					State ZIP Code	
Name of Person Who Knew You	Street Address	Apt. #	City (Country)	State ZIP Code	Telephone Number ( )	

Enter your Social Security Number before going to the next page————————————————▶

11 YOUR EMPLOYMENT ACTIVITIES

List your employment activities, beginning with the present (#1) and working back 7 years. You should list all full-time work, part-time work, military service, temporary military duty locations over 90 days, self-employment, other paid work, and all periods of unemployment. The entire 7-year period must be accounted for without breaks, but you need not list employments before your 16th birthday.

● **Code.** Use one of the codes listed below to identify the type of employment.

1 - Active military duty stations	5 - State Government (Non-Federal employment)	7 - Unemployment (Include name of person who can verify) 9 - Other
2 - National Guard/Reserve	6 - Self-employment (Include business and/or name of person who can verify)	8 - Federal Contractor (List Contractor, not Federal agency)
3 - U.S.P.H.S. Commissioned Corps		
4 - Other Federal employment		

● **Employer/Verifier Name.** List the business name of your employer or the name of the person who can verify your self-employment or unemployment in this block. If military service is being listed, include your duty location or home port here as well as your branch of service. You should provide separate listings to reflect changes in your military duty locations or home ports.

● **Previous Periods of Activity.** Complete these lines if you worked for an employer on more than one occasion at the same location. After entering the most recent period of employment in the initial numbered block, provide previous periods of employment at the same location on the additional lines provided. For example, if you worked at XY Plumbing in Denver, CO, during 3 separate periods of time, you would enter dates and information concerning the most recent period of employment first, and provide dates, position titles, and supervisors for the two previous periods of employment on the lines below that information.

Month/Year Month/Year	Code	Employer/Verifier Name/Military Duty Location			Your Position Title/Military Rank	
#1 To Present						
Employer's/Verifier's Street Address		City (Country)	State	ZIP Code	Telephone Number ( )	
Street Address of Job Location (if different than Employer's Address)		City (Country)	State	ZIP Code	Telephone Number ( )	
Supervisor's Name & Street Address (if different than Job Location)		City (Country)	State	ZIP Code	Telephone Number ( )	

	Month/Year Month/Year	Position Title	Supervisor
PREVIOUS PERIODS OF ACTIVITY *(Block #1)*	Month/Year Month/Year To	Position Title	Supervisor
	Month/Year Month/Year To	Position Title	Supervisor
	Month/Year Month/Year To	Position Title	Supervisor

Month/Year Month/Year	Code	Employer/Verifier Name/Military Duty Location			Your Position Title/Military Rank	
#2 To						
Employer's/Verifier's Street Address		City (Country)	State	ZIP Code	Telephone Number ( )	
Street Address of Job Location (if different than Employer's Address)		City (Country)	State	ZIP Code	Telephone Number ( )	
Supervisor's Name & Street Address (if different than Job Location)		City (Country)	State	ZIP Code	Telephone Number ( )	

	Month/Year Month/Year	Position Title	Supervisor
PREVIOUS PERIODS OF ACTIVITY *(Block #2)*	Month/Year Month/Year To	Position Title	Supervisor
	Month/Year Month/Year To	Position Title	Supervisor
	Month/Year Month/Year To	Position Title	Supervisor

Month/Year Month/Year	Code	Employer/Verifier Name/Military Duty Location			Your Position Title/Military Rank	
#3 To						
Employer's/Verifier's Street Address		City (Country)	State	ZIP Code	Telephone Number ( )	
Street Address of Job Location (if different than Employer's Address)		City (Country)	State	ZIP Code	Telephone Number ( )	
Supervisor's Name & Street Address (if different than Job Location)		City (Country)	State	ZIP Code	Telephone Number ( )	

	Month/Year Month/Year	Position Title	Supervisor
PREVIOUS PERIODS OF ACTIVITY *(Block #3)*	Month/Year Month/Year To	Position Title	Supervisor
	Month/Year Month/Year To	Position Title	Supervisor
	Month/Year Month/Year To	Position Title	Supervisor

Enter your Social Security Number before going to the next page——————▶

YOUR EMPLOYMENT ACTIVITIES *(CONTINUED)*

Month/Year To	Month/Year	Code	Employer/Verifier Name/Military Duty Location		Your Position Title/Military Rank			
#4								

Employer's/Verifier's Street Address		City (Country)	State	ZIP Code	Telephone Number ( )
Street Address of Job Location (if different than Employer's Address)		City (Country)	State	ZIP Code	Telephone Number ( )
Supervisor's Name & Street Address (if different than Job Location)		City (Country)	State	ZIP Code	Telephone Number ( )

	Month/Year To	Month/Year	Position Title	Supervisor
PREVIOUS PERIODS OF ACTIVITY *(Block #4)*	Month/Year To	Month/Year	Position Title	Supervisor
	Month/Year To	Month/Year	Position Title	Supervisor

Month/Year To	Month/Year	Code	Employer/Verifier Name/Military Duty Location		Your Position Title/Military Rank			
#5								

Employer's/Verifier's Street Address		City (Country)	State	ZIP Code	Telephone Number ( )
Street Address of Job Location (if different than Employer's Address)		City (Country)	State	ZIP Code	Telephone Number ( )
Supervisor's Name & Street Address (if different than Job Location)		City (Country)	State	ZIP Code	Telephone Number ( )

	Month/Year To	Month/Year	Position Title	Supervisor
PREVIOUS PERIODS OF ACTIVITY *(Block #5)*	Month/Year To	Month/Year	Position Title	Supervisor
	Month/Year To	Month/Year	Position Title	Supervisor

Month/Year To	Month/Year	Code	Employer/Verifier Name/Military Duty Location		Your Position Title/Military Rank			
#6								

Employer's/Verifier's Street Address		City (Country)	State	ZIP Code	Telephone Number ( )
Street Address of Job Location (if different than Employer's Address)		City (Country)	State	ZIP Code	Telephone Number ( )
Supervisor's Name & Street Address (if different than Job Location)		City (Country)	State	ZIP Code	Telephone Number ( )

	Month/Year To	Month/Year	Position Title	Supervisor
PREVIOUS PERIODS OF ACTIVITY *(Block #6)*	Month/Year To	Month/Year	Position Title	Supervisor
	Month/Year To	Month/Year	Position Title	Supervisor

12   **YOUR EMPLOYMENT RECORD**

Has any of the following happened to you in the last 7 years? If "Yes," begin with the most recent occurrence and go backward, providing date fired, quit, or left, and other information requested.

Yes	No

Use the following codes and explain the reason your employment was ended:

1 - Fired from a job

2 - Quit a job after being told you'd be fired

3 - Left a job by mutual agreement following allegations of misconduct

4 - Left a job by mutual agreement following allegations of unsatisfactory performance

5 - Left a job for other reasons under unfavorable circumstances

Month/Year	Code	Specify Reason	Employer's Name and Address *(Include city/Country if outside U.S.)*	State	ZIP Code

Enter your Social Security Number before going to the next page ——————————➤

13 PEOPLE WHO KNOW YOU WELL
List three people who know you well and live in the United States. They should be good friends, peers, colleagues, college roommates, etc., whose combined association with you covers as well as possible the last 7 years. Do not list your spouse, former spouses, or other relatives, and try not to list anyone who is listed elsewhere on this form.

Name #1	Dates Known Month/Year Month/Year To	Telephone Number Day Night ( )			
Home or Work Address		City (Country)		State	ZIP Code

Name #2	Dates Known Month/Year Month/Year To	Telephone Number Day Night ( )			
Home or Work Address		City (Country)		State	ZIP Code

Name #3	Dates Known Month/Year Month/Year To	Telephone Number Day Night ( )			
Home or Work Address		City (Country)		State	ZIP Code

14 YOUR MARITAL STATUS
Mark one of the following boxes to show your current marital status:

☐ **1** - Never married *(go to question 15)*   ☐ **3** - Separated   ☐ **5** - Divorced

☐ **2** - Married   ☐ **4** - Legally Separated   ☐ **6** - Widowed

Current Spouse   Complete the following about your current spouse.

Full Name	Date of Birth *(Mo./Day/Yr.)*	Place of Birth *(Include country if outside the U.S.)*	Social Security Number

Other Names Used *(Specify maiden name, names by other marriages, etc., and show dates used for each name)*

Country of Citizenship	Date Married *(Mo./Day/Yr.)*	Place Married *(Include country if outside the U.S.)*	State
If Separated, Date of Separation *(Mo./Day/Yr.)*	If Legally Separated, Where is the Record Located? City *(Country)*		State

Address of Current Spouse *(Street, city, and country if outside the U.S.)*	State	ZIP Code

15 YOUR RELATIVES
Give the full name, correct code, and other requested information for each of your relatives, living or dead, specified below.

1 - Mother *(first)*   **3** - Stepmother   **5** - Foster Parent   **7** - Stepchild

2 - Father *(second)*   **4** - Stepfather   **6** - Child *(adopted also)*

Full Name *(If deceased, check box on the left before entering name)*	Code	Date of Birth Month/Day/Year	Country of Birth	Country(ies) of Citizenship	Current Street Address and City *(country)* of Living Relatives	State
☐	1					
☐	2					
☐						
☐						
☐						
☐						
☐						
☐						
☐						
☐						

Enter your Social Security Number before going to the next page————————▶

Page 5

16 YOUR MILITARY HISTORY

		Yes	No
a Have you served in the United States military?		☐	☐
b Have you served in the United States Merchant Marine?		☐	☐

List all of your military service below, including service in Reserve, National Guard, and U.S. Merchant Marine. Start with the most recent period of service (#1) and work backward. If you had a break in service, each separate period should be listed.

●**Code.** Use one of the codes listed below to identify your branch of service:

   1 - Air Force   **2** - Army   **3** - Navy   **4** - Marine Corps   **5** - Coast Guard   **6** - Merchant Marine   **7** - National Guard

●**O/E.** Mark "O" block for Officer or "E" block for Enlisted.

●**Status.** "X" the appropriate block for the status of your service during the time that you served. If your service was in the National Guard, do not use an "X": use the two-letter code for the state to mark the block.

●**Country.** If your service was with other than the U.S. Armed Forces, identify the country for which you served.

Month/Year	Month/Year	Code	Service/Certificate No.	O	E	Status Active	Status Active Reserve	Status Inactive Reserve	Status National Guard (State)	Country
To				☐	☐	☐	☐	☐	☐	
To				☐	☐	☐	☐	☐	☐	

17 YOUR SELECTIVE SERVICE RECORD

	Yes	No
a Are you a male born after December 31, 1959? If "**No**," go to **18**. If "**Yes**," go to b.	☐	☐
b Have you registered with the Selective Service System? If "**Yes**," provide your registration number. If "**No**," show the reason for your legal exemption below.	☐	☐

Registration Number	Legal Exemption Explanation

18 YOUR INVESTIGATIONS RECORD

	Yes	No
a Has the United States Government ever investigated your background and/or granted you a security clearance? If "**Yes**," use the codes that follow to provide the requested information below. If "**Yes**," but you can't recall the investigating agency and/or the security clearance received, enter "**Other**" agency code or clearance code, as appropriate, and "**Don't know**" or "**Don't recall**" under the "**Other Agency**" heading, below. If your response is "**No**," or you don't know or can't recall if you were investigated and cleared, check the "**No**" box.	☐	☐

Codes for Investigating Agency		Codes for Security Clearance Received		
1 - Defense Department **4** - FBI		**0** - Not Required **3** - Top Secret		**6** - L
2 - State Department **5** - Treasury Department		**1** - Confidential **4** - Sensitive Compartmented Information		**7** - Other
3 - Office of Personnel Management **6** - Other *(Specify)*		**2** - Secret **5** - Q		

Month/Year	Agency Code	Other Agency	Clearance Code	Month/Year	Agency Code	Other Agency	Clearance Code

	Yes	No
b To your knowledge, have you ever had a clearance or access authorization denied, suspended, or revoked, or have you ever been debarred from government employment? If "**Yes**," give date of action and agency. **Note:** An administrative downgrade or termination of a security clearance is not a revocation.	☐	☐

Month/Year	Department or Agency Taking Action	Month/Year	Department or Agency Taking Action

19 FOREIGN COUNTRIES YOU HAVE VISITED

List foreign countries you have visited, except on travel under official Government orders, beginning with the most current (#1) and working back 7 years. (Travel as a dependent or contractor must be listed.)

●Use one of these codes to indicate the purpose of your visit: **1** - Business   **2** - Pleasure   **3** - Education   **4** - Other

●Include short trips to Canada or Mexico. If you have lived near a border and have made short (one day or less) trips to the neighboring country, you do not need to list each trip. Instead, provide the time period, the code, the country, and a note ("Many Short Trips").

●Do not repeat travel covered in items 9, 10, or 11.

	Month/Year	Month/Year	Code	Country		Month/Year	Month/Year	Code	Country
#1		To			#5		To		
#2		To			#6		To		
#3		To			#7		To		
#4		To			#8		To		

Enter your Social Security Number before going to the next page ➜

20 **YOUR POLICE RECORD** *(Do not include anything that happened before your 16th birthday.)*

In the last 7 years, have you been arrested for, charged with, or convicted of any offense(s)? (Leave out traffic fines of less than $150.)

		Yes	No

If you answered "Yes," explain your answer(s) in the space provided.

Month/Year	Offense	Action Taken	Law Enforcement Authority or Court *(City and county/country if outside the U.S.)*	State	ZIP Code

21 **ILLEGAL DRUGS**

The following questions pertain to the illegal use of drugs or drug activity. You are required to answer the questions fully and truthfully, and your failure to do so could be grounds for an adverse employment decision or action against you, but neither your truthful responses nor information derived from your responses will be used as evidence against you in any subsequent criminal proceeding.

	Yes	No

a In the last year, have you illegally used any controlled substance, for example, marijuana, cocaine, crack cocaine, hashish, narcotics (opium, morphine, codeine, heroin, etc.), amphetamines, depressants (barbiturates, methaqualone, tranquilizers, etc.), hallucinogenics (LSD, PCP, etc.), or prescription drugs?

b In the last 7 years, have you been involved in the illegal purchase, manufacture, trafficking, production, transfer, shipping, receiving, or sale of any narcotic, depressant, stimulant, hallucinogen, or cannabis, for your own intended profit or that of another?

If you answered "Yes" to "a" above, provide information relating to the types of substance(s), the nature of the activity, and any other details relating to your involvement with illegal drugs. Include any treatment or counseling received.

Month/Year	Month/Year	Controlled Substance/Prescription Drug Used	Number of Times Used
	To		
	To		
	To		

22 **YOUR FINANCIAL RECORD**

	Yes	No

a In the last 7 years, have you, or a company over which you exercised some control, filed for bankruptcy, been declared bankrupt, been subject to a tax lien, or had legal judgment rendered against you for a debt? If you answered "Yes," provide date of initial action and other information requested below.

Month/Year	Type of Action	Name Action Occurred Under	Name/Address of Court or Agency Handling Case	State	ZIP Code

b Are you now over 180 days delinquent on any loan or financial obligation? Include loans or obligations funded or guaranteed by the Federal Government.

	Yes	No

If you answered "Yes," provide the information requested below:

Month/Year	Type of Loan or Obligation and Account #	Name/Address of Creditor or Obligee	State	ZIP Code

After completing this form and any attachments, you should review your answers to all questions to make sure the form is complete and accurate, and then sign and date the following certification and sign and date the release on Page 8.

Certification That My Answers Are True

My statements on this form, and any attachments to it, are true, complete, and correct to the best of my knowledge and belief and are made in good faith. I understand that a knowing and willful false statement on this form can be punished by fine or imprisonment or both. (See section 1001 of title 18, United States Code).

Signature *(Sign in ink)* _____ Date _____

Enter your Social Security Number before going to the next page ⟶

Standard Form 85P
Revised September 1995
U.S. Office of Personnel Management
5 CFR Parts 731, 732, and 736

Form approved:
OMB No. 3206-0191
NSN 7540-01-317-7372
85-1602

UNITED STATES OF AMERICA

AUTHORIZATION FOR RELEASE OF INFORMATION

Carefully read this authorization to release information about you, then sign and date it in ink.

I Authorize any investigator, special agent, or other duly accredited representative of the authorized Federal agency conducting my background investigation, to obtain any information relating to my activities from individuals, schools, residential management agents, employers, criminal justice agencies, credit bureaus, consumer reporting agencies, collection agencies, retail business establishments, or other sources of information. This information may include, but is not limited to, my academic, residential, achievement, performance, attendance, disciplinary, employment history, criminal history record information, and financial and credit information. I authorize the Federal agency conducting my investigation to disclose the record of my background investigation to the requesting agency for the purpose of making a determination of suitability or eligibility for a security clearance.

I Understand that, for financial or lending institutions, medical institutions, hospitals, health care professionals, and other sources of information, a separate specific release will be needed, and I may be contacted for such a release at a later date. Where a separate release is requested for information relating to mental health treatment or counseling, the release will contain a list of the specific questions, relevant to the job description, which the doctor or therapist will be asked.

I Further Authorize any investigator, special agent, or other duly accredited representative of the U.S. Office of Personnel Management, the Federal Bureau of Investigation, the Department of Defense, the Defense Investigative Service, and any other authorized Federal agency, to request criminal record information about me from criminal justice agencies for the purpose of determining my eligibility for assignment to, or retention in a sensitive National Security position, in accordance with 5 U.S.C. 9101. I understand that I may request a copy of such records as may be available to me under the law.

I Authorize custodians of records and other sources of information pertaining to me to release such information upon request of the investigator, special agent, or other duly accredited representative of any Federal agency authorized above regardless of any previous agreement to the contrary.

I Understand that the information released by records custodians and sources of information is for official use by the Federal Government only for the purposes provided in this Standard Form 85P, and that it may be redisclosed by the Government only as authorized by law.

Copies of this authorization that show my signature are as valid as the original release signed by me. This authorization is valid for five (5) years from the date signed or upon the termination of my affiliation with the Federal Government, whichever is sooner.

Signature *(Sign in ink)*	Full Name *(Type or Print Legibly)*	Date Signed
Other Names Used		Social Security Number

Current Address *(Street, City)*	State	ZIP Code	Home Telephone Number *(Include Area Code)* ( )

Page 8

Standard Form 85P
Revised September 1995
U.S. Office of Personnel Management
5 CFR Parts 731, 732, and 736

Form approved:
OMB No. 3206-0191
NSN 7540-01-317-7372
85-1602

UNITED STATES OF AMERICA

AUTHORIZATION FOR RELEASE OF MEDICAL INFORMATION

Carefully read this authorization to release information about you, then sign and date it in black ink.

Instructions for Completing this Release

This is a release for the investigator to ask your health practitioner(s) the three questions below concerning your mental health consultations. Your signature will allow the practitioner(s) to answer only these questions.

I am seeking assignment to or retention in a position of public trust with the Federal Government as a(n)

(Investigator instructed to write in position title.)

As part of the investigative process, **I hereby authorize** the investigator, special agent, or duly accredited representative of the authorized Federal agency conducting my background investigation, to obtain the following information relating to my mental health consultations:

Does the person under investigation have a condition or treatment that could impair his/her judgment or reliability?

If so, please describe the nature of the condition and the extent and duration of the impairment or treatment.

What is the prognosis?

I understand that the information released pursuant to this release is for use by the Federal Government only for purposes provided in the Standard Form 85P and that it may be redisclosed by the Government only as authorized by law.

Copies of this authorization that show my signature are as valid as the original release signed by me. This authorization is valid for 1 year from the date signed or upon termination of my affiliation with the Federal Government, whichever is sooner.

Signature *(Sign in ink)*	Full Name *(Type or Print Legibly)*		Date Signed
Other Names Used			Social Security Number
Current Address *(Street, City)*	State	ZIP Code	Home Telephone Number *(Include Area Code)* ( )

SUMMING IT UP

- The FAA is currently hiring from three groups of applicants: ex-military air traffic controllers, graduates of approved college programs, and the general public. Applicants must pass a rigorous set of exams, including medical, psychological, and aptitude tests, and security and suitability screenings. Applicants who are hired must not only complete training at an FAA academy but must also successfully complete an on-the-job training program.

- Each FAA facility is assigned a pay grade based on the type of traffic it controls. The pay grades determine base salaries for controllers at that facility. Within each pay grade is a pay band—the salary range at each facility based on length of time working—and a cost-of-living locality adjustment.

- Health and life insurance benefits, vacation time, and sick leave for air traffic controllers are similar to those of many U.S. companies.

- The medical, psychological, and security checks you must pass to be hired as an air traffic controller are repeated throughout your employment with the FAA, so it's important to continue meeting these standards to avoid the risk of termination.

PART II

THE U.S. AIR TRAFFIC CONTROL SYSTEM

What You Need to Know About the Air Traffic Control System

chapter 3

OVERVIEW

- **Navigation**

- **Navigation systems**

- **Airways**

- **Communications**

- **Air traffic control surveillance**

- **Air traffic management**

- **Aircraft identification**

- **Summing it up**

In this section of the book, you'll learn about how the air traffic control system operates in the United States. If you are accepted into an air traffic controller training program, it is particularly important that you understand this material before reporting for training and testing.

The U.S. air traffic control system encompasses all of the country's airports and the airspace over the United States. It has four distinct components:

1. Navigation
2. Communications
3. Surveillance
4. Air traffic management

Collectively, these are known as CNS/ATM. Understanding each component of this system is essential to becoming a proficient air traffic controller.

NAVIGATION

07018
AIRPORT DIAGRAM

AL-166 (FAA)

CHICAGO-O'HARE INTL (ORD)
CHICAGO, ILLINOIS

ATIS
135.4　269.9
O'HARE TOWER
126.9(N)　120.75(S)　390.9
127.925　132.7
GND CON
121.9　121.75　348.6
CLNC DEL
121.6

ELEV 653

VAR 2.8° W

JANUARY 2005
ANNUAL RATE OF CHANGE
0.1° W

42°01' N

42°00' N

ELEV 666

FIELD ELEV 668

ELEV 648

1005 X 150

SCENIC HOLD PAD

FIRE STATION

LAHSO

ELEV 660

7500 X 150

7967 X 150

NORTHEAST CARGO RAMP

ELEV 650

41°59' N

092.8°

ELEV 656

LAHSO

LAHSO

CONTROL TOWER 905

ELEV 648

13000 X 200

A21
A20
A19

(H)

EC-3, 18 JAN 2007 to 15 FEB 2007

ELEV 666

092.7°

LAHSO

10144 X 150　←272.7°

ELEV 654

SOUTHWEST CARGO RAMPS

FIRE STATION

LAHSO

ELEV 651

224.3°

41°58' N

ELEV 649

8075 X 150

Rwy 14L ldg 8007'

RWYS 9R-27L, 14R-32L, 14L-32R, 4L-22R
S100, D185, ST175, DT350
RWY　9L-27R
S100, D210, ST175, DT350
RWY　4R-22L
S100, D200, ST175, DT350

044.3°

ELEV 661

41°57' N

CAUTION BE ALERT TO RUNWAY CROSSING CLEARANCES.
READBACK OF ALL RUNWAY HOLDING INSTRUCTIONS IS REQUIRED.

87°56' W　　87°55' W　　87°54' W　　87°53' W

AIRPORT DIAGRAM
07018

CHICAGO, ILLINOIS
CHICAGO-O'HARE INTL (ORD)

A diagram of Chicago O'Hare International, an example of diagrams used by air traffic controllers to direct local airport traffic.

Airport Runways and Taxiways

Air traffic controllers are responsible for separating aircraft operating on the runways and taxiways of airports. However, they are not responsible for aircraft or vehicles operating on the ramps around the hangars and terminals; this is the responsibility of the airport owner and the airlines that operate at that airport.

Only designated runways can be used for takeoff and landings. They are numbered according to their direction. A runway number is its heading, rounded off to the nearest 10 degrees, with the last number dropped from the designation. For example, a runway heading 273 degrees (westward) would be rounded down to 270 degrees, and with the last digit dropped, it becomes runway 27. If two runways operate parallel to one another, they are known as left and right (for example 27L and 27R).

At very large airports where there may be three parallel runways, the middle of the three is logically called the center runway—so using the same example as above, the three runways would be designated 27L, 27C, and 27R. If the airport has more than three parallel runways, two of them are assigned numbers 10 degrees off from the existing set of runways: 27L, 27R, 26L, and 26R.

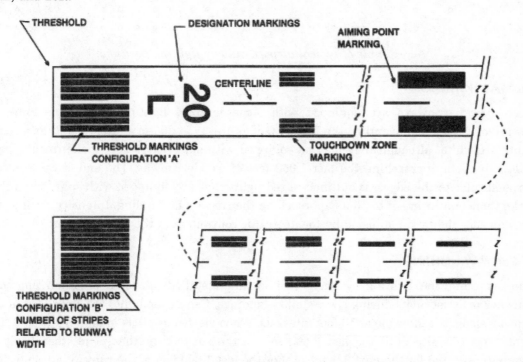

Threshold markings at the landing end of an airport runway

To differentiate runways from other pavements at an airport, runways are always marked with white paint. The edge of every runway is outlined in white, and the centerline is marked with an alternating white stripe, similar to what you see in passing lanes of highways. The landing end of a runway is marked with the runway number and threshold markings. About 1,000 feet from the landing end are large fixed distance markers. Additional markings along the centerline of a runway designate the distance from the landing end.

Airport Lighting Systems

At the end of an instrument approach—that is, when a pilot is making a transition from instrument flying to visual flying—the weather and/or lighting conditions may be such that the runway is difficult to see. This is the reason for runway and approach lighting systems. Airport lighting systems provide visual aids for pilots, especially during very low visibility situations when a pilot may be able to see only the first portion of his or her designated runway, a condition that doesn't allow for safe aircraft navigation and control.

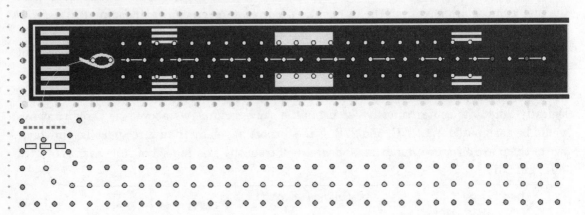

An example of typical airport runway lighting positions

RUNWAY LIGHTING

Most airport runways are equipped with some form of lighting. High-, medium-, or low-intensity edge lights outline the "borders" of a runway at 200-foot intervals. Runway edge lights are white, although they may be equipped with split lenses that make them appear yellow to pilots approaching the last 1,000 feet of usable runway. The end of the runway, perpendicular to the edges, is outlined in red lights that are equipped with split lenses that make them appear green to pilots approaching the runway for landing. Intensity settings for runway edge lights are adjusted by the air traffic controllers in the control tower.

IN-RUNWAY LIGHTING

Runway centerline lighting systems (RCLSs) are installed on some precision approach runways to assist pilots during low-visibility landings. Centerline lights are embedded in the runway along its centerline at 50-foot intervals. When viewed by pilots in landing aircraft, the lights appear white until the last 3,000 feet of the runway. At that point, they begin to alternate with red for the next 2,000 feet. For the last 1,000 feet of the runway, all centerline lights are red.

The landing end of the runway may have touchdown zone lights (TDZL) installed on both sides of the centerline lights, embedded into the runway. TDZL indicates the aircraft's touchdown zone.

TAXIWAY LIGHTING

An airport taxiway is a strip of land on which aircraft can roll (taxi) to or from a hangar, terminal, runway, or other facility. Taxiway lighting is similar to that of runways, but the edge lighting on taxiways is blue. At busy airports, some taxiways are equipped with green centerline lights. Many airports also have flashing yellow lights in areas where a taxiway crosses a runway. These provide additional visual warnings to pilots.

AIRPORT/HELIPORT BEACONS

Most airports and heliports (small airports used only by helicopters) are equipped with rotating light beacons that allow them to be identified from the air. Rotating beacons are high-intensity lights that rotate at a constant speed, producing a regularly spaced flash. Each type of airport has a specific rotating beacon color combination:

- white, green = civilian land airport

- white, yellow = civilian water airport

- white, green, green = military airports

- green, yellow, white = heliports

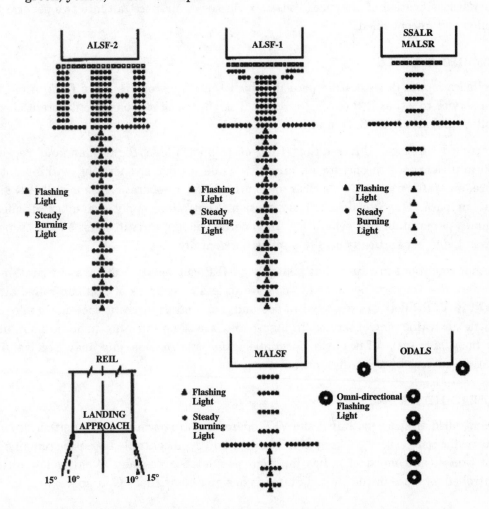

Three examples of approach lighting systems for airport runways

APPROACH LIGHTING SYSTEMS

Approach lights are groups of lights that begin at the end of the runway and extend away from the runway's end to about 2,400 to 3,000 feet. Most approach lighting systems consist of a "light bar" of five high-intensity lights that resemble large automobile high beams, although some consist of a single light or a subset of light bars. Some approach lighting systems include sequenced flashing lights on each light bar; these appear to the pilot as a ball of light traveling towards the runway at high speed. Approach lighting systems can be set at either medium- or high-intensity levels; they are operated by air traffic controllers in the airport control tower.

Airspace

Not all air traffic in the United States is subject to the same level of air traffic control. Depending on the amount and type of air traffic in any given area, airspace is divided into six different categories. The type and level of air traffic control service provided depends on that category's classification of airspace. These six classes of airspace fall into two general types: controlled and uncontrolled.

CONTROLLED AIRSPACE

Controlled airspace describes airspace in which the FAA provides some form of air traffic control service to either IFR or VFR aircraft. The United States has five different classes of controlled airspace: A, B, C, D, and E.

In controlled airspace, IFR requires that each pilot file a flight plan and receive an appropriate clearance to operate an aircraft. While a pilot is operating within controlled airspace, air traffic control issues clearances providing for separation among all IFR aircraft in that airspace. This is called IFR separation. Controllers apply a number of rules and techniques to maintain IFR separation. In general, though, aircraft must be kept separated by either 1,000 feet vertically or 3 to 5 miles horizontally.

If weather conditions are such that pilots flying IFR can see each other and maintain their own separation, they are permitted to operate in less busy areas of that controlled airspace using VFR. VFR pilots are expected to see and avoid other aircraft; they normally require very little air traffic control service. In high-traffic areas, on the other hand (around airports or on busy airways), VFR pilots encounter some restrictions and may receive limited separation services by air traffic controllers.

UNCONTROLLED AIRSPACE

In uncontrolled airspace, both IFR and VFR operations are permitted, but neither are offered any air traffic control services. As you might guess, little uncontrolled airspace remains in the United States, and much of it lies far from populated areas and at fairly low altitudes. Uncontrolled airspace in the United States is designated as Class G airspace.

SPECIAL RULES FOR OTHER AIRSPACE

In addition to standardized controlled and uncontrolled airspace classifications, air traffic controllers have special rules for other blocks of airspace that may be reserved for military or national security uses.

Special Use Airspace

Special use airspace restricts civilian flight operations. This type of airspace might be in use by the military or may be essential to national security. It might also be in areas where special activities are conducted that could be dangerous to aircraft and flight crews—for example, where high-power laser testing occurs. The most common forms of special use airspace include:

- **Prohibited Areas:** Areas within which the flight of all civilian aircraft is expressly prohibited. Prohibited areas are established for security or other reasons and are marked on aeronautical charts. Most of the prohibited areas of U.S. airspace are clustered around the nation's capital, and they're usually quite small and limited.

- **Restricted Areas:** Airspace within which civilian flights are subject to several restrictions. Restricted areas normally cover locations where potentially dangerous operations or exercises are routinely conducted, such as artillery firing, aerial gunnery, or guided missiles exercises. Like prohibited areas, restricted areas are marked on aeronautical charts, which also include restricted area operating times and dimensions. These areas may be active—all civilian aircraft are banned from operating within them—or they may be temporarily inactive. An inactive restricted area may be used for civilian flight operations only with the approval of the controlling military agency.

- **Military Operations Areas:** Airspace where military activities are being conducted that are not particularly dangerous (such as flight training or practice maneuvering), but where the volume of air traffic makes it inadvisable for IFR aircraft to enter. When Military Operation Areas (MOAs) are active, air traffic control keeps all IFR aircraft clear of the airspace. VFR pilots are free to transit MOAs if they can maintain safe visibility and distance from clouds.

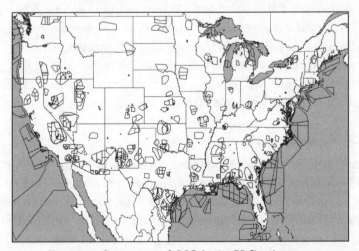

Restricted areas and MOAs in U.S. airspace

NAVIGATION SYSTEMS

Each of the many types of air navigation aids in use today serves a unique purpose. Some have been around for decades and are being slowly phased out; others have been introduced only in the last ten years or so. Each has special capabilities and limitations. Here's a rundown.

Nondirectional Radio Beacon

The nondirectional radio beacon (NDB) is a fairly old air navigation system that operates in the radio frequency band just below commercial AM radio stations. NDBs transmit a single radio signal in all directions, and aircraft equipped with automatic direction finders can navigate to—or "home in on"—these stations. NDB systems can be fairly long range, but they are prone to electronic interference, such as that created by thunderstorms.

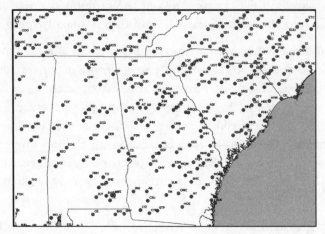

Nondirectional radio beacons currently in use in the southeastern United States

VHF Omni-directional Range

A more modern system than NDBs is the ground-based VHF Omni-directional Range (VOR) system. VORs transmit signals in all directions in the 108.0 to 117.95 MHz frequency band, just above the commercial FM radio band. VORs are not as prone to interference from thunderstorms as NDBs, and they provide the pilot with individual courses, known as radials, to fly either to or from the station that is transmitting. They are much more accurate than the NDB system, although VORs have a range of only 50–200 miles, depending on the altitude of the aircraft. VOR systems provide only the direction from a station (known as bearing or azimuth information); they don't provide distance information.

DISTANCE MEASURING EQUIPMENT

Distance measuring equipment (DME) systems are an add-on to the VOR system. They're designed to provide distance information to properly equipped aircraft. A DME station on the ground responds to pulses transmitted from DME-equipped aircraft. This is called the interrogation pulse. Once the DME ground station receives this pulse, it responds by transmitting a coded return pulse to the aircraft on a different frequency. The time required for the round trip of this signal exchange is measured in nautical miles by the DME unit on the aircraft, and is displayed for the pilot. DME stations are normally located with existing VOR stations. Combined VOR and DME stations are predictably known as VOR/DME systems.

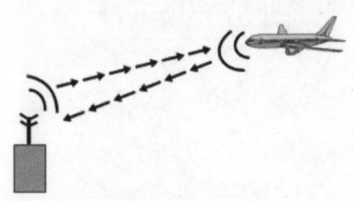

How a distance measuring equipment (DME) system works

TACTICAL AIR NAVIGATION

Tactical Air Navigation (TACAN) is a military version of the VOR/DME system that uses UHF signals. UHF is better suited to the unique operating requirements of the military, such as battlefield or naval operations, and it is incompatible with the VOR navigation system used by civilian pilots and airliners.

VHF Omni-directional Range/Tactical Air Navigation

To provide an integrated navigational system throughout the U.S. military branches, TACAN facilities have been integrated into many civil VOR/DME installations to form a navigational facility known as a VHF Omni-directional Range/Tactical Air Navigation (VORTAC). VORTAC facilities consist of two separate components modified to work together: VOR/DME and TACAN. The VOR component provides directional information to civilian pilots. A component of TACAN provides direction and distance to military aircraft, and another TACAN component provides DME to civilian pilots.

The VOR and TACAN signals are identified by unique three-letter codes and are interlocked, so that pilots using VOR azimuth with TACAN distance receive signals from the same ground station. Civilian pilots simply select the appropriate frequency to receive their signals, while military navigational equipment is set to operate according to channel numbers. In either case, the result is the same: civilian pilots receive separate VOR and DME information for azimuth and distance, and military pilots use just the TACAN signal to receive both types of data.

AIRWAYS

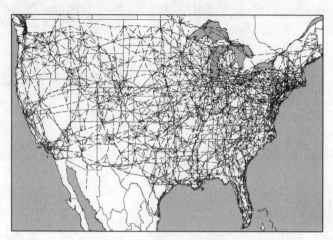

Low-altitude airway structure of the United States (Victor airways)

To provide a unified and logical method of flying cross-country, the FAA has developed a series of numbered airways for use by pilots. A standard system of airways provides an easier way for pilots and controllers to navigate. The airway system in the United States consists of low-altitude airways (known as Victor airways) that operate from ground level to 18,000 feet. At and above 18,000 feet, the airways change numbers and are called jet routes.

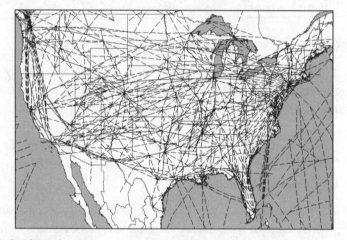

High-altitude airway structure of the United States (jet routes)

Area Navigation

The process of navigating from VORTAC to VORTAC results in airways that are not straight lines, but instead collections of slightly angled routes. A number of navigational systems have been developed to provide point-to-point, straight-line navigation. These systems are collectively known as Area Navigation, or RNAV. They include:

- Long-range navigation-C (LORAN-C)

- Global Navigation Satellite System (GNSS)

- Global Positioning System (GPS)

- Instrument Landing System (ILS)

LONG RANGE NAVIGATION-C

Long-range navigation-C (LORAN-C) is an RNAV system operated by the U.S. Coast Guard (USCG). It was designed to provide reliable, all-weather navigation for marine users along U.S. coasts and around the Great Lakes. In the 1980s, the USCG and the FAA expanded LORAN-C coverage to encompass the entire continental United States.

LORAN-C provides relatively accurate latitude-longitude position information. Pilots using an onboard computer and a database of airport locations can receive reasonably accurate LORAN-C straight-line navigation information between any two locations in the United States.

Technical problems with LORAN-C early in its history kept the system from becoming widely adopted as a navigation standard, but it is still used as a backup. LORAN-C has been super-seded by a more accurate system that provides worldwide coverage: the global navigation satellite system.

GLOBAL NAVIGATION SATELLITE SYSTEM

Global Navigation Satellite System (GNSS) is the worldwide standard for satellite-based navigation. GNSS satellites can be used by the aviation industry, surface transportation interests, surveyors, outdoor enthusiasts, and the general public. The U.S. Department of Defense implemented the first system, known as the Global Positioning System (GPS). It was quickly followed by the former Soviet Union. The European Union is currently planning to launch a GNSS, as are Japan, India, and China.

GLOBAL POSITIONING SYSTEM

As mentioned above, Global Positioning System (GPS) was launched and is still operated by the U.S. government. GPS uses more than two dozen low-earth orbit satellites that provide horizontal positioning accuracy of 100 meters or less. GPS provides accurate latitude-longitude positioning for aircraft. A pilot using an onboard database and computer uses GPS to calculate the distance and bearing to a destination airport. The receiver will display:

- The course to be flown

- The aircraft's current position

- The aircraft's speed over the ground (ground speed)

- Time until it reaches its destination (estimated time en route)

- Whether winds are affecting the aircraft's operation (winds aloft)

At present, GPS is not accurate enough to guide aircraft all the way to the runway in poor weather conditions, but two augmentation systems have been designed to provide this capability:

- The Wide-Area Augmentation System (WAAS), which became operational in 2005, gives properly equipped aircraft non-precision approach capability. It may eventually prove reliable enough to guide aircraft to about one-half mile from the end of the runway, where the pilot is able to perform a visual landing.

- The Local-Area Augmentation System (LAAS), if developed, may allow aircraft to be navigated much closer to the end of the runway than the WAAS. It may also allow autolanding of aircraft. However, LAAS is still under development; it may become operational within the next ten years.

INSTRUMENT LANDING SYSTEM

With the exception of LAAS, none of the navigational systems reviewed so far is sufficiently accurate to navigate aircraft to the runway under low-visibility conditions. However, all of them can be used to provide a non-precision runway approach. This presents a lateral course (left-right) but not vertical guidance.

That's where the Instrument Landing System (ILS) comes in. Developed in the 1950s, the ILS remains the primary method of flying precision instrument approaches—which is defined as a system that provides both lateral and vertical guidance. The ILS transmits horizontal and vertical signals that provide an accurate all-dimensional approach path for aircraft.

ILS ground equipment consists of two directional transmitting systems and one or two marker beacons along the approach path. The directional transmitters are known as the localizer and glideslope transmitters. Depending on the type of ILS equipment installed, accurate navigation to three levels or categories is possible. A Category I ILS, the most common one, provides accurate navigation down to an altitude of about 200 feet from the ground. A more accurate, but also more expensive ILS installation, Category II, permits aircraft to descend to an altitude of 100 feet from the ground before the pilot takes over visually. If the aircraft is properly equipped and pilots receive special training, it's possible to make Category III ILS approaches in a few locations in the United States. Category III approaches are essentially autolandings, in which the aircraft landing system automatically lands and slows the airplane on the runway.

COMMUNICATIONS

The most critical element of air traffic control is the system used to maintain communication between pilots and controllers. Civilian pilots typically use radios operating in the very-high-frequency (VHF) radio band; military pilots use ultra-high-frequency (UHF) radios. The general operating principles and procedures for civilian and military flight are the same, however. The FAA operates more than 5,000 separate communications systems and frequencies.

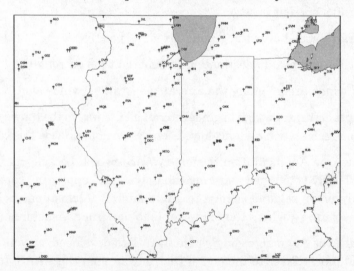

The FAA communications systems in use in the Midwest

In an effort to maintain absolute clarity in radio communications, air traffic controllers and pilots use special jargon, known as phraseology. We'll review this in more detail later in this chapter. An appendix of this book (p. 237) also provides an extensive sampling of the most common air traffic control phraseology.

Facility Identification

Most air traffic control communications include the following four components:

1. The identification of the ATC facility or the intended recipient of the message

2. The location to which the aircraft is cleared to fly (the clearance limit)

3. The altitude at which the aircraft should fly

4. Any other pertinent clearance or weather information

Most air traffic control facilities use the name of the city or airport as their location, then the type of facility as their identification. For example, a control tower in Lafayette, IN, would call itself "Lafayette Tower" over air traffic control radio. Other facilities may use slightly different descriptions. Below are some examples.

Facility	Call Sign
Flight Service Station, Chicago, IL	"Chicago Radio"
Airport Traffic Control Tower, Augusta, GA	"Augusta Tower"
Clearance Delivery, Dallas, TX	"Dallas Clearance Delivery"
Ground Control, Miami, FL	"Miami Ground"
Radar Approach Control, Oklahoma City, OK	"Oklahoma City Approach"
Radar Departure Control, St. Louis, MO	"St. Louis Departure"
Air Route Traffic Control Center, Washington, DC	"Washington Center"

Aircraft Identification

Airline pilots commonly identify themselves using the name of the airline for which they work, followed by the flight number (although some airlines use different call signs). For example, an American Airlines pilot operating Flight 643 would identify as "American 643." Civilian non-commercial flights use an assigned serial number; military flights use the aircraft's serial number and their service name.

The Phonic Alphabet

All air traffic controllers and pilots use a standard phonic alphabet (and number pronunciation) when communicating with one another. This is an internationally recognized system adopted at the end of World War II and affiliated with Morse Code. The proper pronunciations for the letters of the alphabet and numbers 0–9 are shown in the following table.

Character	Morse Code	Telephone	Phonic (Pronunciation)
A	•—	Alfa	(AL-FAH)
B	—•••	Bravo	(BRAH-VOH)
C	—•—•	Charlie	(CHAR-LEE) or (SHAR-LEE)
D	—••	Delta	(DELL-TAH)
E	•	Echo	(ECK-OH)
F	••—•	Foxtrot	(FOKS-TROT)
G	——•	Golf	(GOLF)
H	••••	Hotel	(HOH-TEL)
I	••	India	(IN-DEE-AH)
J	•———	Juliett	(JEW-LEE-ETT)
K	—•—	Kilo	(KEY-LOH)
L	•—••	Lima	(LEE-MAH)
M	——	Mike	(MIKE)
N	—•	November	(NO-VEM-BER)
O	———	Oscar	(OSS-CAH)
P	•——•	Papa	(PAH-PAH)
Q	——•—	Quebec	(KEH-BECK)
R	•—•	Romeo	(ROW-ME-OH)
S	•••	Sierra	(SEE-AIR-RAH)
T	—	Tango	(TANG-GO)
U	••—	Uniform	(YOU-NEE-FORM) or (OO-NEEE-FORM)
V	•••—	Victor	(VIK-TAH)
W	•——	Whiskey	(WISS-KEY)
X	—••—	Xray	(ECKS-RAY)
Y	—•——	Yankee	(YANG-KEY)
Z	——••	Zulu	(ZOO-LOO)
1	•————	One	(WUN)
2	••———	Two	(TOO)
3	•••——	Three	(TREE)

Character	Morse Code	Telephone	Phonic (Pronunciation)
4	● ● ● ● —	Four	(FOW-ER)
5	● ● ● ● ●	Five	(FIFE)
6	— ● ● ● ●	Six	(SIX)
7	— — ● ● ●	Seven	(SEV-EN)
8	— — — ● ●	Eight	(AIT)
9	— — — — ●	Nine	(NIN-ER)
0	— — — — —	Ten	(ZEE-RO)

Standard Phraseology

In addition to the phonic alphabet, controllers and pilots also use a standardized system of identifying headings, altitudes, flight levels, airspeed, and time in an effort to eliminate miscommunications.

DIRECTIONS

All headings, courses, or wind directions are stated as a three-digit number preceded by a description of what the number stands for. For example, a pilot flying an aircraft heading north (360 degrees) would say the aircraft is "heading three six zero." Similarly, a wind from the northeast (40 degrees) would be stated as "wind zero four zero."

ALTITUDES AND FLIGHT LEVELS

In air traffic control, each number in a sequence is usually pronounced individually. If the number is part of an altitude reading, however, the words "hundred" and "thousand" are used.

Number	Air Traffic Control/Pilot Pronunciation
500	five hundred
4,500	four thousand five hundred
10,000	one zero thousand

Altitudes of 18,000 feet or higher are measured slightly different from lower numbers, and they are known as "flight levels." To properly pronounce a flight level reading, you must first say the words "flight level," then speak the first three digits individually (you do not pronounce the last two digits). For example, 18,000 is pronounced "flight level one eight zero."

SPEEDS

Speeds in the air traffic control system are normally measured in knots. One knot equals about 1.15 miles per hour. Each digit of a speed is always pronounced individually—so, for example, 165 knots would be pronounced "one six five knots."

TIME

Aviation follows the military 24-hour clock. For example, 1:00 p.m. is "1300 hours." Also, since it may be impossible for pilots to keep track of each time zone they're flying over, aviation uses what is called Coordinated Universal Time (UTC). To convert from standard time to UTC, you first must convert to military time. Then you add the conversion factor to the military time. The conversion factor number is based on the time zone in which you live. For example:

3:00 p.m. U.S. central = 1500 hours military time

1500 hours military time + conversion (5 hours) = 2000 UTC

To convert from daylight savings time to UTC time, you add one less hour than when converting from standard time.

Standard Time to Coordinated Universal Time	
Eastern daylight time	Add 4 hours
Eastern standard time	Add 5 hours
Central daylight time	Add 5 hours
Central standard time	Add 6 hours
Mountain daylight time	Add 6 hours
Mountain standard time	Add 7 hours
Pacific daylight time	Add 7 hours
Pacific standard time	Add 8 hours
Alaska daylight time	Add 8 hours
Alaska standard time	Add 9 hours
Hawaii daylight time	Add 9 hours
Hawaii standard time	Add 10 hours

AIR TRAFFIC CONTROL SURVEILLANCE

Air traffic controllers in the tower primarily operate visually, meaning that they observe the location and flight direction of each aircraft by sight alone. TRACON and ARTCC controllers, on the other hand, must use electronic surveillance to monitor aircraft. The most common form of surveillance in the air traffic control system is provided by radar (radio detection and ranging). There are two types of radar used in air traffic control:

- **Primary surveillance radar,** invented just before the start of World War II, uses pulsed radio waves to determine an aircraft's position. Radar transmits high-energy pulses focused by an antenna into a narrow beam of radio frequency energy. These pulses are reflected to the radar antenna by objects in the path of the beam, such as aircraft (although heavy weather, birds, and other solid objects also reflect radar energy).

The distance of the aircraft from the radar antenna is determined by measuring the time it takes (at the speed of light) for the radio wave to reach the object and return. The direction of the object relative to the radar station is determined by the direction of the rotating antenna when the reflected portion of the radio wave is received.

- **Secondary surveillance radar,** developed during World War II to correct some of the deficiencies in primary radar, consists of two main components. An interrogator on the ground generates a coded pulse. A transponder on the aircraft receives the signal from the interrogator and "replies."

In air traffic control, a radar display unit combines information from the primary and secondary radar systems and the air traffic control computer system to display aircraft location and other pertinent information. Computers designed primarily for air traffic control process all of this information and use it to monitor each aircraft in the sector. The computers can provide controllers with additional information, including the aircraft's identity, altitude, and speed. It can also predict an aircraft's future location, so that controllers are alerted to possible traffic conflicts.

AIR TRAFFIC MANAGEMENT

ARTCCs primarily provide air traffic service to aircraft operating on IFR flight plans within controlled airspace, and principally during the en route phase of flight. ARTCCs are divided into different sectors, each of which is managed by a team of controllers. Each sector must separate aircraft by an appropriate interval (usually either 1,000 feet of altitude or 5 nautical miles of distance) while organizing the flow of traffic across the United States. Center controllers must maintain this flow, adding new airplanes as they take off and distributing departures to their proper airways. Controllers at ARTCCs must be adept at visualizing three-dimensional flows of traffic and at visualizing future aircraft locations. While they do so, they must also be constantly evaluating current traffic flow and developing strategies to eliminate any potential traffic conflicts—all while each aircraft they monitor flies at nearly 600 mph.

TRACON

As we briefly reviewed in Chapter 1, TRACON controllers are responsible for the safety of aircraft within the immediate vicinity of the airport. In the TRACON, controllers use radar to combine data provided by the ARTCC about inbound flows of aircraft to ensure properly spaced aircraft on final approaches to runways. While doing so, they must also maneuver departing aircraft out of their airspace and handle aircraft flying to multiple airports.

TRACON controllers must see that all aircraft are separated by at least 1,000 feet vertically or 3 miles in trail.

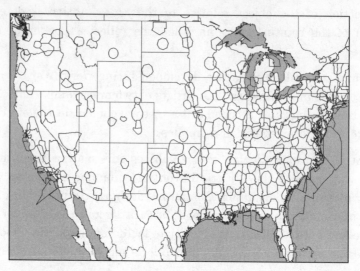

TRACON locations in the United States

Control Tower

Tower controllers monitor the operation of aircraft taxiing in the airport and those that are departing and arriving. If only one runway is available, the local controller arranges to integrate arrivals and departures, using the runway as efficiently as possible. At airports with multiple but crossing runways, the local controller must be sure that runways are used effectively but prevent arriving and departing aircraft from coming too close to one another.

Flight Progress Strips

Although air traffic controllers rely on a number of computers and other electronic equipment to perform their duties, they also use handwritten and computer-generated forms to track aircraft and document changes in any assigned route, altitude, or airspeed. This information is marked on forms called flight progress strips. There are two flight strip formats, adapted for the unique needs of two air traffic control facilities; one is used by ARTCC controllers, and a different one is used by TRACON controllers. Generally, however, the information recorded is the same. Although you're not likely to understand most of what is described in the ARTCC flight progress strip chart below, it can't hurt to become familiar with it if you're planning on a career as an air traffic controller.

ARTCC STRIPS

A flight progress strip in an ARTCC is much larger and contains more information than a TRACON flight strip. Each flight strip has predefined areas for "blocks" of data. Every ARTCC controller must adhere to the same format in filling out a flight progress strip.

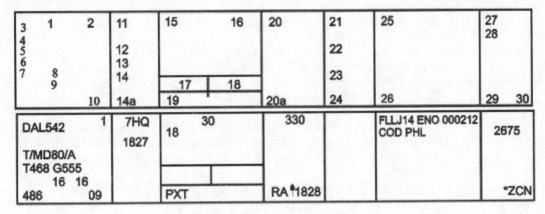

ARTCC flight progress strip

Block Number	Information Recorded
1	Verification symbol (if required)
2	Revision number
3	Aircraft identification
4	Number of aircraft (if more than one), Traffic Alert and Collision Avoidance System (TCAS)/heavy aircraft indicator (if appropriate), type of aircraft, aircraft equipment suffix
5	Filed true airspeed
6	Sector number
7	Computer identification number (if required)
8	Estimated ground speed
9	Revised ground speed or strip request (SR) originator
10	Strip number
11	Previous position fix
12	Estimated time over previous position fix
13	Revised estimated time over previous position fix
14	Actual time over previous position fix, or actual departure time entered on first fix posting after departure

Block Number	Information Recorded
14a	Plus time expressed in minutes from the previous position fix to the posted fix
15	Center-estimated time over position fix (hrs/mins), or clearance information for departing aircraft
16	Arrows to indicate whether aircraft is departing (↑) or arriving (↓)
17	Pilot-estimated time over position fix
18	Actual time over position fix, time leaving holding fix, arrival time at nonapproach control airport, or symbol indicating cancellation of IFR flight plan for arriving aircraft, or departure time (actual or assumed)
19	Position fix. For departing aircraft, add proposed departure time
20	Altitude information (in hundreds of feet)
21	Next posted position fix or coordination fix
22	Pilot's estimated time over next position fix
23	Arrows to indicate north (↑), south (↓), east (→), or west (←) direction of flight (if required)
24	Requested altitude
25	Point of origin, route as required for control and data relay, and destination
26	Pertinent remarks, minimum fuel, point out/radar vector/speed adjustment information or sector/position number
27	Mode 3/A beacon code (if applicable)
28	Miscellaneous control data (expected further clearance time, time cleared for approach, etc.)
29 and 30	Transfer of control data and coordination indicators

TERMINAL FLIGHT PROGRESS STRIPS

The flight progress strips used in towers and TRACONs are smaller than ARTCC flight progress strips and require less data. Three different formats are used for tower and TRACON flight strips, based on the aircraft's status: arrival, departure, and overflight.

AIRCRAFT IDENTIFICATION

Civilian aircraft pilots use FAA-assigned serial numbers to identify themselves. Military aircraft pilots use a serial number and their service name.

Every airline uses its own three-letter abbreviation to identify its aircraft. Here are some of the more common airline abbreviations:

Airline	Aircraft ID
American Airlines	AAL
Continental	COA
Delta	DAL
Federal Express	FDX
JetBlue	JBU
Southwest	SWA
United	UAL
UPS	UPS
U.S. Airways	USA

A suffix code follows every aircraft equipment abbreviation. Here are some of the more common codes:

Suffix	Aircraft Equipment
	No DME
/T	Transponder with no Mode C
/U	Transponder with Mode C
	DME
/B	Transponder with no Mode C
/A	Transponder with Mode C
	TACAN Only
/N	Transponder with no Mode C
/P	Transponder with Mode C
	Area Navigation (RNAV)
/C	LORAN-C, VOR/DME, or Inertial Navigation System (INS), transponder with no Mode C
/I	LORAN-C, VOR/DME, or Inertial Navigation System (INS), transponder with Mode C
	Advanced RNAV with Transponder and Mode C *(If an aircraft is unable to operate with a transponder and/or Mode C, it reverts to appropriate code listed under Area Navigation.)*
/E	Flight Management System (FMS) with DME; DME and Inertial Reference Unit (IRU) position updating
/F	Flight Management System (FMS) with DME; DME position updating
/G	Global Navigation Satellite System (GNSS), including GPS or WAAS, with en route and terminal capability
/R	Required Navigation Performance (RNP). The aircraft meets the RNP type prescribed for the route segment(s), route(s) and/or area concerned

Clearance Abbreviations

The following chart shows some of the more common abbreviations and controller stripmarking symbols used on flight progress strips.

Abbreviation	Meaning
A	Cleared to airport (point of intended landing)
B	Center clearance delivered
C	ATC clears (when clearance is relayed through non-ATC facility)
CAF	Cleared as filed
D	Cleared to depart from the position fix
F	Cleared to the position fix
H	Cleared to hold and instructions issued
L	Cleared to land
N	Clearance not delivered
O	Cleared to the outer marker
PD	Cleared to climb/descend at pilot's discretion
Q	Cleared to fly specified sectors of navigational aid (NAVAID) defined in terms of courses, bearings, radials or quadrants within a designated radius
T	Cleared through (for landing and takeoff through intermediate point)
V	Cleared over the position fix
X	Cleared to cross (airway, route, radial) at [point]
Z	Tower jurisdiction
BC	Back course approach
CT	Contact approach
FA	Final approach
FMS	Flight management system approach
GPS	GPS approach
I	Initial approach
ILS	ILS approach
MA	Missed approach
MLS	Microwave Landing System approach
NDB	Nondirectional radio beacon approach

Abbreviation	Meaning
OTP	VFR conditions on top
PA	Precision approach
PT	Procedure turn
RA	Resolution advisory—pilot-reported Traffic Alert and Collision Avoidance System (TCAS) event
RH	Runway heading
RNAV	Area Navigation approach
RP	Report immediately upon passing (position fix/altitude)
RX	Report crossing
SA	Surveillance approach
SI	Straight-in approach
TA	TACAN approach
TL	Turn left
TR	Turn right
VA	Visual approach
VR	VOR approach

Air Traffic Controller Stripmarking Symbols

Symbols	Meaning
T→ ( )	Depart (direction, if specified)
↑	Climb and maintain
↓	Descend and maintain
→	Cruise
@	At
X	Cross
‑M→	Maintain
⇗	Join or intercept airway/jet route/track or course
=	While in controlled airspace
△	While in control area
⇗△	Enter control area
△⇗	Out of control area
NW⊘ ⊘ NE ⊖→ E	Cleared to enter, depart or through surface area. Indicated direction of flight by arrow and appropriate compass letter. Maintain Special VFR conditions (altitude if appropriate) while in surface area.
250 K	Aircraft requested to adjust speed to 250 knots
-20 K	Aircraft requested to reduce speed 20 knots
+30 K	Aircraft requested to increase speed 30 knots
Ⓦ	Local Special VFR operations in the vicinity of (name) airport are authorized until (time). Maintain special VFR conditions (altitude if appropriate).
>	Before
<	After or Past
<u>170</u> (red)	Inappropriate altitude/flight level for direction of flight. (Underline assigned altitude/flight level in red.)
/	Until
( )	Alternate instructions
<u>Restriction</u>	Restriction
↓̲	At or Below
↑̲	At or Above
-(Dash)	From-to (route, time, etc.)
(Alt)B(Alt)	Indicates a block altitude assignment. Altitudes are inclusive, and the first altitude shall be lower than the second. Example: 310B370.
v <	Clearance void if aircraft not off ground by (time)

NOTE: The absence of an airway route number between two fixes in the route of flight indicates "direct"; no symbol or abbreviation is required.

Air Traffic Controller Stripmarking Symbols *(continued)*

Symbols	Meaning
C̶L	Pilot canceled flight plan
✓	EN ROUTE: Aircraft has reported at assigned altitude. Example: 80 ✓.
✓	TERMINAL/FSS: Information forwarded (indicated information forwarded as required)
◯ (red)	EN ROUTE: Information or revised information forwarded. (Circle, in red, inappropriate altitude/flight level for direction of flight or other control information when coordinated. Also circle, in red, the time (minutes and altitude) when a flight plan or estimate is forwarded. Use method in both inter-center and intra-center coordination.)
⑤⓪	Other than assigned altitude reported (circle reported altitude)
H ¹⁰ ₆	DME holding (use with mileages). (Upper figure indicates distance from station to DME fix, lower figure indicates length of holding pattern.) In this example, the DME fix is 10 miles out with a 6-mile pattern indicated.
(mi.)(dir.)	DME arc of VORTAC, TACAN, or MLS
C̶ (freq.)	Contact (facility) or (freq.), (time, fix, or altitude if appropriate). Insert frequency only when it is other than standard.
R	Radar contact
R	EN ROUTE: Requested altitude (preceding altitude information)
R̸	Radar service terminated
R̸	Radar contact lost
RV	Radar vector
RX	Pilot resumed own navigation
Ⓡ	Radar handoff (circle symbol when handoff completed)
E (red)	EMERGENCY
W (red)	WARNING
P	Point out initiated. Indicate the appropriate facility, sector or position. Example: PZFW.
FUEL	Minimum fuel
NOTE: The absence of an airway route number between two fixes in the route of flight indicates "direct"; no symbol or abbreviation is required.	

SUMMING IT UP

- The U.S. air traffic control system, which encompasses all of the country's airports and the airspace over the United States, has four components: communications, navigation, surveillance, and air traffic management.

- Air traffic controllers are responsible for separating aircraft operating on the runways and taxiways of airports, lighting systems on runways and taxiways, and airport beacons.

- Depending on the amount and type of air traffic in a given area, airspace is divided into six categories. The type and level of air traffic control service provided depends on the airspace classification and whether the airspace is controlled or uncontrolled.

- Navigation systems in use by U.S. air traffic controllers include nondirectional radio beacons (NDBs) and VHF Omni-directional Range (VOR).

- The airway system in the United States consists of low-altitude airways—Victor airways—from ground level to 18,000 feet, and jet routes at 18,000 feet and above.

- Navigational systems that provide straight-line navigation are collectively known as Area Navigation, or RNAV. They include: long-range navigation-C (LORAN-C), Global Navigation Satellite System (GNSS), Global Positioning System (GPS), and Instrument Landing System (ILS).

- The most critical element of air traffic control is the communications systems. The FAA operates more than 5,000 separate communications systems and frequencies.

- Most air traffic control communications include identification of the ATC facility or the intended recipient of the message, the location to which the aircraft is cleared to fly (the clearance limit), the altitude at which the aircraft should fly, and any other pertinent clearance or weather information.

- Air Route Traffic Control Centers (ARTCCs) are divided into different sectors, each of which is managed by a team of controllers. Each sector must separate aircraft by an appropriate interval while organizing the flow of traffic across the United States.

- Controllers at ARTCCs must be adept at visualizing three-dimensional flows of traffic and at visualizing future aircraft locations. While they do so, they must also be constantly evaluating current traffic flow and developing strategies to eliminate potential traffic conflicts.

Weather and
Air Traffic Control

chapter 4

OVERVIEW

- **Weather forecasting services**

- **FAA facilities for disseminating weather reports**

- **Weather observations**

- **Interpreting the aviation routine weather report**

- **Aviation weather forecasts**

- **Terminal aerodrome forecasts**

- **Aviation area forecasts**

- **In-flight aviation weather advisories**

- **Convective outlook**

- **Severe weather watch bulletins**

- **CWSU products**

- **Summing it up**

Weather has more influence on aviation and air traffic control than perhaps any other variable. Although air traffic controllers are not directly involved in weather forecasting, they must disseminate weather information to pilots and plan for its effects on navigation. This requires that controllers understand the basics of the weather navigation system and how weather is reported and forecast in the United States.

WEATHER FORECASTING SERVICES

Providing weather services to aviation is a joint effort of the National Weather Service (NWS) and the FAA, with the aid of other aviation-oriented groups and companies. It is the role of the NWS to make all official forecasts and observations across the country, and the organization owns and operates most of the weather observation and forecasting equipment in the United States. The NWS collects and analyzes meteorological data and prepares forecasts for aviation users and others. It gathers surface observations from automated and human-operated stations, weather radars, and satellites. Different organizations within the NWS use this data to issue current weather observations and develop and issue forecasts, warnings, and outlooks. The NWS offices most directly involved in aviation and air navigation are:

- The Storm Prediction Center (SPC)
- The Aviation Weather Center (AWC)
- The Weather Forecast Office (WFO)

Storm Prediction Center

The NWS Storm Prediction Center (SPC) in Norman, OK, is responsible for monitoring and forecasting severe weather throughout the United States. Severe weather outlooks, severe weather forecasts, and weather watches are developed and issued by storm predication meteorologists at the SPC.

Aviation Weather Center

The Aviation Weather Center (AWC) in Kansas City, MO, issues warnings, forecasts, and analyses of hazardous weather specifically for aviation purposes. The AWC identifies existing or imminent weather hazards to in-flight aircraft and issues alerts and warnings to aviation workers. It also produces operational forecasts of weather conditions expected during the upcoming two days that may affect domestic and international air travel.

Weather Forecast Offices

Each Weather Forecast Office (WFO) listed here gathers observations over a large region and issues public and aviation forecasts and warnings for its area of responsibility. In particular, WFOs issue terminal aerodrome forecasts (TAFs) for larger airports located in their regions. They also issue weather watches and warnings to the general public.

Weather Forecast Offices

ALABAMA
Birmingham
Huntsville
Mobile

ALASKA
Anchorage
Fairbanks
Juneau

AMERICAN SAMOA
Pago Pago

ARIZONA
Flagstaff
Phoenix
Tucson

ARKANSAS
Little Rock

CALIFORNIA
Eureka
Los Angeles
Sacramento
San Diego
San Francisco Bay Area
San Joaquin Valley

COLORADO
Denver/Boulder
Grand Junction
Pueblo

FLORIDA
Jacksonville
Key West
Melbourne
Miami
Tallahassee
Tampa Bay Area

GEORGIA
Atlanta

GUAM
Guam

HAWAII
Honolulu

IDAHO
Boise
Pocatello/Idaho Falls

ILLINOIS
Central Illinois
Chicago

INDIANA
Indianapolis
Northern Indiana

IOWA
Des Moines
Quad Cities

KANSAS
Dodge City
Goodland
Topeka
Wichita

KENTUCKY
Jackson
Louisville
Paducah

LOUISIANA
Lake Charles
New Orleans/Baton Rouge
Shreveport

MAINE
Caribou
Portland

MARYLAND
Baltimore/Washington

MASSACHUSETTS
Boston

MICHIGAN
Detroit
Grand Rapids
Marquette
North Central Lower Michigan

MINNESOTA
Duluth
Minneapolis

MISSISSIPPI
Jackson

MISSOURI
Kansas City/Pleasant Hill
St. Louis
Springfield

MONTANA
Billings
Glasgow
Great Falls
Missoula

NEBRASKA
Hastings
North Platte
Omaha

NEVADA
Elko
Las Vegas
Reno

NEW JERSEY
Philadelphia (PA)/Mt. Holly

NEW MEXICO
Albuquerque

NEW YORK
Albany
Binghamton
Buffalo
New York City

NORTH CAROLINA
Newport/Morehead City
Raleigh/Durham
Wilmington

NORTH DAKOTA
Bismarck
Eastern North Dakota

OHIO
Cincinnati
Cleveland

OKLAHOMA
Oklahoma City
Tulsa

OREGON
Medford
Pendleton
Portland

PENNSYLVANIA
Central Pennsylvania
Philadelphia/Mt. Holly (NJ)
Pittsburgh

PUERTO RICO
San Juan

SOUTH CAROLINA
Charleston
Columbia
Greenville/Spartanburg

SOUTH DAKOTA
Aberdeen
Rapid City
Sioux Falls

TENNESSEE
Knoxville/Tri-Cities
Memphis
Nashville

TEXAS
Amarillo
Austin/San Antonio
Brownsville
Corpus Christi
Dallas/Fort Worth
El Paso
Houston/Galveston
Lubbock
Midland/Odessa
San Angelo

UTAH
Salt Lake City

VERMONT
Burlington

VIRGINIA
Baltimore/Washington
Roanoke
Wakefield

WASHINGTON
Seattle/Tacoma
Spokane

WEST VIRGINIA
Charleston

WISCONSIN
Green Bay
La Crosse
Milwaukee

WYOMING
Cheyenne
Riverton

FAA FACILITIES FOR DISSEMINATING WEATHER REPORTS

The FAA is part of the U.S. Department of Transportation (DOT); the NWS is part of the U.S. Department of Commerce. Nonetheless, the two organizations work closely to provide meteorological information to pilots and controllers. The precise role of the FAA in this respect is to disseminate the weather products developed by the NWS to specific aviation users. The FAA facilities primarily responsible for weather dissemination are Flight Service Stations (FSS) and weather service units located in larger air traffic control facilities.

Flight Service Stations

The FAA is in the process of modernizing the Flight Service Station (FSS) program. In late 2005, FSS operations were contracted to the Lockheed-Martin Corporation, which plans to significantly upgrade, modernize, and consolidate the network. At present, FSSs are the primary sources of aviation weather briefing services for general aviation pilots before and during flights. In addition to providing pre-flight and in-flight briefings, they supply recorded weather briefings, scheduled and unscheduled weather broadcasts, and weather support to flights in their areas. Currently, the United States has about 100 FSSs; however, Lockheed-Martin's contract with the FAA stipulates that many of these stations will be consolidated into hub facilities.

Direct User Access Terminal Service

Many pilots begin their weather briefing with the Direct User Access Terminal Service (DUATS) provided by the FAA, or with similar systems operated by commercial vendors. DUATS provides current FAA weather and flight plan filing services to certified pilots. The computer-based system receives and stores updated weather reports and forecasts, airport conditions, and navigation aid conditions. Pilots using personal computers with Internet access can log on to request specific types of weather briefings and other pertinent data for planned flights. Pilots may also file, amend, or cancel flight plans using DUATS online. Many pilots, after self-briefing using DUATS, will call the FSS by phone for a more detailed weather briefing.

Once in flight, a pilot can contact the FSS by radio to activate or cancel flight plans or to inquire about actual or forecast weather conditions. In an effort to readily disseminate important safety-of-flight information, the FSSs operate two in-flight advisory systems: the Hazardous In-flight Weather Advisory Service (HIWAS) and the En Route Flight Advisory Service (EFAS).

Hazardous In-flight Weather Advisory Service

Hazardous In-flight Weather Advisory Service (HIWAS) is a continuous recorded broadcast of in-flight weather advisories accessible to a pilot at any time. HIWAS broadcasts 24 hours a day, with no interruptions except during emergency situations. Each report includes a summary of in-flight weather advisories, center weather advisories, severe weather watch bulletins, and reports on any other weather not included in current hazardous weather advisories. Whenever a HIWAS broadcast is updated, it is announced on all communication and navigation frequencies to advise pilots of the revision.

En Route Flight Advisory Service

The En Route Flight Advisory Service (EFAS), also called Flight Watch, is provided by selected FSSs on a common frequency: 122.0 MHz below flight level 180 (18,000 feet), and on assigned discrete frequencies to aircraft at flight levels 180 and above. The purpose of EFAS is to provide en route aircraft with timely and pertinent weather data tailored to the aircraft's altitude and route using the most current available sources of aviation meteorological information. To take advantage of the service, pilots request a report by contacting Flight Watch on the common frequency. The FSS closest to the pilot's reported position immediately responds to the request. EFAS can provide real-time information such as position and intensity of approaching storms and weather and airport conditions.

Center Weather Unit Specialists

You will probably not be surprised to learn that weather is the most common reason for air traffic delays and re-routings. The ATCSCC in Virginia, the ARTCCs, and some larger TRACONs are supported by Center Weather Unit Specialists, who are responsible for disseminating meteorological information pertaining to air traffic flow management. Controllers need timely weather information to perform their duties as efficiently as possible. Within each ARTCC, a Center Weather Service Unit (CWSU) provides weather consultation, forecasts, and advice to air traffic managers and controllers. These weather units are staffed by NWS meteorologists and FAA traffic management personnel.

WEATHER OBSERVATIONS

The most basic required component of all weather services is the station weather observation. Weather observations are measurements and estimates of existing weather conditions at the surface and aloft. When recorded and transmitted, an observation becomes a report; these reports are the basis of all weather analyses, forecasts, advisories, and briefings in aviation. They include the following:

- **Upper-air observations:** Upper-air weather data is received from sounding balloons (known as radiosonde observations) and pilot weather reports. Upper-air observations provide forecasters with temperature, humidity, pressure, and wind data at the upper altitudes.

- **Radar observations:** The NWS, in cooperation with the Department of Defense, operates a network of high-powered Doppler weather radars across the United States. These modern weather radars provide detailed information about precipitation, winds, and weather systems in the surrounding 250 miles of each radar station. Doppler technology allows the radar to provide measurements of winds at different heights within a storm, making it possible for forecasters to detect severe weather such as wind shear, hail, and tornadoes.

- **Terminal Doppler weather radars:** In addition to the primary weather radar network, the FAA has begun installing a limited number of terminal Doppler weather radars (TDWRs) near several major U.S. airports. TDWRs alert and warn airport controllers of approaching wind shear, gust fronts, and heavy precipitation that could create hazardous conditions for landing and departing aircraft. The NWS can also use FAA airport surveillance radars primarily designed for air traffic control purposes. Newer air traffic control radars are capable of displaying six different precipitation intensity levels to controllers and weather service personnel.

- **Satellite systems:** NWS forecasters have access to a number of orbiting satellites belonging either to the United States or to international partners. The satellites provide visible, infrared (IR), and other types of images of current weather around the world. These images are available on an almost real-time basis to NWS and FAA facilities for use in air traffic control situations.

- **Surface aviation weather observations:** Surface aviation weather observations, or aviation routine weather reports (METARs), are specially designed for the aviation industry, so they differ from weather observations provided to the general public. In particular, METARs focus on safety-specific information, such as cloud type and height, visibility, wind speed and direction, and hazardous weather conditions. A network of airport weather observations supplies routine up-to-date surface weather information to pilots and controllers. These stations typically report once per hour, but they are available at any time for special weather observations.

INTERPRETING THE AVIATION ROUTINE WEATHER REPORT

A METAR is a description of weather conditions at a given site and time. METARs are not only used by pilots and air traffic controllers to determine whether VFR or IFR flights can be conducted, but they also provide input for the forecaster to develop aviation-related forecasts. The METAR code structure has been standardized internationally; however, each country is allowed to make modifications or exceptions as it sees fit. The United States, for example, chooses to report temperature and dew point in degrees Celsius, but still usees statute miles and hundreds of feet to measure cloud height and visibility. (Other countries use metric equivalents.)

A METAR is a simple one- or two-line report composed of coded data elements separated by character spaces (the exception is the temperature and dew point data, which are separated by a slash). When an element does not occur or cannot be observed, it is omitted from the report. In general, however, a METAR report contains the following twelve elements:

1. Type of report
2. International Civil Aviation Organization (ICAO) station identifier
3. Date and time of report
4. Modifier (if needed)
5. Wind speed
6. Visibility
7. Runway visual range (RVR) (if available)
8. Weather phenomena

(9) Sky condition

(10) Temperature/dew point group

(11) Altimeter setting

(12) Remarks (if any)

What follows are descriptions of each of these elements, with their positions in a typical METAR highlighted for reference.

Type of Report

METAR KLAX 140651Z AUTO 27010KT 1SM R35L/4500V6000FT -RA BR BKN030 10/08 A2990 RMK AO2

There are two types of METAR reports: regularly scheduled and nonroutine aviation selected special weather reports (SPECI). Regularly scheduled METARs are observed hourly between 45 minutes after the hour and the next hour. A SPECI is a nonroutine METAR made whenever weather conditions change enough to meet SPECI change criteria. In general, if the weather changes abruptly or conditions shift from VFR to IFR navigation or vice versa, a SPECI observation is transmitted. This example is a standard METAR report.

ICAO Station Identifier

METAR **_KLAX_** 140651Z AUTO 27010KT 1SM R35L/4500V6000FT -RA BR BKN030 10/08 A2990 RMK AO2

METARs use International Civil Aviation Organization (ICAO) four-letter station identifiers to note where the observation is made. In the continental United States, the more commonly used three-letter airport identifier is prefixed with the letter K. For example, in the example above, the code for Los Angeles airport (LAX) becomes KLAX. Outside the U.S. mainland, the first one or two letters of the ICAO identifier indicate in which region of the world and country (or state) the station is located. Pacific U.S. locations such as Alaska, Hawaii, and the Mariana Islands begin with the letter P, followed by an A, H, or G, respectively. Here are a few more examples:

- Chicago (ORD) becomes KORD

- Anchorage (ANC) becomes PANC

- Honolulu (HNL) becomes PHNL

Canadian station identifiers always start with the letter C, followed by a Y and a two-letter code identifying the specific airport:

- Toronto becomes CYYZ

- Montreal becomes CYMZ

- Vancouver becomes CYVR

Mexican and western Caribbean station identifiers start with the letter M, followed by a country identifier and a two-letter code identifying the specific airport. The identifier for the eastern Caribbean is T, followed by a country identifier, then a two-letter code that identifies the specific airport:

- Mexico City (Mexico) becomes MMMX

- Guantanamo (Cuba) becomes MUGT

- Santo Domingo (Dominican Republic) becomes MDGM

- Nassau (the Bahamas) becomes MYNN

- San Juan (Puerto Rico) becomes TJSJ

Date and Time of Report

METAR KLAX **_140651Z_** AUTO 27010KT 1SM R35L/4500V6000FT -RA BR BKN030 10080 A2990 RMK AO2

The date and time of an observation is recorded in a METAR as a six-digit date/time group, appended with the letter Z to denote UTC time. The first two digits are the date (no month is recorded); the second two are the hour; the final two digits are minutes. The weather conditions listed in the example above were observed on the 14th day of the month at 6:51 UTC time.

Modifier

METAR KLAX 140651Z **_AUTO_** 27010KT 1SM R35L/4500V6000FT -RA BR BKN030 10/08 A2990 RMK AO2

When needed, a modifier follows the date/time element. The modifier shown above—AUTO—identifies the report as an automated weather report, with no human intervention. When AUTO appears as a modifier, the code "AO1" or "AO2" will also appear in the remarks section of the report (which we'll cover in a bit). These indicate the type of precipitation sensor used at the station.

If AUTO is absent from the report, it means that it was either observed by a human or that the automated report had human input. (The modifier COR identifies a corrected report sent out to replace an earlier report that contained an error.)

Wind Speed

METAR KLAX 140651Z AUTO **_27010KT_** 1SM R35L/4500V6000FT -RA BR BKN030 10/08 A2990 RMK AO2

Wind speed is reported as a five-digit code—six digits if wind speed is higher than 99 knots. The first three digits represent the direction from which the wind is blowing in tens of degrees off true north. Directions less than 100 degrees are preceded with a zero. The wind in the example above is blowing from 270 degrees (west) at 10 knots.

The next two digits represent the average wind speed in knots, measured or estimated. If wind speed is higher than 99 knots, average wind speed appears as the fourth, fifth, and sixth digits. For example, if average wind speed in the above METAR were 105 knots instead of 10 knots, the wind code above would read: 270105KT. If wind speed is less than 3 knots, the wind speed is reported in all zeros. The wind code above would read: 00000KT. If the wind is gusty, with speeds of 10 knots or more between peaks and lulls, a METAR will include the letter "G" (denoting "gust") after the numbers in the wind speed code, followed by the highest gust reported. In the above example, if winds were gusting to 20 knots, the code would read: 27010G20KT.

The abbreviation KT is appended to the wind speed code to denote the use of knots as the unit of measurement for wind speed. Other countries may use kilometers per hour or meters per second. If the wind direction is variable by 60 degrees or more and the speed is greater than 6 knots, a variable group consisting of the extremes of the wind directions separated by the letter "V" (denoting "variable") will follow the wind group. If this were the case in the above example, it would read: 27010G20KT 040V120. The wind direction may also be considered variable if the wind speed is 6 knots or less and varies in direction. This is indicated with the contraction VRB; for example, VRB04KT.

WIND REMARKS

Facilities with a wind recorder and automated weather reporting systems include peak wind (PK WND) in the remarks element whenever peak wind exceeds 25 knots. The peak wind remark includes three digits for direction and two or three digits for speed, followed by the time of occurrence in hours and minutes. (If the hour can be inferred from the report time, only the minutes are reported.) For example, PK WND 28045/15 means that at 15 minutes past the hour, the highest wind gust of 45 knots from 280 degrees was observed.

If a windshift has occurred, WSHFT will be included in the remarks element, followed by the time the windshift began (only minutes are reported if the hour can be inferred from time of observation). A windshift is indicated by a change in wind direction of 45 degrees or more in less than 15 minutes with sustained winds of 10 knots or more throughout the windshift. The code "FROPA" may be entered following the time if the windshift is the result of a frontal passage. For example, WSHFT 30 FROPA means that at 30 minutes past the hour, the wind shifted as a weather front passed through the airport.

Visibility

METAR KLAX 140651Z AUTO 27010KT **1SM** R35L/4500V6000FT -RA BR BKN030 10/08 A2990 RMK AO2

Prevailing visibility is reported in statute miles (followed by a space and then fractions of statute miles if needed) and the letters "SM." Other countries may use meters or kilometers rather than statute miles. Prevailing visibility, which is considered representative of visibility conditions at the observing site, is defined as the greatest visibility equaled or exceeded throughout at least one-half of the horizon circle, which need not be continuous. When visibilities are less than 7 miles, the restriction to visibility is noted in the weather element of a METAR. The only exception to this rule occurs if volcanic ash, low-drifting dust, sand, or snow is observed. These are reported even if they do not restrict visibility to less than 7 miles. In the example above, visibility is one statute mile.

VISIBILITY REMARKS

If tower or surface visibility is less than 4 statute miles, the lesser of the two values is reported in the body of the report and the greater is reported in the remarks. For example, if tower visibility is 1 1/2 statute miles and surface visibility is 2 statute miles, the METAR would read TWR VIS 1 1/2, with SFC VIS 2 in the remarks.

Since automated visibility-measuring equipment can measure only visibilities between 0.25 and 10 statute miles, any visibility less than one-quarter of a statute mile is reported as M1/4SM and visibilities greater than 10 statute miles are reported as 10SM.

If the prevailing visibility rapidly increases or decreases by one-half of a statute mile or more during observation and the average prevailing visibility is less than 3 statute miles, visibility is considered variable. Variable visibility is recorded in the remarks with the minimum and maximum visibility values separated by a "V": VIS 1/2V2.

Runway Visual Range

METAR KLAX 140651Z AUTO 27010KT 1SM *R35L/4500V6000FT* –RA BR BKN030 10/08 A2990 RMK AO2

The automated runway visual range (RVR) measures visibility in hundreds of feet at a specific runway. If RVR is available at an airport, it is shown in a METAR only if the prevailing visibility is 1 statute mile or less and/or the RVR value is 6,000 feet or less. The RVR code follows the visibility element in the METAR and is recorded by following these four designations:

1 R = identifies the group

2 Runway number

3 Parallel runway designator (if needed)

4 Slash followed by measured visual range in feet (FT)

If the RVR varies by more than one reportable value, the lowest and highest values are recorded, separated by the letter "V." For example:

R35L/4500V6000FT

In this element, RVR measured visibility varies between 4,500 and 6,000 feet. The RVR equipment is measuring the visibility on runway 35 Left.

When the observed RVR is above the maximum value that can be detected by the system (6,000 feet), it is reported as P6000. When the observed RVR is below the minimum value detectable by the system (usually 600 feet), it is reported as M0600.

Observed Weather Phenomena

METAR KLAX 140651Z AUTO 27010KT 1SM R35L/4500V6000FT *–RA BR* BKN030 10/08 A2990 RMK AO2

Observed weather phenomena follow the visibility elements on a METAR. It can be divided into two categories: qualifiers and weather phenomena.

QUALIFIERS

Some forms of precipitation, primarily rain and snow, are assigned additional attributes, called qualifiers. These measure intensity levels ranging from light to heavy. The intensity qualifier is a plus or minus sign (+ or −) preceding the type of precipitation. The minus sign denotes low-intensity (or light) precipitation; moderate precipitation has no qualifier; and the plus sign denotes high-intensity (or heavy) precipitation. Other codes include "BL" for blowing, "SH" for showers, and "FZ" for freezing. "TS" indicates that thunder accompanies the precipitation. In the example, light rain (−RA) is recorded.

WEATHER PHENOMENA

The next element denotes the type of weather that is reducing visibility. If more than one type is observed, the appropriate contractions are combined into a single code, with the predominant type first. These can include:

- Precipitation type

- Visibility obscurations

- Weather beginning or ending

Precipitation Type

For air traffic control purposes, precipitation includes any form of water particle—liquid or solid—that falls from the atmosphere and reaches the ground. Here are a few examples of precipitation types and associated codes:

- RA: rain

- SN: snow

- DZ: drizzle

The code "UP" means "unknown precipitation." This is used only at automated sites, and it is recorded when light precipitation is falling but the precipitation discriminator cannot determine the type. This usually happens when rain and snow are falling at the same time.

Visibility Obscurations

Anything in the atmosphere other than precipitation that reduces horizontal visibility is termed visibility obscuration. Some examples:

- Mist restricting visibility code (BR) is used only when visibility ranges from 5/8 mile to 6 miles

- Fog restricting visibility code (FG) is used only when fog limits visibility to less than 5/8 mile

- Haze code (HZ) is used to indicate the presence of atmospheric moisture, dust, smoke, or humidity that diminishes visibility

Refer to the table below for a complete list of weather phenomena codes used in METARs.

Qualifiers	Precipitation	Obscuration	Other
+ Heavy	DZ Drizzle	BR Mist	PO Dust/sand whirls
– Light	RA Rain	FG Fog	SQ Squalls
BL Blowing	SN Snow	DU Dust	FC Funnel cloud
SH Showers	SG Snow grains	SA Sand	+FC Tornado or waterspout
TS Thunder	IC Ice crystals	HZ Haze	SS Sandstorm
FZ Freezing	PL Ice pellets	PY Spray	DS Dust storm
	GR Hail	VA Volcanic ash	
	GS Small hail or snow pellets	FU Smoke	
	UP Unknown precipitation		

Weather Beginning or Ending

When rain or thunder begins or ends during the hour previous to the METAR observation, the remarks element should show the beginning and ending times. Types of precipitation may be combined if beginning or ending times are the same. For example, RAB05E30SNB30E45 means that rain began at 5 minutes past the hour and ended at 30 minutes past the hour, and snow began at 30 minutes past the hour and ended at 45 minutes past the hour. A remark of TSB05E45 would indicate that a thunderstorm began at 05 minutes past the hour and ended at 45 minutes past the hour.

Sky Condition

```
METAR KLAX 140651Z AUTO 27010KT 1SM R35L/4500V6000FT –RA BR BKN030 10/08
A2990 RMK AO2
```

Sky condition reports the height of the clouds above the observation site and records what percentage of the sky is cloud-covered. It is always reported as a fraction of sky cover and the height of the clouds. In certain circumstances, cloud type is also reported.

SKY COVER AND CLOUD HEIGHT

A clear sky, layer of clouds, or an obscuring phenomenon is reported by one of the six sky cover codes shown here. When more than one layer of cloud exists, the layers are reported in ascending order of height. For each layer above a lower layer or layers, the sky cover for that higher layer is considered the total sky cover that includes all lower layers. In other words, the total of the cloud layers below and at the reported height determines what sky cover is reported. The amount of sky cover is reported in eighths of the sky, using the contractions listed below.

Abbreviation	Description	Sky Coverage
*SKC or CLR	Clear	0 or 0 below 12,000
FEW	Few	> 0 but < 2/8 of sky
SCT	Scattered	3/8–4/8 of sky
BKN	Broken	5/8–7/8 of sky
OVC	Overcast	8/8 (all) of sky
VV	Vertical visibility (indefinite ceiling)	8/8 (all) of sky

* SKC is used only at non-automated stations. The abbreviation CLR is always used at automated stations, since these stations do not detect clouds above 12,000 feet.

In METAR reports, the base of the cloud layers is reported and measured in hundreds of feet above ground level. For example, SCT020 means that a scattered (3/8 to 4/8 sky coverage) layer of clouds has been observed 2,000 feet above the ground. If a layer of clouds is observed at 2,000 feet and covering 3/8 of the sky and another layer of clouds covering 2/8 of the sky is observed at 4,000 feet, the *total* sky coverage at and below 4,000 feet would be 5/8, which qualifies as broken. Therefore, the METAR report would read as follows: SCT020 BKN040.

CLOUD TYPE

If towering cumulus clouds (TCU) or cumulonimbus clouds (CB) are present, they are reported as the height representing their base. For example, SCT040TCU describes scattered towering cumulus clouds with a base height of 40 feet, and BKN025CB describes broken cumulonimbus clouds with a base height of 25 feet. TCU indicates that the atmosphere is unstable and conducive to turbulence. A CB, or thunderstorm cloud, contains aviation weather hazards such as turbulence, icing, hail, and low-level wind shear (LLWS), and must be reported.

INDEFINITE CEILING/HEIGHTS (VERTICAL VISIBILITY)

An indefinite ceiling means that a cloud essentially extends to the ground (heavy fog, mist, or drizzle), and all that can be measured is the distance one can see looking straight up before fog, mist, or drizzle obscures visibility. The height into an indefinite ceiling is preceded with the code "VV" followed by three digits indicating the vertical visibility in hundreds of feet above ground level. It is read as "indefinite ceiling" and indicates total obscuration. For example, the code VV002 denotes that the vertical visibility is only 200 feet.

Temperature and Dew Point Group

```
METAR KLAX 140651Z AUTO 27010KT 1SM R35L/4500V6000FT -RA BR BKN030 10/08
A2990 RMK AO2
```

Temperature and dew point are reported in two-digit format in whole degrees Celsius, separated by a slash. Temperatures below zero are prefixed with the letter M. If the temperature is available but the dew point is missing, the temperature is recorded followed by a slash and a blank space. If the temperature is missing, the entire group is omitted from the report. In the example, the temperature is 10 degrees Celsius and the dew point is 8 degrees Celsius.

Altimeter Setting

METAR KLAX 140651Z AUTO 27010KT 1SM R35L/4500V6000FT -RA BR BKN030 10/08 **_A2990_** RMK AO2

The altimeter setting element of a METAR follows the temperature/dew point group and is the last required element in the body of the report. It measures the atmospheric pressure in inches of mercury adjusted for non-standard conditions.

The altimeter setting is usually somewhere around 30.00 inches of mercury. In a METAR, the decimal point is not reported or stated. Instead, it is recorded as a four-digit number representing the pressure to hundredths of an inch of mercury, prefixed with the letter A.

If the pressure is rising or falling rapidly at the time of observation, the remarks element should read PRESRR or PRESFR, respectively. Some stations also include sea-level pressure, which is different from the altimeter setting. This is recorded in the remarks element as "SLP," followed by the sea-level pressure in hectopascals (h/Pa)—a unit of measurement equivalent to millibars (mb). Sea-level pressure is not normally used in air traffic control, but the information is useful to weather forecasters reading the METAR.

Remarks

METAR KLAX 140651Z AUTO 27010KT 1SM R35L/4500V6000FT -RA BR BKN030 10/10 A2990 **_RMK AO2_**

Remarks are included in a METAR to clarify preceding elements or to add information that does not fit into the standard code of an element. If remarks are necessary, the code "RMK" follows the altimeter setting element. Time entries are shown as minutes past the hour if the time reported occurs during the same hour the observation is taken. (If the hour is different, hours and minutes are shown.) Location of phenomena within 5 statute miles of the point of observation will be reported as occurring at the station. Anything occurring between 5 and 10 statute miles from the station is recorded as "in the vicinity" (VC). If it is farther than 10 statute miles from the station, it is recorded as "distant" (DSNT). The direction of phenomena is indicated using the eight main points of the compass: N, NE, E, SE, S, SW, W, NW. Distance remarks are in statute miles except automated lightning remarks, which are recorded in nautical miles. Movements of clouds or weather are indicated by the direction toward which the phenomenon is moving.

The remark in the example above is connected with the "AUTO" modifier, as we saw earlier. An AO1 remark indicates that the report originates at a station that does not have a precipitation discriminator; an AO2 remark indicates that the report originates from a station that has a precipitation discriminator. (A discriminator is an automatic system that detects the type of precipitation present.) In this case, the AUTO modifier means that the information was collected by automated equipment without human input, and the remark clarifies that the station issuing the METAR has a precipitation discriminator.

Many types of remarks appear in METARs—too many to include here. You can obtain a complete list from the National Weather Service, but we've provided examples of the more common ones below, along with their plain-language equivalents.

METAR Remark	Translation
TORNADO B13 6 NE	Tornado observed beginning 13 minutes past the hour 6 miles northeast of the airport.
PK WND 28045/15	The peak wind observed since the last METAR was from 280 degrees at 45 knots. This was observed at 15 minutes past the hour.
WSHFT 30 FROPA	The wind shifted at 30 minutes past the hour and a frontal passage was observed.
OCNL LTGICCG OHD	Occasional lightning in cloud and cloud-to-ground is observed directly overhead.
FRQ LTGICCCCG W	Frequent lightning in cloud, cloud-to-cloud, and cloud-to-ground is observed to the west.
RAB05E30SNB20E55	Rain began at 5 minutes past the hour and ended at 30 minutes past the hour. Snow began at 20 minutes past the hour and ended at 55 minutes past the hour.
TSB05E30	Thunder began at 5 minutes past the hour and ended at 30 minutes past the hour.
TS SE MOV NE	Thunderstorms were observed southeast of the airport moving to the northeast.
CIG 005V010	The ceiling varies between 500 and 1,000 feet above the ground.
BKN014 V OVC	The clouds at 1,400 feet above the ground vary between broken and overcast.
PRESRR	The barometric pressure is rising rapidly.
PRESFR	The barometric pressure is falling rapidly.

Examples and Explanations of METAR Reports

The following examples present weather reports, explanations of the codes used, and the phraseology that an air traffic controller would use to relay the report to a pilot. The phrases or words shown in parentheses would not normally be spoken but are assumed. Review the examples and practice finding the correct phraseology before checking the answers.

Example 1

METAR KMKL 021250Z 33018KT 290V360 1/2SM R31/2600FT SN BLSN FG VV008 00/M03 A2991 RMK RAESNB42

METAR	aviation routine weather report
KMKL	Jackson, TN
021250Z	date 02, time 1250 UTC
33018KT	wind 330 degrees at 18 knots
290V360	wind direction variable between 290 and 360 degrees
1/2SM	visibility one-half statute mile
R31/2600FT	runway 31, RVR 2600
SN	moderate snow
BLSN FG	blowing snow and fog
VV008	indefinite ceiling 800 feet
00/M03	temperature 0°C, dew point −3°C
A2991	altimeter 29.91
RMK	remarks
RAESNB42	rain ended at 42 minutes past the hour, snow began at 42

Jackson (Tennessee), (one two five zero observation), wind three three zero at one eight, wind variable between two niner zero and three six zero, visibility one-half, runway three one RVR, two thousand six hundred, heavy snow, blowing snow, fog, indefinite ceiling eight hundred, temperature zero, dew point minus three, altimeter two niner niner one.

Example 2

METAR KSFO 031453Z VRB02KT 7SM MIFG SKC 15/14 A3012 RMK SLP993

METAR	aviation routine weather report
KSFO	San Francisco, CA
031453Z	date 03, time 1453 UTC
VRB02KT	wind variable at 2 knots
7SM	visibility 7 statute miles
MIFG	shallow fog
SKC	clear
15/14	temperature 15°C, dew point 14°C
A3012	altimeter 30.12
RMK	remarks
SLP993	sea-level pressure 999.3 hectopascals

San Francisco (one four five three observation), wind variable at two, visibility seven, shallow fog, clear, temperature one five, dew point one four, altimeter three zero one two.

Example 3

SPECI KORD 312228Z 28024G36KT 3/4SM +TSRA SQ BKN008 OVC020CB 28/23 A3000 RMK TSB24 TS OHD MOV E

SPECI	aviation selected special weather report
KORD	Chicago O'Hare
312228Z	date 31, time 2228 UTC
28024G36KT	wind 280 at 24 knots, gusts 36 knots
3/4SM	visibility three-quarters statute mile
+TSRA SQ	thunderstorm with heavy rain and squalls
BKN008 OVC020CB	ceiling 800 feet broken, 2,000 feet overcast, cumulonimbus
28/23	temperature 28°C, dew point 23°C
A3000	altimeter 30.00
RMK	remarks
TSB24	thunderstorm began at 24 minutes past the hour
TS OHD MOV E	thunderstorm overhead moving east

Covington (Kentucky) special report, two eight observation, wind two eight zero at two four, gusts three six, visibility three-quarters, thunderstorm, heavy rain, squall, ceiling eight hundred broken, two thousand overcast, cumulonimbus, temperature two eight, dew point two three, altimeter three zero zero zero, thunderstorm began two four, thunderstorm overhead, moving east.

Example 4

METAR KLAX 140651Z AUTO 00000KT 10SM −RA SCT080 12/05 A2990 RMK AO2

METAR	aviation routine weather report
KLAX	Los Angeles, CA
140651Z	date 14, time 0651 UTC
AUTO	automated site
00000KT	calm winds
10SM	visibility 10 statute miles
−RA	light rain
SCT080	8,000 feet scattered
12/05	temperature 12°C, dew point 5°C
A2990	altimeter 29.90
RMK	remarks
AO2	automated observation with precipitation discriminator

Los Angeles zero six five one automated observation, wind calm, visibility one zero, light rain, eight thousand scattered, temperature one two, dew point five, altimeter two niner niner zero.

Example 5

*SPECI KDEN 241310Z 09014G35KT 1/4SM +SN FG VV002 01/01 A2975 RMK AO2
TWR VIS 1/2 RAE08SNB08*

SPECI	aviation selected special weather report
KDEN	Denver, CO
241310Z	date 24, time 1310 UTC
09014G35KT	wind 090 at 14, gusts to 35 knots
1/4SM	visibility one-quarter statute mile
+SN FG	heavy snow and fog
VV002	indefinite ceiling 200 feet
01/01	temperature 1°C, dew point 1°C
A2975	altimeter 29.75
RMK	remarks
AO2	automated observation with precipitation discriminator
TWR VIS 1/2	tower visibility one-half statute mile
RAE08SNB08	rain ended and snow began at 8 minutes after the hour

Denver special report, one three one zero observation, wind zero niner zero at one four, gusts three five, visibility one quarter, heavy snow, fog, indefinite ceiling two hundred, sky obscured, temperature one, dew point one, altimeter two niner seven five. Tower visibility one half, rain ended at zero eight, snow began at zero eight.

Example 6

*METAR KSPS 301656Z 06014KT 020V090 3SM –TSRA FEW040 BKN060CB 12/ A2982
RMK OCNL LTGICCG NE TSB17 TS E MOV NE PRESRR SLP093*

METAR	aviation routine weather report
KSPS	Wichita Falls, TX
301656Z	date 30, time 1656 UTC
06014KT 020V090	wind 60 deg. at 14 knots varying between 20 and 90 deg.
3SM	visibility 3 statute miles
–TSRA	thunderstorm with light rain
FEW040 BKN060CB	few clouds at 4,000 ft., ceiling 6,000 ft. broken, cumulonimbus
12/	temperature 12°C (dew point missing)
A2982	altimeter 29.82
RMK	remarks
OCNL LTGICCG NE	occasional lightning in cloud, cloud-to-ground northeast
TSB17	thunderstorm began 17 minutes after the hour
TS E MOV NE	thunderstorm east moving northeast
PRESRR	pressure rising rapidly
SLP093	sea-level pressure 1,009.3 hectopascals

Sheppard Air Force Base one six five six observation, wind zero six zero at one four, wind variable zero two zero to zero niner zero, visibility three, light rain, thunderstorms, few at four thousand, ceiling six thousand broken, temperature one two, altimeter two niner eight two, occasional lightning in cloud and cloud-to-ground northeast, thunderstorm east moving northeast, pressure rising rapidly.

Example 7

SPECI KBOS 051237Z VRB02KT 3/4SM R15R/4000FT BR OVC004 05/05 A2998 RMK AO2 CIG 002V006

SPECI	aviation selected special weather report
KBOS	Boston, MA
051237Z	date 5, time 1237 UTC
VRB02KT	variable wind at 2 knots
3/4SM	visibility three-quarters statute mile
R15R/4000FT	runway visual range on runway 15R 4,000 feet
BR	mist
OVC004	ceiling 400 feet overcast
05/05	temperature 5°C, dew point 5°C
A2998	altimeter 29.98
RMK	remarks
AO2	automated observation with precipitation discriminator
CIG 002V006	ceiling variable 200 to 600 feet

Boston Logan airport special report, one two three seven observation, wind variable at two knots, visibility three quarters, mist, ceiling four hundred overcast, temperature five, dew point five, altimeter two niner niner eight, ceiling variable two hundred to six hundred, runway one five right visibility four thousand.

AVIATION WEATHER FORECASTS

The National Weather Service offers an array of forecasting products. The ones most commonly used in aviation are:

- Terminal aerodrome forecasts (TAFs)
- Significant meteorological information (SIGMET)
- Airman's meteorological information (AIRMET)
- Convective outlook (AC)
- Severe Weather Watch Bulletins (WWs)
- Center Weather Service Unit (CWSU)

TERMINAL AERODROME FORECASTS

A terminal aerodrome forecast describes the weather conditions expected on and around an airport during a 24-hour period. TAFs use the same general weather codes as METAR weather reports. A TAF contains the following eleven forecast elements in order:

1. Type of report

2. ICAO station identifier

3. Date and time of origin

4. Valid period date and time

5. Wind forecast

6. Visibility forecast

7. Significant weather forecast

8. Sky condition forecast

9. Nonconvective low-level wind shear forecast (optional data)

10. Forecast change indicators

11. Probability forecast

Here's how to interpret terminal aerodrome forecasts.

Report Type Header

TAF
```
KPIR 111140Z 111212 13012KT P6SM BKN100 WS020/35035KT TEMPO 1214 5SM BR
FM1500 16015G25KT P6SM SCT040 BKN250
FM0000 14012KT P6SM BKN080 OVC150 PROB40 0004 3SM TSRA BKN030CB
FM0400 14008KT P6SM SCT040 OVC080 TEMPO 0408 3SM TSRA OVC030CB
BECMG 0810 32007KT=
```

The report type header will always appear as the first element in a TAF. There are two types of TAF reports: a routine forecast (TAF) and an amended forecast (TAF AMD). An amended TAF is issued when a forecaster believes that the TAF is not representative of the current or expected weather conditions. The equal sign at the end of a TAF signifies the end of the report.

ICAO Station Identifier

```
TAF
KPIR 111140Z 111212 13012KT P6SM BKN100 WS020/35035KT TEMPO 1214 5SM BR
FM1500 16015G25KT P6SM SCT040 BKN250
FM0000 14012KT P6SM BKN080 OVC150 PROB40 0004 3SM TSRA BKN030CB
FM0400 14008KT P6SM SCT040 OVC080 TEMPO 0408 3SM TSRA OVC030CB
BECMG 0810 32007KT=
```

The TAF forecast uses the same ICAO four-letter location identifiers used in METAR reports. In this example, the TAF originates from Pierre, SD (PIR).

Date and Time of Origin

```
TAF
KPIR 111140Z 111212 13012KT P6SM BKN100 WS020/35035KT TEMPO 1214 5SM BR
FM1500 16015G25KT P6SM SCT040 BKN250
FM0000 14012KT P6SM BKN080 OVC150 PROB40 0004 3SM TSRA BKN030CB
FM0400 14008KT P6SM SCT040 OVC080 TEMPO 0408 3SM TSRA OVC030CB
BECMG 0810 32007KT=
```

This element is the date and coordinated universal time (UTC) when the forecast was prepared. As with METARs, this is recorded as a two-digit date and four-digit time, followed by the letter Z. Routine TAFs are prepared and filed approximately one-half hour before scheduled issuance times. In the TAF listed above, the forecast was prepared on the eleventh day of the month at 11:40 a.m. UTC.

Valid Period Date and Time

```
TAF
KPIR 111140Z 111212 13012KT P6SM BKN100 WS020/35035KT TEMPO 1214 5SM BR
FM1500 16015G25KT P6SM SCT040 BKN250
FM0000 14012KT P6SM BKN080 OVC150 PROB40 0004 3SM TSRA BKN030CB
FM0400 14008KT P6SM SCT040 OVC080 TEMPO 0408 3SM TSRA OVC030CB
BECMG 0810 32007KT=
```

The valid period of a TAF is represented by a two-digit date followed by the two-digit beginning and two-digit ending hours in UTC time. Routine TAFs are valid for 24 hours and are issued four times daily at 0000Z, 0600Z, 1200Z, and 1800Z. The above TAF is valid from 12Z on the eleventh day of the month until 12Z on the twelfth day of the month.

An amended, canceled, or delayed forecast will show valid periods of less than 24 hours. They normally end at the same time the original unamended forecast was scheduled to end. For example, 231512 on a TAF means that the forecast was valid from the 23rd day at 15Z to the 24th day at 12Z.

Forecast Meteorological Conditions

```
TAF
KPIR 111140Z 111212 13012KT P6SM BKN100 WS020/35035KT TEMPO 1214 5SM BR
FM1500 16015G25KT P6SM SCT040 BKN250
FM0000 14012KT P6SM BKN080 OVC150 PROB40 0004 3SM TSRA BKN030CB
FM0400 14008KT P6SM SCT040 OVC080 TEMPO 0408 3SM TSRA OVC030CB
BECMG 0810 32007KT=
```

The surface wind forecast is the wind direction in degrees from true north (the first three digits) and the mean speed in knots (the last two or three digits if wind is 100 knots or greater). As with METARs, "KT" denotes wind speed as measured in knots, and wind gusts are noted with a "G" appended to the mean wind speed, followed by the highest expected gust. Likewise, calm winds are reported as 00000KT and a variable wind is encoded as VRB when wind direction fluctuates because of convective activity or low wind speeds (3 knots or less).

In the above example, 13012KT indicates that the wind is from the southeast (130 degrees) at an average speed of 12 knots. 16015G25KT means that the wind is from 160 degrees at 15 knots, occasionally gusting to 25 knots.

Prevailing Visibility

```
TAF
KPIR 111140Z 111212 13012KT P6SM BKN100 WS020/35035KT TEMPO 1214 5SM BR
FM1500 16015G25KT P6SM SCT040 BKN250
FM0000 14012KT P6SM BKN080 OVC150 PROB40 0004 3SM TSRA BKN030CB
FM0400 14008KT P6SM SCT040 OVC080 TEMPO 0408 3SM TSRA OVC030CB
BECMG 0810 32007KT=
```

The prevailing visibility forecast appears in whole and fractional numbers of statute miles followed by "SM" denoting the unit of measurement. Statute miles followed by fractions of statute miles are separated by a letter space: 1 1/2SM. Forecast visibility greater than 6 statute miles is indicated by P6SM. If prevailing visibility is 6 statute miles or less, one or more weather phenomena must be included in the significant weather forecast. In the example above, P6SM means more than 6 statute miles of visibility, and 3SM means that the visibility is forecast at 3 statute miles.

Significant Weather

```
TAF
KPIR 111140Z 111212 13012KT P6SM BKN100 WS020/35035KT TEMPO 1214 5SM BR
FM1500 16015G25KT P6SM SCT040 BKN250
FM0000 14012KT P6SM BKN080 OVC150 PROB40 0004 3SM TSRA BKN030CB
FM0400 14008KT P6SM SCT040 OVC080 TEMPO 0408 3SM TSRA OVC030CB
BECMG 0810 32007KT=
```

Expected weather phenomena are coded in TAFs using the same format, qualifiers, and contractions as in METARs. Visibility obscurations are always listed when visibility is forecast to be 6 statute miles or less. Precipitation and volcanic ash are always included in TAFs regardless of the visibility forecast. In the example above, BR denotes mist; TSRA represents thunderstorms and rain showers.

Sky Condition Forecast

```
TAF
KPIR 111140Z 111212 13012KT P6SM BKN100 WS020/35035KT TEMPO 1214 5SM BR
FM1500 16015G25KT P6SM SCT040 BKN250
FM0000 14012KT P6SM BKN080 OVC150 PROB40 0004 3SM TSRA BKN030CB
FM0400 14008KT P6SM SCT040 OVC080 TEMPO 0408 3SM TSRA OVC030CB
BECMG 0810 32007KT=
```

TAF sky condition forecasts use the same abbreviations and format as in METAR observations, but cumulonimbus clouds (CB) are the only cloud type forecast in TAFs. In the example above, SCT040 BKN250 means that a scattered layer of clouds is forecast at 4,000 feet above ground with a higher, broken layer located at 25,000 feet. BKN080 OVC150 means that a broken layer at 8,000 feet with a higher overcast at 15,000 feet is predicted. BKN030CB means that a broken layer of clouds at 3,000 feet is forecast and that the clouds are predicted to be cumulonimbus.

When the sky is obscured because of a surface-based phenomenon, vertical visibility (VV) into the obscuration is noted on a TAF. The VV is followed by a three-digit height in hundreds of feet.

Forecast Change Indicators

```
TAF
KPIR 111140Z 111212 13012KT P6SM BKN100 WS020/35035KT TEMPO 1214 5SM BR
FM1500 16015G25KT P6SM SCT040 BKN250
FM0000 14012KT P6SM BKN080 OVC150 PROB40 0004 3SM TSRA BKN030CB
FM0400 14008KT P6SM SCT040 OVC080 TEMPO 0408 3SM TSRA OVC030CB BECMG
0810 32007KT=
```

If a significant change in the weather is expected during the 24 hours of a TAF, a new time period with the changes is added to the TAF. The change indicators identify whether a rapid, gradual, or temporary change is expected in the forecast meteorological conditions.

FROM (FM) GROUP

The FM group is used when a rapid and significant change in weather conditions, usually occurring in less than 1 hour, is expected. Appended to the FM indicator is the four-digit hour and minute when the change is expected to begin. This change to the forecast is valid until the next change group in the forecast or until the end of the valid forecast period.

Each FM group marks the beginning of a new line in a TAF report, and each new FM group contains a forecast of wind, visibility, weather (if significant), sky condition, and wind shear (if warranted).

Example 1

```
FM1500 16015G25KT P6SM SCT040 BKN250
```

Beginning at 1500Z, the weather is forecast as follows: winds from 160 at 15 knots gusting to 25 knots, visibility greater than 6 statute miles, a layer of scattered clouds at 4,000 feet above ground level (AGL) with a higher layer of broken clouds at 25,000 feet AGL.

Example 2

```
FM0000 14012KT P6SM BKN080 OVC150
```

Beginning at 0000Z, the weather is forecast as follows: wind from 140 at 12 knots, visibility greater than 6 miles, broken clouds at 8,000 feet AGL with a higher, overcast layer at 15,000 feet AGL.

BECOMING GROUP

The becoming code (BECMG) is similar to FM and is used when a gradual change in conditions is expected over a period not exceeding 2 hours. The time period when the change is expected to occur is denoted by a four-digit number containing the beginning and ending hours of the change that follows the BECMG indicator. The gradual change will occur at an unspecified time within that period. Only the changing forecasted meteorological conditions are included in BECMG groups. Omitted conditions are carried over from the previous time group.

FM0400 14008KT P6SM SCT040 OVC080 TEMPO 0408 3SM TSRA OVC030CB ***BECMG***
0810 32007KT=

The BECMG portion of the TAF above describes a gradual change in wind to 320 degrees at 7 knots. This change will gradually occur between 0800Z and 1000Z. Other than the change in wind speed and direction, the rest of the forecast weather conditions remain in effect. Refer to the previous forecast group, in this case the FM0400 group, for the prevailing visibility, weather, and sky conditions. The forecast after 10Z will be 32007KT P6SM SCT040 OVC080.

TEMPORARY GROUP

The temporary code (TEMPO) is used for temporary fluctuations in wind, visibility, weather, and sky condition that are expected to last for less than an hour at a time and expected to occur during less than one-half the time period covered. The TEMPO indicator is followed by a four-digit code that supplies the beginning and ending hours of the time period during which the temporary conditions are expected.

Only changing forecast conditions are included in TEMPO groups. The omitted conditions are carried over from the previous time group. For example:

FM1000 27005KT P6SM SKC TEMPO 1216 3SM BR

This TAF indicates that even though the forecasted sky conditions are clear and greater than 6 statute miles visibility between 12Z and 16Z, occasionally the visibility will be 3 miles because of mist.

Probability Forecast

The probability forecast describes the probability of thunderstorms or other precipitation occurring during a given time period, along with associated weather conditions (wind, visibility, and sky conditions). The PROB30 or PROB40 group is used when the occurrence of thunderstorms or precipitation is between 30 and 39 percent or between 40 and 50 percent, respectively. If the thunderstorms or precipitation chance is higher than 50 percent, it is considered a prevailing weather condition and is included in the significant weather section or the TEMPO change indicator group.

PROB30 or PROB40 is followed by a four-digit code supplying the beginning and ending hours of the time period during which the precipitation is expected. For example, the following TAF shows that there is 30 to 39 percent chance of 1-mile visibility in moderate rain, and a broken cloud layer (ceiling) at 1,500 feet between 1000Z and 1400Z:

FM0600 0915KT P6SM BKN020 ***PROB30 1014 1SM RA BKN015***

The following example states that there is a 40 to 50 percent chance of visibility of 3 statute miles, thunderstorms with moderate rain showers, and a broken cloud layer at 3,000 feet with cumulonimbus clouds between 0000Z and 0400Z:

FM0000 14012KT P6SM BKN080 OVC150 ***PROB40 0004 3SM TSRA BKN030CB***

Examples and Explanations of TAF Reports

The following examples present weather reports and explanations of the codes used in TAFs.

Example 1

```
TAF
KPIR 111140Z 111212 13012KT P6SM BKN100 WS020/35035KT TEMPO 1214 5SM BR
FM1500 16015G25KT P6SM SCT040 BKN250
FM0000 14012KT P6SM BKN080 OVC150 PROB40 0004 3SM TSRA BKN030CB
FM0400 14008KT P6SM SCT040 OVC080 TEMPO 0408 3SM TSRA OVC030CB
BECMG 0810 32007KT=
```

TAF	Aviation terminal forecast
KPIR	Pierre, South Dakota
111140Z	prepared on the 11th at 1140Z
111212	valid period from the 11th at 1200Z until the 12th at 1200Z
13012KT	wind 130 at 12 knots
P6SM	visibility greater than 6 statute miles
BKN100	ceiling 10,000 broken
WS020/35035KT	wind shear at 2,000 feet, wind (at 2,000 feet) from 350 at 35 knots
TEMPO 1214	temporary conditions between 1200Z and 1400Z
5SM	visibility 5 statute miles
BR	mist
FM1500	from 1500Z
16015G25KT	wind 160 at 15 knots gusting to 25 knots
P6SM	visibility greater than 6 statute miles
SCT040 BKN250	4,000 feet scattered, ceiling 25,000 feet broken
FM0000	from 0000Z
14012KT	wind 140 at 12 knots
P6SM	visibility greater than 6 statute miles
BKN080 OVC150	ceiling 8,000 feet broken, 15,000 feet overcast
PROB40 0004	40 percent probability of precipitation between 0000Z and 0400Z
3SM	visibility 3 statute miles
TSRA	thunderstorm with moderate rain showers
BKN030CB	ceiling 3,000 feet broken with cumulonimbus
FM0400	from 0400Z
14008KT	wind 140 at 8 knots
P6SM	visibility greater than 6 statute miles
SCT040 OVC080	4,000 feet scattered, ceiling 8,000 feet overcast
TEMPO 0408	temporary conditions between 0400Z and 0800Z
3SM	visibility 3 statute miles
TSRA	thunderstorms with moderate rain showers
OVC030CB	ceiling 3,000 feet overcast with cumulonimbus
BECMG 0810	becoming between 0800Z and 1000Z
32007KT	wind 320 at 7 knots
=	end of TAF

Example 2

```
TAF AMD
KEYW 131555Z 131612 VRB03KT P6SM VCTS SCT025CB BKN250 TEMPO 1618 2SM
TSRA
BKN020CB
FM1800 VRB03KT P6SM SCT025 BKN250 TEMPO 2024 1SM TSRA OVC010CB
FM0000 VRB03KT P6SM VCTS SCT020CB BKN120 TEMPO 0812 BKN020CB=
```

TAF AMD	Amended aviation terminal forecast
KEYW	Key West, Florida
131555Z	prepared on the 13th at 1555Z
131612	valid period from the 13th at 1600Z until the 14th at 1200Z
VRB03KT	wind variable at 3 knots
P6SM	visibility greater than 6 statute miles
VCTS	thunderstorms in the vicinity
SCT025CB BKN250	2,500 feet scattered with cumulonimbus, ceiling 25,000 feet broken
TEMPO 1618	temporary conditions between 1600Z and 1800Z
2SM	visibility 2 statute miles
TSRA	thunderstorms with moderate rain showers
BKN020CB	ceiling 2,000 feet broken with cumulonimbus
FM1800	from 1800Z
VRB03KT	wind variable at 3 knots
P6SM	visibility greater than 6 statute miles
SCT025 BKN250	2,500 feet scattered, ceiling 25,000 feet broken
TEMPO 2024	temporary conditions between 2000Z and 0000Z
1SM	visibility 1 statute mile
TSRA	thunderstorms with moderate rain showers
OVC010CB	ceiling 1,000 overcast with cumulonimbus
FM0000	from 0000Z
VRB03KT	variable wind at 3 knots
P6SM	visibility greater than 6 statute miles
VCTS	thunderstorms in the vicinity
SCT020CB BKN120	2,000 feet scattered with cumulonimbus, ceiling 12,000 feet broken
TEMPO 0812	temporary conditions between 0800Z and 1200Z
BKN020CB	ceiling 2,000 broken with cumulonimbus
=	end of TAF

Example 3

TAF
KCRP 111730Z 111818 19007KT P6SM SCT030 TEMPO 1820 BKN040
FM2000 16011KT P6SM VCTS FEW030CB SCT250
FM0200 14006KT P6SM FEW025 SCT250
FM0800 VRB03KT 5SM BR SCT012 TEMPO 1012 1/2SM FG BKN001
FM1500 17007KT P6SM SCT025=

TAF	Aviation terminal forecast
KCRP	Corpus Christi, Texas
111730Z	prepared on the 11th at 1730Z
111818	valid period from the 11th at 1800Z until the 12th at 1800Z
19007KT	wind 190 at 7 knots
P6SM	visibility greater than 6 statute miles
SCT030	3,000 feet scattered
TEMPO 1820	temporary conditions between 1800Z and 2000Z
BKN040	ceiling 4,000 feet broken
FM2000	from 2000Z
16011KT	wind 160 at 11 knots
P6SM	visibility greater than 6 statute miles
VCTS	thunderstorms in the vicinity
FEW030CB SCT250	3,000 few with cumulonimbus, 25,000 feet scattered
FM0200	from 0200Z
14006KT	wind 140 at 6 knots
P6SM	visibility greater than 6 statute miles
FEW025 SCT250	2,500 few, 25,000 scattered
FM0800	from 0800Z
VRB03KT	wind variable at 3 knots
5SM	visibility 5 statute miles
BR	mist
SCT012	1,200 feet scattered
TEMPO 1012	temporary conditions between 1000Z and 1200Z
1/2SM	visibility one-half statute mile
FG	fog
BKN001	ceiling 100 feet broken
FM1500	from 1500Z
17007KT	wind 170 at 7 knots
P6SM	visibility greater than 6 statute miles
SCT025	2,500 scattered
=	end of TAF

Example 4

TAF
KACK 112340Z 120024 29008KT P6SM SKC BECMG 1618 22015KT=

TAF	Aviation terminal forecast
KACK	Nantucket, Massachusetts
112340Z	prepared on the 11th at 2340Z
120024	valid period from the 12th at 0000Z until the 13th at 0000Z
29008KT	wind 290 at 8 knots
P6SM	visibility greater than 6 statute miles
SKC	sky clear
BECMG 1618	becoming between 1600Z and 1800Z
22015KT	wind 220 at 15 knots
=	end of TAF

Example 5

TAF
KMWH 200535Z 200606 NIL=

TAF	Aviation terminal forecast
KMWH	Moses Lake, Washington
200535Z	prepared on the 20th at 0535Z
200606	valid period from the 20th at 0600Z to the 21st at 0600Z
NIL	no TAF
=	end of TAF

AVIATION AREA FORECASTS

The TAF is a highly localized, very specific forecast. It is difficult, however, to get a good idea of the "big picture" by interpreting multiple TAFs. Most pilots and controllers use the Aviation Area Forecast (FA) as a means of quickly determining the overall weather pattern and forecast for a large area. The FA is a detailed forecast of meteorological conditions, clouds, and general weather conditions over an area the size of several U.S. states. An FA is made up of four sections:

1 Communications and product header

2 Precautionary statements

3 Synopsis

4 Visual Flight Rules (VFR) clouds/weather

This is an example of a partial FA:

DFWC FA 120945
SYNOPSIS AND VFR CLDS/WX
SYNOPSIS VALID UNTIL 130400
CLDS/WX VALID UNTIL 122200...OTLK VALID 122200-130400 OK TX AR TN LA MS AL AND
CSTL WTRS
.
SEE AIRMET SIERRA FOR IFR CONDS AND MTN OBSCN.
TS IMPLY SEV OR GTR TURB SEV ICE LLWS AND IFR CONDS.
NON MSL HGTS DENOTED BY AGL OR CIG.
.
SYNOPSIS...LOW PRES TROF 10Z OK/TX PNHDL AREA FCST MOV EWD INTO CNTRL-SWRN
OK BY 04Z. WRMFNT 10Z CNTRL OK-SRN AR-NRN MS FCST LIFT NWD INTO NERN OKNRN
AR XTRM NRN MS BY 04Z.
.
S CNTRL AND SERN TX
AGL SCT-BKN010. TOPS 030. VIS 3-5SM BR. 14-16Z BECMG AGL SCT030. 19Z AGL SCT050.
OTLK...VFR.
.
OK
PNHDL AND NW...AGL SCT030 SCT-BKN100. TOPS FL200. 15Z AGL SCT040 SCT100. AFT 20Z
SCT TSRA DVLPG...FEW POSS SEV. CB TOPS FL450. OTLK...VFR.
SWRN OK...CIG BKN020. TOPS 050. VIS 3-5SM BR. 14Z AGL SCT-BKN040. 18Z CIG BKN060.
TOPS FL180. 22Z SCT TSRA DVLPG..FEW POSS SEV. CB TOPS ABV FL450.
OTLK...VFR.
NERN QTR...CIG BKN020 OVC050. VIS 3-5SM NMRS TSRA...FEW POSS SEV. CB TOPS ABV
FL450. 15Z AGL SCT030 SCT-BKN100. TOPS FL250. 18Z AGL SCT040.
OTLK...VFR.
SERN QTR...AGL SCT-BKN020. TOPS 050. 18Z AGL SCT040. OTLK...VFR.
.
CSTL WTRS
LA MS AL WTRS...SCT025 SCT-BKN080. TOPS 150. ISOL -TSRA. CB TOPS FL350.
OTLK...VFR.
TX WTRS...SCT CI. OCNL SCT030. OTLK...VFR. ....

Communications and Product Header

The communications and product header identifies the office from which the FA is issued, the date and time of issuance, the name of the forecasting product used, the valid times when the forecast is in effect, and the states and/or areas covered by the FA. The following is the communications and product header for the example provided on the facing page:

```
DFWC FA 120945
SYNOPSIS AND VFR CLDS/WX
SYNOPSIS VALID UNTIL 130400
CLDS/WX VALID UNTIL 122200...OTLK VALID 122200-130400 OK TX AR TN LA MS
AL AND
CSTL WTRS
```

On the first line, "DFW" is the three-letter airport/navigation aid code for which the FA is valid (Dallas-Forth Worth). The "C" after the three-letter code indicates VFR clouds and weather. As with METARs and TAFs, "FA" indicates what type of forecast it is, and "120945" represents the date (12th day of the month) and time (0945Z) that the FA was issued.

On the second line, SYNOPSIS AND VFR CLDS/WX gives a broad description of the weather patterns expected. SYNOPSIS VALID UNTIL 130400 means that the synopsis section of this FA is valid until the 13th day of the month at 0400Z.

On the fourth line, "CLDS/WX VALID UNTIL 122200...OTLK VALID 122200-130400" indicates that the forecast section of this FA is valid until the 12th of the month at 2200Z, while the outlook portion is valid from the 12th of the month at 2200Z until the 13th at 0400Z. "OK TX AR TN LA MS AL AND CSTL WTRS" describes the area for which this FA forecast is valid: Oklahoma, Texas, Arkansas, Tennessee, Louisiana, Mississippi, Alabama, and coastal waters.

Precautionary Statements

After the communications/product header in the example above are precautionary statements. The first statement, "SEE AIRMET SIERRA FOR IFR CONDS AND MTN OBSCN," alerts users that IFR conditions and/or mountain obscurations may be occurring or may be forecast to occur in a portion of the FA area.

The second statement, "TS IMPLY SEV OR GTR TURB SEV ICE LLWS AND IFR CONDS," warns users of hazards inherent in all thunderstorm situations: "Thunderstorms imply possible severe or greater turbulence, severe icing, low-level wind shear, and Instrument Flight Rules conditions."

The third statement in the example, "NON MSL HGTS DENOTED BY AGL. OR CIG.," reminds the user that heights stipulated in an FA are, for the most part, measured above mean sea level (MSL) in hundreds of feet. Any height measured above ground level will be noted using the contraction "CIG" (ceiling). Ceiling is always measured above ground level. The code "AGL" is another way to indicate that the cloud height being referenced is above ground level.

Synopsis

The synopsis is a brief summary of the location and movement of weather fronts, pressure systems, and other circulation features for the next 18-hour period. References to low ceilings and/or visibilities, strong winds, or any other phenomena the forecaster considers useful may also be included. The following is the synopsis section for the example provided earlier:

```
SYNOPSIS...LOW PRES TROF 10Z OK/TX PNHDL AREA FCST MOV EWD INTO CNTRL-
SWRN OK BY 04Z. WRMFNT 10Z CNTRL OK-SRN AR-NRN MS FCST LIFT NWD INTO
NERN OKNRN AR XTRM NRN MS BY 04Z
```

It states that a low-pressure trough at 10Z was over the Oklahoma/Texas panhandle area. The front is forecast to move eastward into central-southwestern OK by 04Z. At 10Z, a warm front was located from central OK to southern Arkansas (AR) to northern Mississippi (MS). This warm front will lift northward into northeastern OK, northern AR, to extreme northern MS by 04Z.

VFR Clouds and Weather

This section of the FA contains a 12-hour specific forecast followed by a 6-hour categorical outlook, covering the FA's total forecast period of 18 hours. It is usually several paragraphs long. It may be broken down by states or by well-known geographical areas.

The specific forecast section gives a general description of clouds and weather that cover an area greater than 3,000 square miles and are significant to VFR flight operations. Surface visibility and obscurations to vision are included when the forecast visibility is between 3 and 5 statute miles. Precipitation, thunderstorms, and sustained winds of 20 knots or more are always included.

The abbreviation OCNL (occasional) describes clouds and visibilities that may affect VFR flights and is used when the probability of a phenomenon occurring is higher than 50 percent, but is likely for less than one-half of the forecast period. The area coverage terms ISOL (isolated), WDLY SCT (widely scattered), SCT or AREAS (scattered), and NMRS or WDSPRD (numerous or widespread) indicate the area coverage of thunderstorms or showers. The term ISOL may also be used to describe areas of ceilings or visibilities that are expected to affect areas of less than 3,000 square miles.

```
CSTL WTRS
LA MS AL WTRS...SCT025 SCT-BKN080. TOPS 150. ISOL -TSRA. CB TOPS FL350.
OTLK...VFR TX WTRS...SCT CI. OCNL SCT030. OTLK...VFR. ....
```

This part of the VFR clouds/weather section is the forecast for the coastal waters of any coastal states in the FA; in this case, Louisiana (LA), Mississippi (MS), Alabama (AL), and Texas (TX). For the coastal waters of LA, MS, and AL, the base of the scattered layer is 2,500 feet MSL. The second layer is scattered to broken at 8,000 feet MSL with the tops of the clouds at 15,000 feet MSL. Also during this time, isolated (ISOL) thunderstorms with light rain showers are expected, with the tops of the thunderstorms (CB) at flight level (FL) 350. (Remember that "FL" is used only for altitudes 18,000 feet and higher.) The visibility is expected to be greater than 6 statute miles and the winds less than 20 knots; otherwise the forecast would expressly state them. The weather conditions along the TX coastal waters are expected to be scattered cirrus clouds with occasional (OCNL) scattered layers at 3,000 feet MSL.

A categorical outlook, identified by "OTLK," is included for each area breakdown in an FA. In this example, the coastal areas have outlooks of VFR conditions. "OTLKàVFR BCMG MVFR CIG F AFT 09Z" means that the weather is expected to be VFR, becoming marginal VFR (MVFR) due to low ceilings, and that visibilities will be restricted by fog after 0900Z. "WND" is included in the outlook if winds, whether sustained or gusty, are expected to be 20 knots or more.

IN-FLIGHT AVIATION WEATHER ADVISORIES

In-flight Aviation Weather Advisories advise en route aircraft of the development of potentially hazardous weather. All in-flight aviation weather advisories in the continental United States are issued by the Aviation Weather Center (AWC) in Kansas City, MO; the WFO in Honolulu issues advisories for the Hawaiian islands; and the Alaska Aviation Weather Unit (AAWU) issues in-flight aviation weather advisories in that state. All heights in these advisories are referenced to MSL altitudes, except in the case of a ceiling, which is always reported as above ground level.

There are three types of in-flight aviation weather advisories:

1. Significant meteorological information (SIGMET)
2. Convective SIGMET
3. Airman's meteorological information (AIRMET)

All of these advisories use the same location identifiers (VORs, airports, or well-known geographic areas) to describe the hazardous weather regions.

SIGMETs

A SIGMET advises of nonconvective (non-thunderstorm) weather that is potentially hazardous to all aircraft, regardless of size. SIGMETs are issued when needed and are usually valid for 4 hours. Updates and corrections are issued as necessary. In the continental United States, SIGMETs are issued when any of the following four phenomena occur or are expected to occur:

1. Severe icing not associated with thunderstorms
2. Severe or extreme turbulence or clear air turbulence (CAT) not associated with thunderstorms
3. Dust storms or sandstorms lowering surface or in-flight visibilities to below 3 miles
4. Volcanic ash

In Alaska and Hawaii, SIGMETs are also issued for four weather conditions:

1. Tornadoes
2. Lines of thunderstorms
3. Embedded thunderstorms
4. Hail greater than or equal to 3/4 inch in diameter

SIGMETs are identified by the alphabetic designators November through Yankee, excluding Sierra and Tango. (Sierra, Tango, and Zulu are reserved for AIRMETs.) The first issuance of a SIGMET will be labeled "UWS" (Urgent Weather SIGMET). Subsequent issuances are at the forecaster's discretion. Issuance for the same phenomenon will be sequentially numbered, using the original designator until the phenomenon ends. For example, the first issuance in the Chicago (CHI) FA area for weather moving from the Salt Lake City (SLC) FA area would be "SIGMET Papa 3" if the previous two issuances, "Papa 1" and "Papa 2," had been in the SLC FA area. No two phenomena across the country can have the same alphabetic designator at the same time.

Here's an example of a SIGMET:

```
BOSR WS 050600
SIGMET ROMEO 2 VALID UNTIL 051000
ME NH VT
FROM CAR TO YSJ TO CON TO MPV TO CAR
MOD TO OCNL SEV TURB BLW 080 EXP DUE TO STG NWLY FLOW. CONDS CONTG BYD
1000Z.
```

SIGMETS DECODED

The first line of a SIGMET denotes the issuing NWS office and the date/time code. The second line identifies the SIGMET by name and states how long the SIGMET is to be considered valid. In the example above, SIGMET Romeo 2 was issued at 0600Z on the fifth day of the month, and it is valid until 1000Z on the same day.

The next line identifies which states are affected by the SIGMET. Note that the entire state may not be affected, but this line makes it easier to sort through numerous SIGMETS to determine which ones require closer scrutiny.

The fourth line of a SIGMET can be confusing. A series of locations are listed as three-letter airport/navigation aid identifier codes. If you were to draw a line on a map from the first fix noted to the last, you'd have a circle. Notice that this SIGMENT starts and finishes at "CAR" (Caribou, ME). That means that this SIGMET applies to the area located in a circle whose limits extend from CAR to "CYSJ" (St. John, New Brunswick) to "CON" (Concord, NH) to "MPV" (Montpelier, VT), and then back to CAR.

The remaining lines of a SIGMET describe the weather conditions, using standard NWS contractions, which have prompted its issuance. In the example above, the weather conditions read:

```
MOD TO OCNL SEV TURB BLW 080 EXP DUE TO STG NWLY FLOW. CONDS CONTG BYD
1000Z
```

This translates to: "Moderate to occasionally severe turbulence is expected below 8,000 MSL due to strong northwesterly wind. It is expected that these conditions will continue beyond the expiration time of the SIGMET at 1000Z."

Convective SIGMETs

Convective SIGMETs are issued in the continental United States for particularly severe weather conditions that are commonly found around large thunderstorms or active weather fronts. A convective SIGMET will be issued for any of the following four situations:

1. Severe thunderstorm due to surface winds greater than or equal to 50 knots and/or hail at the surface greater than or equal to 3/4 inch in diameter and/or tornadoes

2. Embedded thunderstorms

3. A line of thunderstorms

4. Thunderstorms producing precipitation greater than or equal to heavy precipitation affecting 40 percent or more of an area of at least 3,000 square miles

A convective SIGMET implies severe or greater turbulence, severe icing, and low-level wind shear. A convective SIGMET may be issued for any convective situation that the forecaster feels is hazardous to all categories of aircraft. Convective SIGMETs are routinely issued for any of three areas of the continental United States: western (W), central (C), and eastern (E). (Convective SIGMETs are not issued for Alaska and Hawaii.) These three areas are separated at 87 and 107 degrees W longitude with sufficient overlap to cover most cases when the phenomenon crosses the boundaries.

Convective SIGMETs are issued every hour at 55 minutes past the hour. Special bulletins are issued at any time they are needed. If no criteria meeting convective SIGMET requirements are observed or forecast, the message "CONVECTIVE SIGMET... NONE" is issued for each of the three areas at 55 past each hour.

Individual convective SIGMETs for the western, central, and eastern United States are numbered sequentially beginning with number 1 each day at 00Z. The text of the bulletin consists either of an observation and a forecast or a forecast alone. The forecast is valid for up to 2 hours. Here are a few examples of convective SIGMETs:

Example 1

```
MKCC WST 251655
CONVECTIVE SIGMET 54C
VALID UNTIL 1855Z
WI IL
FROM 30E MSN-40ESE DBQ
DMSHG LINE TS 15 NM WIDE MOV FROM 30025KT. TOPS TO FL450. WIND GUSTS TO
50 KT POSS.
```

Example 2

```
CONVECTIVE SIGMET 55C
VALID UNTIL 1855Z
WI IA
FROM 30NNW MSN-30SSE MCW
DVLPG LINE TS 10 NM WIDE MOV FROM 30015KT. TOPS TO FL300.
```

Example 3

```
CONVECTIVE SIGMET 56C
VALID UNTIL 1855Z
MT ND SD MN IA MI
LINE TS 15 NM WIDE MOV FROM 27020KT. TOPS TO FL380.
OUTLOOK VALID 151855-252255
FROM 60NW ISN-INL-TVC-SBN-BRL-FSD-BIL-60NW ISN
IR STLT IMGRY SHOWS CNVTV CLD TOP TEMPS OVER SRN WI HAVE BEEN WARMING
STEADILY INDCG A WKNG TREND. THIS ALSO REFLECTED BY LTST RADAR AND LTNG
DATA. WKNG TREND OF PRESENT LN MAY CONT... HWVR NEW DVLPMT IS PSBL ALG
OUTFLOW BDRY AND/OR OVR NE IA/SW WI BHD CURRENT ACT.
A SCND TS IS CONTG TO MOV EWD THRU ERN MT WITH NEW DVLPMT OCRG OVR CNTRL
ND. TS EXPD TO INCR IN COVERAGE AND INTSTY DURG AFTN HRS.
```

AIRMETs

AIRMETs, or WAs, are advisories of significant weather phenomena that describe conditions at intensities lower than those requiring SIGMET issuance. AIRMETs are intended to be disseminated to all pilots in the preflight and en route phases to enhance safety.

AIRMET bulletins are issued on a scheduled basis every 6 hours. Unscheduled updates and corrections are issued as necessary. Each AIRMET bulletin contains any current AIRMET in effect and an outlook for conditions expected after the AIRMET valid period. AIRMETs contain details about IFR weather, extensive mountain obscuration, turbulence, strong surface winds, icing, and freezing levels.

There are three categories of AIRMETs:

1. Sierra—describes IFR conditions and/or extensive mountain obscurations

2. Tango—describes moderate turbulence, sustained surface winds of 30 knots or greater, and/or nonconvective low-level wind shear

3. Zulu—describes moderate icing and provides freezing level heights

After the first of each type of AIRMET issuance each day, scheduled or unscheduled bulletins issued thereafter are numbered sequentially for easier identification.

Example of AIRMET Sierra

```
CHIS WA 121345
AIRMET SIERRA UPDT 3 FOR IFR AND MTN OBSCN VALID UNTIL 122000 .
AIRMET IFR...SD NE MN IA MO WI LM MI IL IN KY
FROM 70NW RAP TO 50W RWF TO 50W MSN TO GRB TO MBS TO FWA TO CVG TO HNN
TO TRI TO ARG TO 40SSW BRL TO OMA TO BFF TO 70NW RAP OCNL CIG BLW 010/
VIS BLW 3SM FG/BR. CONDS ENDG 15Z-17Z.

AIRMET MTN OBSCN...KY TN
FROM HNN TO TRI TO CHA TO LOZ TO HNN
MTNS OCNL OBSC CLDS/PCPN/BR. CONDS ENDG TN PTN AREA 18Z- 20Z..CONTG KY
BYD 20Z..ENDG 02Z.
```

Example of AIRMET Tango

```
AIRMET TANGO UPDT 2 FOR TURB VALID UNTIL 122000 .
AIRMET TURB...NV UT CO AZ NM
FROM LKV TO CHE TO ELP TO 60S TUS TO YUM TO EED TO RNO TO LKV OCNL MOD
TURB BLW FL180 DUE TO MOD SWLY/WLY WNDS. CONDS CONTG BYD 20Z THRU 02Z.

AIRMET TURB...NV WA OR CA CSTL WTRS
FROM BLI TO REO TO BTY TO DAG TO SBA TO 120W FOT TO 120W TOU TO BLI
OCNL MOD TURB BTWN FL180 AND FL400 DUE TO WNDSHR ASSOCD WITH JTSTR.
CONDS CONTG BYD 20Z THRU 02Z.
```

Example of AIRMET Zulu

```
SFOZ WA 121345
AIRMET ZULU UPDT 2 FOR ICE AND FRZLVL VALID UNTIL 122000 .
AIRMET ICE...WA OR ID MT NV UT
FROM YQL TO SLC TO WMC TO LKV TO PDT TO YDC TO YQL
LGT OCNL MOD RIME/MXD ICGICIP BTWN FRZLVL AND FL220. FRZLVL 080-120.
CONDS CONTG BYD 20Z THRU 02Z.

AIRMET ICE...WA OR
FROM YDC TO PDT TO LKV TO 80W MFR TO ONP TO TOU TO YDC
LGT OCNL MOD RIME/MXD ICGICIP BTWN FRZLVL AND FL180. FRZLVL 060-080.
CONDS CONTG BYD 20Z THRU 02Z.

FRZLVL...WA...060 CSTLN SLPG 100 XTRM E.
OR...060-070 CASCDS WWD. 070-095 RMNDR.
NRN CA...060-100 N OF A 30N FOT-40N RNO LN SLPG 100-110 RMNDR.
```

CONVECTIVE OUTLOOK

The convective outlook (AC) is a national forecast of thunderstorms and other convective activity. The convective outlook is composed of two forecasts: Day 1 convective outlook (first 24 hours) and Day 2 convective outlook (the following 24 hours). These forecasts describe areas in which there is a slight, moderate, or high risk of severe thunderstorms, as well as areas of general (non-severe) thunderstorms. The severe thunderstorm criteria include:

- Winds equal to or greater than 50 knots at the surface
- Hail measuring 3/4 inch or greater at the surface
- Tornadoes

ACs are produced by the Storm Prediction Center (SPC). They provide another flight planning tool for air traffic controllers and pilots, to help them predict the location and severity of convective activity.

Here's an example of an AC:

```
MKC AC 291435
CONVECTIVE OUTLOOK... REF AFOS NMCGPH940.
VALID 291500Z-301200Z
THERE IS A SLGT RISK OF SVR TSTMS TO THE RIGHT OF A LINE FROM 10 NE JAX
35 NNW AYS AGS 15 E SPA 30 NE CLT 25 N FAY 30 ESE EWN.
GEN TSTMS ARE FCST TO THE RIGHT OF A LINE FROM 55 ESE YUM 30 NE IGM 15 S
CDC 30
SW U24 25 ESE ELY 40 W P38 DRA 50 SW DRA 50 NW NID SAC 30 E ACV 25 E ONP
40 E BLI.
...SEVERE THUNDERSTORM FORECAST DISCUSSION...
.SERN U.S...
COOL FRONT CONTS SC/NC BORDER. VERY MOIST AND UNSTBL AMS ALONG AND S OF
FRONT E OF APLCHNS WITH CAPES TO REACH TO 4000 J/KG WITH AFTN HEATING.
ALTHOUGH WIND PROFILES ARE WK...COMB OF FRONTAL CNVGNC COUPLED WITH SEA
BREEZE FRONT WILL INITIATE PULSE SVR TSTMS VCNTY AND S OF FRONT THIS
AFTN/EVE. PRIMARY SVR EVENTS WILL BE WET DOWNBURST TO PUSH SWD FROM
CNTRL RCKYS EWD TO MID ATLC CST. E OF APLCNS FRONT NOW LCTD VCNTY WND
DMG.

...GENERAL THUNDERSTORM FORECAST DISCUSSION...
...GULF CST AREA INTO SRN PLNS...
SFC FNT CURRENTLY LOCATED FM THE CAROLINAS WWD INTO PARTS OF OK WL CONT
TO SAG SLOWLY SWD ACRS THE SRN APLCNS/LWR MS VLY THRU THE REMAINDER OF
THE PD. S OF THE BNDRY...A VRY MOIST AMS RMNS IN PLACE AS DWPNTS ARE IN
THE MID TO UPR 70S. WHILE SOME CLDNS IS PRESENT ACRS THE AREA...SUF
HEATING SHOULD OCR TO ALLOW FOR MDT TO STG AMS DSTBLZN DURG THE LATE
MRNG/ERY AFTN. AS A RESULT...SFC BASED CAPE VALUES SHOULD BE AOA 2000
J/KG THIS AFTN. BNDRYS FM OVERNIGHT CNVTN AS WELL AS SEA BREEZE
CIRCULATIONS SHOULD BE SUF TO INITIATE SCT TO NMRS TSTMS ACRS THE AREA.
MID TO UPR LVL FLOW IS RELATIVELY WK...SO THIS SUG ORGANIZED SVR TSTM
ACTVTY IS NOT LIKELY.
```

SEVERE WEATHER WATCH BULLETINS

A Severe Weather Watch Bulletin (WW) defines areas of possible severe thunderstorm or tornado activity. The bulletins are issued by the SPC in Norman, OK. WWs are unscheduled and issued when required. A severe thunderstorm watch describes areas of expected severe thunderstorms. (As noted above, severe thunderstorm criteria include hail measuring 3/4 inch or larger and/or wind gusts of 50 knots or greater.) A tornado watch describes areas where the threat of tornadoes exists. A WW is issued in the following four-step format:

① Type of severe weather watch, watch area, valid time period, type of severe weather possible, watch axis, meaning of a watch, and a statement that persons should be on the lookout for severe weather

② Other watch information (e.g., references to previous watches)

③ Phenomena, intensities, hail size, wind speed (knots), maximum CB tops, and estimated cell movement (mean wind vector)

④ Cause of severe weather

Here's an example of a WW:

```
BULLETIN - IMMEDIATE BROADCAST REQUESTED
TORNADO WATCH NUMBER 381
STORM PREDICTION CENTER NORMAN OK
556 PM CDT MON JUN 2 1997
THE STORM PREDICTON CENTER HAS ISSUED A TORNADO WATCH FOR PORTIONS OF
NORTHEAST NEW MEXICO TEXAS PANHANDLE

EFFECTIVE THIS MONDAY NIGHT AND TUESDAY MORNING FROM 630 PM UNTIL
MIDNIGHT CDT.

TORNADOES... HAIL TO 2 3/4 INCHES IN DIAMETER... THUNDERSTORM WIND GUSTS
TO 80 MPH... AND DANGEROUS LIGHTNING ARE POSSIBLE IN THESE AREAS.

THE TORNADO WATCH AREA IS ALONG AND 60 STATUTE MILES NORTH AND SOUTH OF
A LINE FROM 50 MILES SOUTHWEST OF RATON NEW MEXICO TO 50 MILES EAST OF
AMARILLO TEXAS.

REMEMBER... A TORNADO WATCH MEANS CONDITIONS ARE FAVORABLE FOR TORNADOES
AND SEVERE THUNDERSTORMS IN AND CLOSE TO THE WATCH AREA. PERSONS IN
THESE AREAS SHOULD BE ON THE LOOKOUT FOR THREATENING WEATHER CONDITIONS
AND LISTEN FOR LATER STATEMENTS AND POSSIBLE WARNINGS. OTHER WATCH
INFORMATION... CONTINUE.. WW 378... WW 379... WW 380

DISCUSSIONà THUNDERSTORMS ARE INCREASING OVER NE NM IN MOIST
SOUTHEASTERLY UPSLOPE FLOW. OUTFLOW BOUNDARY EXTENDS EASTWARD INTO THE
TEXAS PANHANDLE AND EXPECT STORMS TO MOVE ESE ALONG AND NORTH OF THE
BOUNDARY ON THE N EDGE OF THE CAP. VEERING WINDS WITH HEIGHT ALONG WITH
INCREASING MID LVL FLOW INDICATE A THREAT FOR SUPERCELLS. AVIATION...
TORNADOES AND A FEW SEVERE THUNDERSTORMS WITH HAIL SURFACE AND ALOFT TO
2 3/4 INCHES. EXTREME TURBULENCE AND SURFACE WIND GUSTS TO 70 KNOTS. A
FEW CUMULONIMBI WITH MAXIMUM TOPS TO 550. MEAN STORM MOTION VECTOR
28025.
```

CWSU PRODUCTS

CWSU products are issued by meteorologists located in the ARTCCs. They are primarily for use by pilots and air traffic controllers operating within ARTCC airspace and include the Meteorological Impact Statement (MIS) and center weather advisories.

Meteorological Impact Statements

A Meteorological Impact Statement (MIS) is an unscheduled flow control and flight operations planning forecast valid for 2 to 12 hours after issuance. MISs are used internally at ARTCCs; they are issued if any one of the following conditions occur, are forecast to occur, or if previously forecasted are no longer expected to occur:

- Convective SIGMET issuance

- Moderate or greater icing and/or turbulence

- Heavy or freezing precipitation

- Low IFR conditions

- Surface winds/gusts 30 knots or greater

- Low-level wind shear within 2,000 feet of the surface

- Volcanic ash, dust, or sandstorm

Example 1

```
ZOA MIS 01 VALID 041415-041900
... FOR ATC PLANNING PURPOSES ONLY...
FOR SFO BAY AREA
DNS BR/FG WITH CIG BLO 005 AND VIS OCNL BLO 1SM TIL 19Z.
```

The example above is an MIS from the Oakland ARTCC. It is the first of the day, issued at 1415Z on the fourth of the month, and it is valid until 1900Z on the fourth. The forecast, which is for the San Francisco Bay Area, calls for dense fog/mist with ceilings below 500 feet and visibilities occasionally below 1SM until 19Z.

Example 2

```
ZOA MIS 02 VALID 041650
... FOR ATC PLANNING PURPOSES ONLY...
FOR SFO BAY AREA
CANCEL ZOA MIS 01. DNS BR/FG CONDS HAVE IPVD ERYR THAN FCST.
```

The above MIS from Oakland ARTCC cancels the previously issued MIS. Specifically, it states that dense fog/mist conditions have improved earlier than was previously forecast.

Example 3

```
ZID MIS 03 VALID 041200-042330
... FOR ATC PLANNING PURPOSES ONLY...
FROM IND TO CMH TO LOZ TO EVV TO IND
FRQ MOD TURBC FL310-390 DUE TO JTSTR... CONDS DMSHG IN INTSTY AFT 21Z.
```

This MIS originates with the Indianapolis ARTCC and was issued at 1200Z on the fourth of the month. It is valid until the same day at 2330Z. The forecast describes an area from Indianapolis, IN, to Columbus, OH, to London, KY, to Evansville, IN, and back to Indianapolis. It describes frequent moderate turbulence between flight levels 310–390 feet caused by the jet stream. Conditions will diminish in intensity after 21Z.

Center Weather Advisories

A Center Weather Advisory (CWA) is an aviation warning to air crews to anticipate and avoid adverse weather conditions in en route and terminal environments. The CWA is not a flight planning product; instead, it reflects current conditions expected at the time of issuance. It is a short-range forecast for conditions expected to begin within the next 2 hours. CWAs are valid for a maximum of 2 hours. If conditions are expected to continue beyond the 2-hour valid period, a statement will be included in the CWA.

Example

```
ZME1 CWA 081300
ZME CWA 101 VALID UNTIL 081500
```

```
FROM MEM TO JAN TO LIT TO MEM
AREA SCT VIP 5-6 (INTENSE/EXTREME) TS MOV FROM 26025KT. TOPS TO FL450.
```

The CWA above was issued by the Memphis, TN, ARTCC. The 1 after the ZME in the first line denotes that this CWA was issued for the first weather phenomenon to occur for that day. It was written on the eighth at 1300Z. The 101 in the second line denotes the phenomenon number again (1) and the issuance number (01) for this phenomenon. The CWA is valid until the eighth of the month at 1500Z. The area for which it was issued is bounded by Memphis, TN; Jackson, MS; Little Rock, AR; and back to Memphis. Within the CWA is an area with scattered VIP 5–6 (meaning intense/extreme) thunderstorms moving from 260 degrees at 25 knots. Tops of the thunderstorms are at FL450.

SUMMING IT UP

- Because air traffic controllers provide weather information to pilots and plan for its effects on navigation, they are required to understand basic weather navigation systems and the methods by which weather is reported and forecast in the United States.

- The National Weather Service (NWS) and the FAA are the primary providers of weather services to aviation workers. The NWS makes all official forecasts and observations and owns and operates most of the U.S. weather observation and forecasting equipment.

- NWS offices most directly involved in aviation are the Storm Prediction Center, the Aviation Weather Center, and individual weather forecast offices throughout the country.

- FAA facilities primarily responsible for weather dissemination are Flight Service Stations (FSSs) and weather service units located in larger air traffic control facilities.

- For aviation purposes, weather observations are measurements and estimates of existing weather conditions both on the ground and aloft. They include upper air observations, radar observations, terminal Doppler weather radar stations (TDWR), satellite systems, and surface aviation weather observations.

- A METAR, a one- or two-line coded report, describes weather conditions at a given site and time. METARs are used by the aviation community to determine whether Visual Flight Rules (VFR) or Instrument Flight Rules (IFR) flights can be conducted and to provide information for developing aviation-related weather forecasts. The METAR code structure has been standardized internationally, although countries make allowances or modifications.

- A terminal aerodrome forecast (TAF) is similar to a METAR, but it describes the weather conditions expected at and around an airport during a 24-hour period. TAFs use the same general weather abbreviations and codes found in METAR weather reports.

- SIGMETs are short-term reports advising of non-thunderstorm weather. AIRMETs are scheduled bulletins that advise on weather phenomena at intensities lower than those requiring a SIGMET. Severe Weather Watch Bulletins (WWs) define areas of possible severe thunderstorm or tornado activity. Center Weather Service Unit (CWSU) products issued by Air Route Traffic Control Centers (ARTCCs) are intended primarily for pilots and controllers operating within ARTCC airspace.

Charting and Air Traffic Control

OVERVIEW

- **Mapping airspace**

- **Navigation aids**

- **Airways**

- **Airport information**

- **Weather information and communication features**

- **Terminal instrument procedure publications**

- **Instrument approach procedures charts**

- **Summing it up**

MAPPING AIRSPACE

Charts are a graphic way to depict the structure of the national airspace system. Air traffic controllers and pilots use a number of charts, but the ones most commonly used by VFR pilots are sectional charts. IFR pilots use a combination of en route charts and approach and departure charts.

Sectional Charts

Sectional aeronautical charts are designed for visual navigation. These charts show topographic information and visual checkpoints, such as populated places, roads, railroads, lakes and rivers, and other distinctive landmarks visible from the air. The aeronautical information on these charts includes visual and radio aids to navigation, airports, controlled airspace, restricted areas, obstructions, and related data.

chapter 5

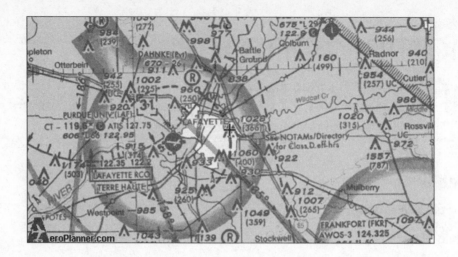

IFR Charts

IFR pilots use a combination of en route and approach and departure charts. En route charts are useful for pilots flying from airport to airport. Approach and departure charts assist the pilot in making the transition to and from the airway structure.

En route high-altitude charts provide aeronautical information for IFR flights at or above 18,000 feet. These charts include jet routes, identification and frequencies of radio aids,

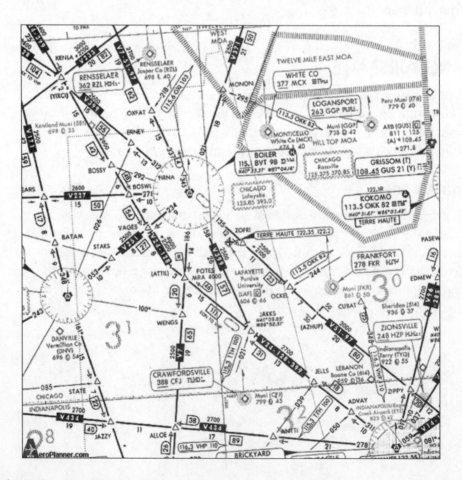

selected airports, distances, time zones, special-use airspace, and related information. Scales vary from 1 inch = 45 nautical miles (NM) to 1 inch = 18 NM. The charts are revised every 56 days.

IFR low-altitude en route charts are similar and depict the airspace from the earth's surface up to but not including 18,000 feet above sea level. Some of the more commonly used symbols and information found on en route charts are explained below.

NAVIGATION AIDS

- **Very-high-frequency Omni-directional Ranges (VORs):** these are the principal navigational aids (NAVAIDs) found on en route charts. The symbol looks like this:

- **Nondirectional radio beacons (NDBs):** NDBs are used as temporary replacements for VORs; they are also still in use for some oceanic en route navigation. The symbol looks like this:

- **Distance measuring equipment (DME):** allows the pilot to measure distance from the location of the DME transmitter. The first symbol denotes DME fix (distance same as airway/route mileage). In the second symbol, the encircled number denotes mileage, which is shown when it's not otherwise obvious:

- **VOR/DME:** this is a facility that combines a VOR and DME transmitter. The symbol looks like this:

- **Tactical Air Navigation (TACAN):** a military navigation system that provides bearing and distance information. The symbol for a TACAN system looks like this:

- **VORTAC:** the international standard navigational system that combines the civilian VOR/DME with the military TACAN system to create one transmitting station. VORTACs are indicated with this symbol:

AIRWAYS

Most airways measure 8 nautical miles wide. They connect VORs to one another. The U.S. air system has low- and high-altitude airways. The names for low-altitude airways (below 18,000 feet) are called Victor airways and are prefixed with the letter "V." High-altitude airways, called jetways, extend upward from 18,000 feet; their names are prefixed with the letter "J." Airways are depicted on en route charts as blue lines. The radial defining the airway and extending from each VOR is indicated where the airway joins the VOR.

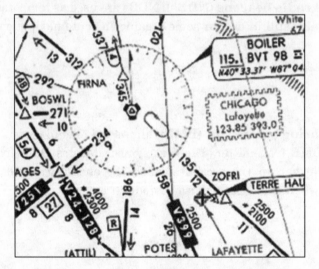

Identifying Intersections

Identifying intersections along an airway route are established by a variety of NAVAIDs. An open triangle indicates the location of an ATC reporting point or intersection. NDBs, localizers, and off-route VORs can be used to establish intersections. Off-route VORs are one of the most common means of identifying intersections.

Another means of identifying an intersection is with a DME. A hollow arrowhead indicates that a DME is authorized for intersection identification. Offset arrows next to the intersection symbol indicate which NAVAID should be used for identification.

VOR Changeover Points

VOR changeover points (COPs) are depicted on charts by this symbol:

The numbers indicate the distance at which VOR frequency is changed. The frequency change might be required because of poor signal reception or conflicting frequencies. If a COP does not appear on an airway, radio frequency should be changed midway between facilities. Occasionally, an "x" will appear at a separated segment of an airway that is not an intersection. The "x" represents a mileage breakdown or computer navigation fix and indicates a course change.

Holding Patterns

Holding patterns are designated locations where air traffic control has deemed it necessary to occasionally hold aircraft to temporarily restrict traffic flow. The symbol for a holding pattern is an elongated horizontal oval with arrows indicating the direction in which the aircraft should fly. If a number appears inside the oval, it represents indicated airspeed.

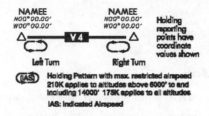

Charted Altitudes

En route charts depict scores of mandatory and minimum altitudes that pilots must comply with. They include the following altitude types.

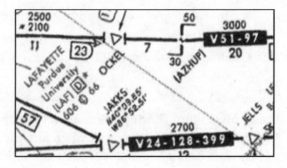

MINIMUM EN ROUTE ALTITUDE

A minimum en route altitude (MEA) is the lowest published altitude between radio fixes that ensures acceptable navigational signal coverage and meets obstacle clearance requirements between those fixes. The MEA is shown just above the airway designation.

MEAs are not normally shown on high-altitude charts unless they are at or above 18,000 feet MSL. The minimum en route altitude ensures a navigation signal strong enough for **adequate** reception by the aircraft navigation receiver and adequate obstacle clearance along the airway. Communication is not necessarily guaranteed with MEA compliance.

The obstacle clearance, within the limits of the airway, is typically 1,000 feet in non-mountainous areas and 2,000 feet in designated mountainous areas. MEAs can be authorized with breaks in signal coverage; if this occurs, the en route chart notes "MEA GAP" parallel to the affected airway. MEAs are usually bidirectional but they are occasionally unidirectional. Arrows indicate the direction to which the MEA applies.

MINIMUM OBSTRUCTION CLEARANCE ALTITUDE

A minimum obstruction clearance altitude (MOCA) is the lowest published altitude in effect between radio fixes on VOR airways, off-airway routes, or en route segments meeting obstacle clearance requirements for the entire route segment and ensuring acceptable navigational signal coverage only within 25 statute miles (22 nautical miles) of a VOR. Like MEAs, MOCAs are not normally shown on high-altitude charts unless the MEA is at or above 18,000 feet MSL. MOCA, as the name suggests, provides the same obstruction clearance as an MEA; however, the navigational (NAV) signal reception is ensured only within 22 nautical miles of the closest navigation aids (NAVAID) defining the route. The MOCA is listed below the MEA and above the airway designation, and it is preceded by an asterisk.

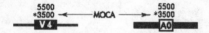

MINIMUM RECEPTION ALTITUDE

Minimum reception altitude (MRA) identifies an intersection from an off-course NAVAID. If the reception is line-of-sight based, signal coverage will only extend to the MRA or above. However, if the aircraft is equipped with distance measuring equipment (DME) and the chart indicates that the intersection can be identified with such equipment, the pilot can define the fix without attaining the MRA. On charts, the MRA is indicated by the following symbol:

MRA 4500

The number "4500" in this example represents the MRA.

MINIMUM CROSSING ALTITUDES

Minimum crossing altitudes (MCAs) are charted when a pilot is approaching a higher MEA route segment. An MCA is usually indicated on a chart when aircraft are approaching steeply rising terrain and obstacle clearance and/or signal reception is compromised. In this case, the pilot is required to initiate a climb, so that the MCA is reached by the time the intersection is crossed. On charts, the MCA is indicated by the symbol, the Victor airway number, and the direction to which it applies. Here's an example:

MCA
V6 4000 SW

MAXIMUM AUTHORIZED ALTITUDE

Maximum authorized altitude (MAA) is the highest altitude at which a pilot can fly an airway without receiving conflicting navigation signals from NAVAIDs operating on the same frequency. A chart depiction of an MAA for 15,000 feet, for example, would read "MAA-15000."

When an MEA, MOCA, and/or MAA changes on an airway at a point other than at a navigation aid, a sideways "T" (with the head in either direction) appears on the chart. When a change of MEA to a higher MEA is required, the climb may commence at that break, ensuring obstacle clearance.

AIRPORT INFORMATION

Airport information is provided in a legend on a navigation chart. The symbols for the airport name, elevation, and runway length are similar to those in a sectional chart. Instrument approaches at airports are noted with blue or green symbols; a brown symbol denotes an airport that does not have approved instrument approaches. Asterisks indicate whether tower operations, lighting facilities, and airspace classifications are part-time (not operating continuously).

ARTCC boundaries on a chart indicate each ARTCC's jurisdiction. They appear on charts as blue serrated lines. The name of the controlling facility is printed on the corresponding side of the division line.

ARTCC remote radio sites are depicted as boxes with blue serrated borders; the boxes contain the center name, sector name, and sector frequency.

WEATHER INFORMATION AND COMMUNICATION FEATURES

As the name suggests, pilots use en route NAVAIDs to obtain weather information while en route. When a NAVAID appears on a chart as a shadowed box, a Flight Service Station (FSS) of the same name is directly associated with the facility. If an FSS is located without an associated NAVAID, the shadowed box is smaller and contains only the name and identifier. FSS frequencies are provided on top of the box.

Remote Communications Outlet

A remote communications outlet (RCO) is a radio transmitter/receiver directly linked to an FSS. If it is co-located with a NAVAID, it is designated by a finely outlined box with the controlling FSS frequency above and the name below. If no associated facility exists, the RCO box contains the FSS name and remote frequency.

HIWAS and TWEB

Hazardous In-flight Weather Advisory Service (HIWAS) and Transcribed Weather En Route Broadcast (TWEB) reports are continuously transmitted over selected NAVAIDs. On charts, they are depicted in the NAVAID box: a HIWAS is represented by a white "H" in a black circle in the upper left corner of the box, and a TWEB broadcast is represented by a white "T" in a black circle in the upper right corner of the box.

TERMINAL INSTRUMENT PROCEDURE PUBLICATIONS

Just as en route charts provide information for pilots to navigate from one airport to another, terminal procedures assist them when they are moving the aircraft to and from an airway.

Arrival routes switch pilots over from airway procedures to the beginning of an instrument approach procedure (IAP). IAPs guide the pilot toward the airport to a minimum altitude for landing, at which point the pilot can see the runway and safely land the aircraft. Departure procedures (DPs) provide an obstacle-free path for aircraft that have just departed and are climbing to minimum airway altitudes.

Departure Procedures

Departure procedures (DPs) provide obstacle clearance protection to aircraft in instrument meteorological conditions while reducing delays in communications and departure. DPs are published in text and/or charted graphic form, but regardless of the format, they all provide ways for pilots to depart an airport and make a safe transition to the en route structure.

Standard Terminal Arrival Route

Standard Terminal Arrival Route (STAR) depicts prescribed routes to help an instrument pilot make the transition from the en route structure to a fix in the terminal area, from which an instrument approach can be conducted. Departure procedures and STAR charts use the same general symbols used on en route charts. The only addition is the name(s) of the airports served and a textual description of the route flown.

INSTRUMENT APPROACH PROCEDURES CHARTS

Instrument approach procedure (IAP) charts provide pilots with approved procedures to descend and land safely in low-visibility conditions. The FAA established the use of IAPs after thorough analyses of obstructions, terrain features, and navigational facilities. Maneuvers—including altitude changes, course corrections, and other limitations—are prescribed in IAPs. The charts reflect the criteria associated with the U.S. Standard for terminal instrument approach procedures (TERPs), which prescribes specific methods for use in designing instrument flight procedures.

The instrument approach chart is divided into five main sections:

1. Margin identification

2. Plan view

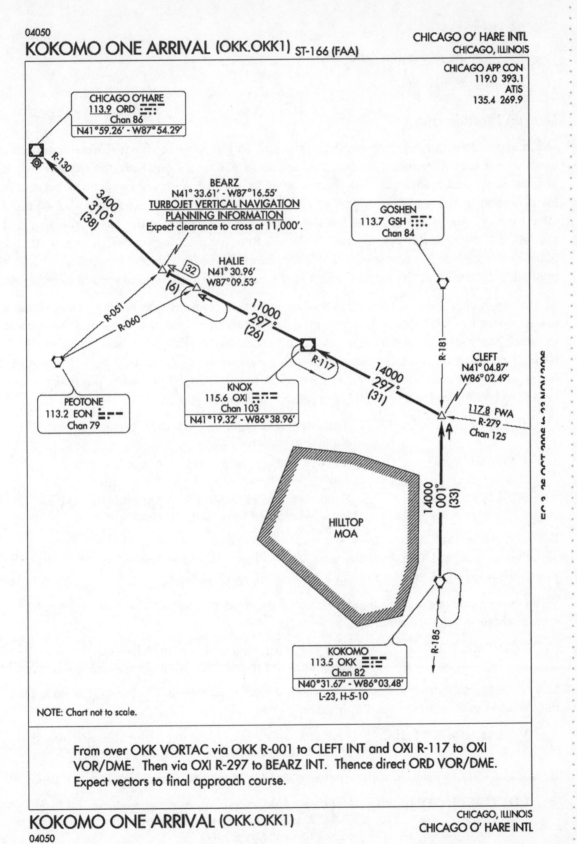

04050

KOKOMO ONE ARRIVAL (OKK.OKK1) ST-166 (FAA)

CHICAGO O' HARE INTL
CHICAGO, ILLINOIS

CHICAGO APP CON
119.0 393.1
ATIS
135.4 269.9

CHICAGO O'HARE
113.9 ORD
Chan 86
N41°59.26' - W87°54.29'

R-130

3400
310°
(38)

BEARZ
N41° 33.61' - W87°16.55'
**TURBOJET VERTICAL NAVIGATION
PLANNING INFORMATION**
Expect clearance to cross at 11,000'.

GOSHEN
113.7 GSH
Chan 84

HALIE
N41° 30.96'
W87°09.53'

32

(6)

11000
297°
(26)

R-051

R-060

R-117

14000
297°
(31)

R-181

CLEFT
N41° 04.87'
W86° 02.49'

117.8 FWA
R-279
Chan 125

PEOTONE
113.2 EON
Chan 79

KNOX
115.6 OXI
Chan 103
N41°19.32' - W86°38.96'

HILLTOP
MOA

14000
001°
(33)

R-185

KOKOMO
113.5 OKK
Chan 82
N40°31.67' - W86°03.48'
L-23, H-5-10

NOTE: Chart not to scale.

From over OKK VORTAC via OKK R-001 to CLEFT INT and OXI R-117 to OXI
VOR/DME. Then via OXI R-297 to BEARZ INT. Thence direct ORD VOR/DME.
Expect vectors to final approach course.

KOKOMO ONE ARRIVAL (OKK.OKK1)

CHICAGO, ILLINOIS
CHICAGO O' HARE INTL

04050

Example of a terminal instrument approach procedure publication

③ Profile view

④ Landing minimums (and notes)

⑤ Airport diagram

Margin Identification

IAP margin identification, located at the top and bottom of each chart, depicts the airport location and procedure identification. The approach plates are organized by city first, then airport name, and then state. The chart's amendment status appears above the procedure identification in the top margin and below in the bottom margin, along with the volume's effective date. (Dates are noted as five-digit numbers incorporating the day of the year and the last two digits of the year. For example, the date notation for the 167th day of 2007 is noted as "07167.") At the center of an IAP's top margin is the FAA chart reference number and approving authority; at the bottom center is the airport's latitude and longitude coordinates.

The means of identification for each procedure is derived from the type of navigational facility that provides the final approach course guidance for straight-in approaches, and the runway to which the course is aligned. As we discussed earlier in this book, some airports have parallel runways and simultaneous approach procedures, so the letters "L," "R," and "C" following "RWY" denote whether the runway is the left, right, or center parallel runway, respectively. Here are some examples of procedure identifications:

ILS RWY 19	An Instrument Landing System is in use; the course is aligned to runway 19
RNAV RWY 29	An Area Navigation system is in use; the course is aligned to runway 29
NDB RWY 16R	Nondirectional radio beacon approach is in use; the course is aligned to runway 16 right

For approaches that do not meet straight-in criteria, a letter from the beginning of the alphabet is assigned (e.g., VOR-A or LDA-B). The letter designation signifies that the procedure is expected to culminate in a circling approach to land.

When more than one navigational system is required to conduct the final approach, the system abbreviations are separated by a slash:

VOR/DME RWY 31	VHF Omni-directional Range and distance measuring equipment are in use; the course is aligned to runway 31

More than one navigational system separated by "or" indicates that either type of equipment may be used to execute the final approach:

VOR or GPS RWY 15C	VHF Omni-directional Range or Global Positioning System is in use; the course is aligned to runway 15 center

Helicopters have special IAPs, designated with COPTER in the procedure identification:

COPTER LOC/DME 25L	Helicopter instrument approach procedure: ILS localizer and distance measuring equipment in use; the course is aligned to runway 25 left

Plan View

The plan view provides a graphical overhead view of the instrument approach procedure and depicts the routes that guide the pilot from the en route segments to the initial approach fix (IAF). During the initial approach, the aircraft has departed the en route phase of flight and is maneuvering to enter an intermediate or final segment of the instrument approach.

An instrument approach can be made along prescribed routes within the terminal area, which may run along an arc, radial, course, heading, radar vector, or a combination thereof. Features of the plan view include:

- The procedure turn

- Obstacle elevation

- Minimum safe altitude (MSA)

- Procedure track

The majority of IAP charts contain a reference or distance circle with a radius of 10 nautical miles. Normally, approach features within the plan view are shown to scale; however, only the data within the reference circle is *always* drawn to scale. The circle is centered on an approach fix and has a radius of 10 NM, unless otherwise indicated.

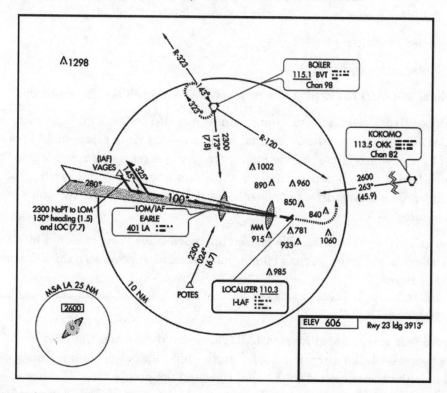

The primary airport depicted in the plan view is drawn with enough detail to show the runway orientation and final approach course alignment. Airports other than the primary approach airport are not depicted in the plan view.

Known spot elevations and obstacles are indicated on the plan view in MSL altitudes. The largest dot and number combination indicate the highest elevation. An inverted "V" with a dot in the center depicts an obstacle. The highest obstacle is indicated with a bolder, larger version of the same symbol. Two interlocking inverted Vs signify a group of obstacles.

In the top left or right corner of the plan view is the communications area. Communication frequencies are generally listed in the order in which they would be used during aircraft arrival. Frequencies for weather and related facilities are noted where applicable. They include Automatic Terminal Information Service (ATIS), Automated Surface Observing System (ASOS), Automated Weather Observing System (AWOS), and FSSs.

The MSA circle appears in the plan view. This information is provided for emergency purposes only, and it guarantees 1,000 feet of obstruction clearance in the sector indicated, with reference to the bearing in the circle. For conventional navigation systems, the MSA is normally based on the primary omnidirectional facility on which the IAP is predicated. The MSA depiction on the approach chart contains the facility identifier of the NAVAID used to determine the MSA altitudes. The MSL altitudes appear in boxes within the circle, which typically represents a radius of 25 NM unless otherwise indicated.

NAVAIDs noted in the plan view are necessary for completing the instrument procedure. They include:

- Facility name

- Radio frequency

- Letter identifier

- Morse code sequence

A heavy-lined NAVAID box depicts the primary NAVAID used for the approach.

Intersections, fixes, radials, and course lines describe route and approach sequencing information. The main procedure—or final approach—course is represented by a thick solid line. A DME arc, which is part of the main procedure course, is also represented as a thick, solid line. A feeder route is represented by a medium line; it provides heading, altitude, and distance information. All three components must be designated on the chart to provide a navigable course.

Radials are shown by thin lines. The missed approach track is represented by a thin dashed line with a directional arrow. A visual flight path segment appears as a thick dashed line with a directional arrow.

COURSE REVERSAL

Course reversals are included in each IAP. These are used when the pilot needs to reverse direction to establish the aircraft inbound on the final approach course. Components of the required procedure are depicted in the plan view and the profile view. The maneuver must be completed within the distance and at the minimum altitude specified in the profile view. The most common form of a course reversal is a procedure turn.

A procedure is indicated on the plan view as a barbed arrow indicating the direction or side of the outbound course on which the procedure turn is made. Headings are provided for course reversal using a 45-degree procedure turn. The point at which the turn may be commenced and the type and rate of turn are left to the pilot's discretion. The absence of a turn symbol in a plan view indicates that a turn is not authorized for that procedure.

TERMINAL ARRIVAL AREA CONCEPT

A new way to construct instrument approaches, known as the Terminal Arrival Area (TAA) concept, is currently being implemented across U.S. airspace. The design objective of TAA procedures is to provide a transitional method for arriving aircraft using GPS/RNAV equipment. TAAs will eliminate or reduce the need for feeder routes, departure extensions, and procedure turns or course reversal. The TAA is established in conjunction with standard or modified RNAV approach configurations.

The standard TAA has three areas: straight-in, left base, and right base. The arc boundaries of the three areas of the TAA are published portions of the approach. They allow pilots to make the transition from an en route structure direct to the nearest IAF. When crossing the boundary of each of these areas, a pilot is expected to proceed directly to the appropriate waypoint IAF for the approach area being flown. In all areas, pilots have the option of proceeding directly to the holding pattern.

The TAA has a "T" formation that normally allows no procedure turn for aircraft using the approach. It provides the pilot and air traffic controllers with an efficient method of routing traffic from the en route to the terminal structure. The TAA formation aligns the procedure on runway centerline, with the missed approach point (MAP) located at the threshold, the final approach fix (FAF) 5 nautical miles from the threshold, and the intermediate fix 5 nautical miles from the FAF.

Profile View

A profile view is a side-view drawing of instrument approach procedure. It illustrates vertical approach path altitudes, headings, distances, and fixes. The view includes the minimum altitude and maximum distance for the procedure turn, altitudes over prescribed fixes, distances between fixes, and the missed approach procedure. The profile view helps pilots interpret the IAP, but it's not drawn to scale.

- The precision approach glideslope intercept altitude is the minimum altitude for glideslope interception after completion of the procedure turn. It's illustrated by an altitude number and a zigzagged line. Precision approach profiles also depict the glideslope angle of descent, threshold crossing height (TCH), and glideslope altitude at the outer marker (OM).

- In non-precision approaches, a final descent is initiated at the FAF or after the pilot completes the procedure turn and establishes inbound on the procedure course. The FAF is clearly identified by a Maltese cross in the profile view.

- A stepdown fix may be required in the final segment to gain lower minimums. Stepdown fixes in non-precision procedures are provided between the FAF and the airport for authorizing a lower minimum descent altitude (MDA) after passing an obstruction. They can be identified by NAVAID, NAVAID fix, waypoint, and/or radar. They are depicted by a vertical dashed line. Typically there is only one stepdown fix between the FAF and the MAP, but it's possible to have several. If the stepdown fix cannot be identified, the minimum altitude at the stepdown fix becomes the MDA for the approach.

- The visual descent point (VDP) is a defined point on the final approach course of a non-precision straight-in approach procedure. A pilot may begin normal descent from the MDA to the runway touchdown point, provided he or she establishes visual reference. The VDP is identified on the profile view of the approach chart by the symbol "V."

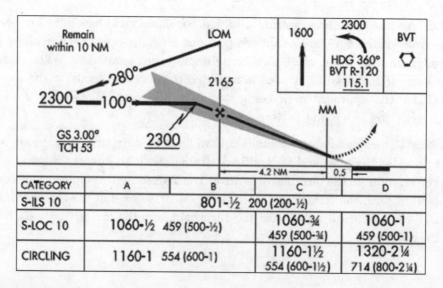

- The missed approach point (MAP) varies depending upon the approach flown. For the ILS, the MAP is at the decision altitude/decision height (DA/DH). In non-precision procedures, the pilot determines the MAP by timing from FAF when the approach aid is well away from the airport, by a fix or NAVAID when the navigation facility is located on the field, or by waypoints as defined by GPS or VOR/DME RNAV.

  A complete description of the missed approach procedure appears in the profile view. A pilot who is initiating a missed approach will be directed by the air traffic controller to climb straight ahead (e.g., "Climb to 2,500"), or to commence a turning climb to a specified altitude (e.g., "Climbing left turn to 2,500"). In some cases, the procedure will direct the pilot to climb straight ahead to an initial altitude, then turn or enter a climbing turn to the holding altitude. For example, the air traffic controller will instruct the pilot to "Climb to 900, then climbing right turn to 2,500 direct ABC VOR and hold."

In addition to these elements, the profile view also depicts minimum, maximum, recommended, and mandatory block altitudes used in approaches.

- The minimum altitude is represented by an underscored number. On final approaches, aircraft are required to maintain an altitude at or above the depicted altitude until reaching the subsequent fix.

- The maximum altitude is represented by an overscored number. Aircraft must remain at or below the depicted altitude.

- Mandatory altitudes are represented by an underscored and overscored altitude number. This means that the altitude noted must be maintained at the stated value.

- Recommended altitudes are advisory altitudes and are not overscored or under-scored.

Landing Minimums (and Notes)

Minimums are specified for various aircraft approach categories based upon a value 1.3 times the stalling speed of the aircraft in the landing configuration at maximum certified gross landing weight. If it is necessary to maneuver at speeds in excess of the upper limit of a speed range for a category, the minimums for the next higher category are used. The minimums for straight-in and circling appear directly under each aircraft category notation. When no solid division line appears between minimums for each category on the rows for straight-in or circling, the minimums apply to those two or more undivided categories.

Precision and non-precision approaches use different terms to describe minimum approach altitudes. Precision approaches use decision altitude (DA), measure in feet MSL, and are followed on the chart by the decision height (DH). DH is measured in feet above threshold elevation of the runway or height above touchdown (HAT).

Non-precision approaches define altitude in terms of minimum descent altitude (MDA). This is measured in feet above mean sea level, followed by a notation of the altitude in feet above the runway touchdown zone. Any figures listed in parentheses are intended for military pilots; they are not used in civil aviation.

Visibility figures are provided either in statute miles or as runway visual range (RVR), which is reported in hundreds of feet. Visibility figures are depicted after the DA/DH or MDA in the minimums section. If visibility in statute miles is indicated, an altitude number, hyphen, and a whole or fractional number appear. For example, the notation "530–1" indicates 530 feet MSL and 1 statute mile visibility as the minimums for this approach. If the runway is so equipped, the RVR value is separated from the minimum altitude with a slash; for example, "1065/24" indicates 1,065 feet MSL and an RVR of 2,400 feet.

Airport Diagram

The airport diagram, located on the bottom right side of the IAP chart, includes many helpful features. For some larger airports, this diagram may take up an entire page. Information on runway orientation, lighting, final approach bearings, airport beacon, and obstacles all provide guidance to pilots in the final phases of flight.

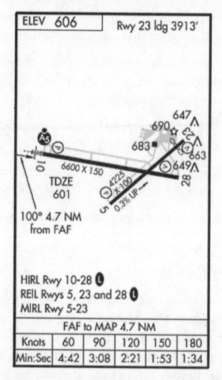

The diagram above shows the runway configuration in solid black. Taxiways and aprons are shaded gray. Other runway environment features include the runway identification, dimensions, magnetic heading, displaced threshold, arresting gear, usable length, and slope.

Airport elevation is indicated in a separate box at the top left of the airport diagram box. The touchdown zone elevation (TDZE), which is the highest elevation within the first 3,000 feet of the runway, is designated at the approach end of the runway.

Beneath the airport diagram is the time and speed table. The table provides the distance and amount of time required to go from the FAF to the MAP for selected ground speeds. The approach lighting systems and the visual approach lights are depicted on the approach chart, as are runway lighting aids.

SUMMING IT UP

- Charts depict the structure of the national airspace system. Air traffic controllers and pilots most commonly use sectional charts (VFR) or a combination of en route charts and approach and departure charts (IFR).

- Sectional charts for visual navigation show topographic information and visual checkpoints. En route charts for IFR are useful for pilots flying from airport to airport. Approach and departure charts assist in making the transition to and from the airway structure.

- Navigation aids (NAVAIDs) include very-high-frequency Omni-directional Ranges (VORs), the principal NAVAIDs on en route charts; nondirectional radio beacons (NDBs); distance measuring equipment (DME); VOR/DMEs; Tactical Air Navigation (TACAN); and VORTAC, the international standard navigational system that combines the civilian VOR/DME with the military TACAN system to create one transmitting station.

- Airways connect VORs to one another. They appear on en route charts as blue lines. The radial defining the airway and extending from each VOR is indicated where the airway joins the VOR. Instrument approach procedure (IAP) charts contain notations for identifying intersections, VOR changeover points, holding patterns, and charted altitudes.

- Airport information is provided in a legend on a navigation chart. The legend includes symbols for the airport name, elevation, runway length, instrument approaches (if present), and whether tower operations, lighting facilities, and airspace classifications are part-time. Air Route Traffic Control Center (ARTCC) boundaries and remote radio sites are also depicted.

- Weather information and communication features on navigational charts include the presence of remote communications outlets, hazardous in-flight weather advisory service, and transcribed weather broadcasts.

- Terminal procedures that assist pilots moving aircraft to and from an airway include departure procedures and standard terminal arrival routes.

- IAP charts provide pilots with approved procedures to descend and land safely in low-visibility conditions. IAP charts include airport location and procedure identification, a plan view, profile view, landing minimums, and airport diagrams.

PART III

THE AIR TRAFFIC SELECTION AND TRAINING TEST (AT-SAT)

CHAPTER 6   Taking the AT-SAT

Taking the AT-SAT

OVERVIEW

- **How to prepare for the AT-SAT**

- **What's on the exam?**

- **How the AT-SAT is scored**

- **What's next: air traffic controller training**

- **Summing it up**

Every applicant for an air traffic control position must eventually pass the Air Traffic Selection and Training Test (AT-SAT) before being considered for employment by the FAA. The FAA is the *only* organization that administers the AT-SAT, and you cannot take the exam until you are well along in the application process.

The AT-SAT has no set test dates, unlike many other standardized tests. If your application is accepted, the FAA contacts you at the appropriate time to arrange a date and location for you to take the exam.

HOW TO PREPARE FOR THE AT-SAT

The AT-SAT is an 8-hour test taken on a computer. It is designed to evaluate the following:

- The ability to reason and prioritize

- A tolerance for high-intensity workloads

- Composure under pressure

- The ability to plan and execute

- The ability to think ahead

- A willingness to take charge

- The ability to work cooperatively with others

- Decisiveness, problem solving, and visualization skills

- Arithmetic and angle calculation skills

131

The AT-SAT is not meant to test you on what you know about air traffic control. So how do you prepare?

First, try to read as much as possible about air traffic control in the weeks before the exam date. (You've made substantial headway if you've made it through this book.) It may sound contradictory, but even though you don't have to know specific terms and details of air traffic control, it will help you to be familiar with the field.

You might want to pick up a copy of *Fundamentals of Air Traffic Control* by Michael S. Nolan (the author of this test-prep guide). Also, be sure to review the FAA's *Aeronautical Information Manual*. The manual is available as a downloadable PDF or online in an HTML version at http://www.faa.gov/airports_airtraffic/air_traffic/publications.

Although neither of these publications specifically address the questions you will encounter on the AT-SAT, they do explain aviation and air traffic control terminology, theory, and practice. Reading them and reviewing the explanatory chapters in this book will help you familiarize yourself with terms and concepts you'll need to know to become an air traffic controller.

Helpful Tips

- Try to get a good night's sleep the night before the exam. On the morning of the exam, be sure to get up early enough so that you can eat a good breakfast and get to the exam center with plenty of time to spare.

- Dress comfortably but professionally. This is not a job interview and you don't want to feel uncomfortable during the exam, but you do want to give a good impression.

- Arrive for the testing session on time. If you're unfamiliar with the test center location, make a "practice run" a few days before the test date.

- During the 8-hour exam, you will have two scheduled 15-minute rest breaks and a 45-minute lunch break. Take the rest breaks. Some of the AT-SAT test sections can be mentally taxing. The breaks are intended to help you stay alert and keep your concentration level up. If you don't know whether food and drinks are available at or near the test center, think about packing a lunch. You may want to bring reading material, an MP3 player, or some other form of distraction for your lunch break.

- *Read all directions.* Among the most common reasons for wrong answers are inattention to directions or failure to read them.

- Test administrators cannot answer questions about the test questions or the rules provided.

WHAT'S ON THE EXAM?

The AT-SAT is computer-based. Computer prompts will lead you through each section of the exam. The program first introduces the topic on which you will be tested and provides a review of the proper method for inputting answers. It will then lead you through a brief practice session before administering the actual exam.

The AT-SAT consists of eight sections:

1. Scan
2. Dial Reading
3. Angles
4. Applied Math
5. Experience Questionnaire
6. Analogies
7. Letter Factory
8. Air Traffic Scenario

Scan

During the scanning section of the AT-SAT, multiple blocks of data appear at random on your computer screen. The numbers in the data blocks will either be inside or outside a specific range, which is displayed at the bottom of the screen. This section of the test is scored according to how quickly and accurately you can identify the data blocks with numbers outside the specified range.

Here's a tip for doing well on the scanning section: Make certain you remember what the range is, and keep in mind that you are looking for data that is *outside* the range, not within it.

Dial Reading

Air traffic controllers must be able to see and perceive visual information quickly and accurately. Much of this information comes from gauges, dials, and digital and analog readouts. The dial reading section of the AT-SAT assesses your ability to read simulated dials quickly and accurately. The only thing you need to keep in mind for this section is that you must be sure you are accurately reading the scale on each dial.

Angles

Air traffic controllers must be able to recognize angles and perform calculations on them quickly and accurately. The angles section of the AT-SAT measures your ability to perform these tasks. You will be asked a series of questions about the general and relative size of angles presented on your computer screen. Some questions may provide an angular measurement and ask you to pick the drawing that matches the measurement. Another type of question you'll see in this section will provide the drawing and ask you to estimate its angle.

Applied Math

The applied math section of the AT-SAT evaluates your ability to apply simple mathematical functions to air traffic control. All of the questions involve calculating time, distance, and speed, based on information supplied in the problem, and all questions relate to the movement of aircraft. For example, a question may provide an aircraft's speed and the distance to be flown, and require you to determine its travel time.

To complete this section, it helps to be familiar with a few aviation conventions:

- Air traffic controllers use the 24-hour military clock. This means that a.m. time notations remain the same, but you must add 12 hours to those times to get p.m. time notations. For example, 2:15 p.m. civilian time is 1415 in military time.

- In air traffic control, time is referenced as Consolidated Universal Time (UTC), the standard based in Greenwich, England, and used around the world. In aviation, this time is often called Zulu (for "zero") time.

- Distance measurements in aviation are often given in nautical miles; resulting speed in nautical miles per hour is noted in knots.

Keep in mind that all of these aviation-related terms may be distracters to the math questions. After all, 1 hour of time is always 60 minutes, regardless of whether you are using a 24-hour clock, a 12-hour clock, or Zulu time. As long as the mileage and speeds are both noted in nautical miles, you would calculate a problem just as if they were noted in statute miles.

TIME-SPEED-DISTANCE FORMULAS

A working knowledge of the basic "time-speed-distance" formula is invaluable in the applied math section of the AT-SAT. Become familiar with the following formulas—all variations of the same calculation—and your chances of answering math questions correctly will be much higher.

$$distance \div time = speed$$

$$speed \times time = distance$$

$$distance \div speed = time$$

When applying these formulas to math problems, first make sure that all your time figures are in minutes (not hours); then multiply by 60 if necessary to get the number of hours.

Example 1

Let's say that a question on the exam provides you with the time it takes to fly a specific distance in an aircraft and then asks you to determine that aircraft's speed:

If an aircraft flies 145 miles in 35 minutes, how fast is it going (in standard miles per hour)?

Using the first formula above, *distance* ÷ *time* = *speed*, you plug in the time and distance values to divide the distance flown by the time *in minutes*:

$$145 \div 35 = 4.14 \text{ miles per minute}$$

Now you want to convert the speed to standard miles per hour, so you multiply the answer by 60.

$$4.14 \times 60 = 248 \text{ mph}$$

If the distance is given in nautical miles—meaning that the answer must be in knots (nautical miles per hour)—use the same procedure. Perform the calculations just as you did above, and you will have the results in knots.

Example 2

Now, let's say that the problem provides you with speed and time values and you need to calculate the distance. Here's where the second version of the formula, *speed × time = distance,* comes in.

> An aircraft is traveling at 248 miles per hour and reaches its destination in 35 minutes. How far has it flown when it reaches its destination?

Before using the time-speed-distance formula, you must convert the time into the decimal equivalent of an hour by multiplying by 60:

> 35 minutes × 60 = 0.584 hour

Now that you have the time in minutes, multiply this fraction of an hour by the speed to come up with distance flown:

> 0.584 × 248 mph = 145 miles

Example 3

In this example, you've been provided with the distance an aircraft has flown and the speed at which it traveled. You must determine the time it took to fly that route. Here's where you'll use the third version of the time-speed-distance formula, *distance ÷ speed = time.*

> An aircraft travels 145 miles at a speed of 248 mph. How long did it take to travel this route?

To answer this question, you simply divide the distance by the speed:

> 145 ÷ 248 = 0.584

This will give you the flight time. Remember, this figure is the decimal equivalent of fractions of an hour, so you must multiply by 60 (the number of minutes in an hour) to get the flight time in minutes:

> 0.584 × 60 = 35 minutes

Example 4

Some questions on the AT-SAT are presented as word problems with multiple steps. Some have distracters as well. For instance, a question might read:

> If the distance between point A and point B is 560 miles and if the aircraft departed point A at 0800 Zulu and flew at 400 kts, what time would the aircraft cross point B?

Here, the mention of Zulu time and the "kts" abbreviation (for knots) are distracters. You don't need them to arrive at the correct answer. You have been provided with the distance and speed values, so you need to calculate the missing element—time—using the formula *time = distance ÷ speed*:

$$560 \text{ mi} \div 400 \text{ knots} = 1.4 \text{ hrs}$$

Again, multiply by 60 to get the answer in minutes:

$$60 \times 1.4 = 84 \text{ minutes}$$

$$84 \text{ minutes} = 1:24 \text{ (1 hour and 24 minutes)}$$

Since the aircraft departed point A at 0800Z, you must add the 1:24 flight time to the departure time to get an arrival time:

$$0800 + 0124 = 0924$$

The flight arrived at 0924Z.

Experience Questionnaire

Air traffic controllers must possess certain work-related attributes to perform their jobs well. The experience questionnaire section of the AT-SAT attempts to determine whether you have these attributes by asking about your past experiences. The FAA emphasizes that there are no correct or incorrect answers on this section of the test. Each test-taker will respond in his or her own way to the questions on this section, based on what is true for that person.

Obviously, there's no way of preparing for the experience questionnaire section of the AT-SAT. The best you can do is to respond truthfully to each question.

Analogies

Air traffic controllers must be able to determine very quickly whether specific rules apply to a given situation—and must then apply those rules correctly. The analogies portion of the AT-SAT is meant to measure your ability to apply previously unknown rules to solving a given problem.

This section consists of verbal and visual items that may not be related to air traffic control. Typically, you will be provided with an example that has a rule-based solution, but you will not be given the rule itself. You must determine what rule is implied by the example, and then use that rule to answer the question correctly.

Letter Factory

The complex operations section of the AT-SAT, more commonly known as the letter factory, is a simulation developed by the FAA to assess three abilities:

1. Planning and deciding what action to take in a given situation
2. Thinking ahead to avoid problems before they occur
3. Maintaining awareness of the work setting

During this simulation, you will be provided with the rules you need to operate your "factory" of alphabetical letters, including how to operate the facility, how to control various processes, how to order and/or dispose of items, and how to summon help. In the beginning of the simulation, letters move down several conveyor belts, and you must place the correctly colored letter in the correct color box at the bottom of the diagram using the computer mouse. You must also move empty boxes from the storage area to the loading area, order new boxes when supplies become low, and call Quality Control when "defective" letters appear. During the simulation, the program pauses at various times to present a multiple-choice question about the letter factory display.

It is impossible to prepare for this section as you might for a math or vocabulary test. The best method for success is to make sure that you operate your factory according to the rules provided. It's a good idea to occasionally scan the entire screen to remember what is going on as a whole—but don't spend too much time doing this. Scan just long enough so that you can answer questions about the scenario when they arise.

As with similarly formatted exams, it's probably best to go with your first answer on letter factory questions. Trust your abilities, and don't waste time trying to memorize.

Air Traffic Scenario

The final section of the AT-SAT is a series of simulated air traffic control situations. These measure your ability to safely and efficiently guide airplanes. Don't panic: This section doesn't require prior knowledge of air traffic control. It employs simple rules that are relatively easy to follow.

In fact, in some cases previous knowledge of air traffic control might not be completely helpful. Many standard air traffic control concepts, such as precise headings and altitudes, are not used in this section. Instead, you'll see a highly simplified radar display, and you will be prompted to direct each aircraft to specified points or airports while maintaining appropriate separation of the aircraft. As a new aircraft appears on the screen, you must route it safely to an appropriate exit or airport.

This section is scored based on how quickly and accurately you direct the aircraft to their destinations. Before the scored scenario, you will be presented with practice sessions to become accustomed to the program.

HOW THE AT-SAT IS SCORED

You will not know your AT-SAT score when you leave the test center. Your score will be sent to you by mail after it is graded. At present, if you receive a score of 70 (out of 100) or higher, your application remains active and will most likely be processed further. A score below 70 disqualifies you for consideration; your application process will then be terminated.

One point to keep in mind: The FAA is currently in the process of determining whether to raise the passing score from 70 to 80. It's best to check with the FAA before you take the AT-SAT.

Whether you eventually get a position as an air traffic controller depends on the number of applicants the FAA has received and their test scores relative to yours. Generally, a score of 90 or higher places you in the uppermost group of applicants—those most likely to be hired. Even if you are not in the 90 or higher group, you could still be offered a position, but you may have to wait a little longer.

WHAT'S NEXT: AIR TRAFFIC CONTROLLER TRAINING

So you have scored high on the AT-SAT, and you have passed all of the other tests administered by the FAA and outlined in Chapter 2 (the medical, psychological, and aptitude tests and the security and suitability screenings). This process typically takes between twelve and twenty-four months. Let's assume you have been offered a job as an air traffic controller. What's next?

The job offer is a provisional one—this means that you must still complete the FAA's multiyear training program. Still, if you accept the job offer, you will become a paid FAA employee while you undergo training.

Training for air traffic controllers is a combination of formal and on-the-job instruction. Once you have been selected for employment, you are to present yourself to the FAA's Training Academy in Oklahoma City. Based on your experience, you attend the Academy for up to twelve weeks. The academy program includes academics; task training; and full-fledged, high-fidelity simulator training.

Once you are attending the Academy, you will be tested on your knowledge of basic air traffic control information. This information can be obtained from a variety of sources. (See Appendix B for a list.) This exam will be given during the first portion of the training program. You must pass this exam or risk being terminated by the FAA.

The seven practice tests in this book present the types of questions you will be required to answer on your academy exam. Be sure to work through these practice tests before reporting to duty at the academy.

Once you have completed the academy training program, you are assigned to your first FAA facility. After a period of study in which you learn local procedures, memorize charts and maps, and learn the specific requirements of your job, you will begin to work with fellow controllers in on-the-job training. This training process will last at least two years, based on the complexity of the facility, before you are certified as a controller and able to work on your own.

At airports, new air traffic controllers begin by supplying pilots with basic flight data and airport information. You can advance to the position of ground controller, then local controller, departure controller, and finally arrival controller. At an air route traffic control center, new controllers will first be assigned to delivering printed flight plans to teams, but gradually you can advance to radar associate controller and then to radar controller.

After a period of time, you may request a transfer to another facility if you desire, but you are required to complete an on-the-job training process all over again at the new location. Opportunities are limited for a controller to switch from an en route center position to a tower position; however, you can advance to supervisory positions, including management or staff jobs in air traffic control and top administrative jobs with the FAA.

SUMMING IT UP

- The AT-SAT is an 8-hour computerized test of your abilities, personality strengths, work habits, math and calculation skills, and other qualities essential to becoming an air traffic controller. Only the FAA administers the exam, and you must be invited to take it.

- The AT-SAT consists of eight sections: Scan, Dial Reading, Angles, Applied Math, Experience Questionnaire, Analogies, Letter Factory, and Air Traffic Scenario. Scoring 70 or higher will keep your application active. Whether you are actually offered a position as an air traffic controller depends on the number of applicants the FAA has received and their test scores relative to yours.

- If you score high on the AT-SAT and pass the FAA's medical, psychological, and aptitude tests and the security and suitability screenings, you may be offered a job, but you are still required to complete the FAA training program.

- Air traffic controller training is a combination of formal and on-the-job instruction. You attend the FAA Training Academy in Oklahoma City for up to twelve weeks to study academic subjects and receive task completion and simulator training. You will be tested on your knowledge of basic air traffic control information. The test includes questions similar to those in the practice tests of this book. You must pass this exam or risk termination.

- After you complete academy training, you are assigned to an air traffic control facility, where you continue training on the job for at least two years, after which you are certified as a controller. From that point, you are eligible to request a transfer to another facility, or you can eventually advance to a supervisory position.

PART IV

SEVEN PRACTICE TESTS

PRACTICE TEST 1

PRACTICE TEST 2

PRACTICE TEST 3

PRACTICE TEST 4

PRACTICE TEST 5

PRACTICE TEST 6

PRACTICE TEST 7

ANSWER SHEET PRACTICE TEST 1

1. Ⓐ Ⓑ Ⓒ
2. Ⓐ Ⓑ Ⓒ
3. Ⓐ Ⓑ Ⓒ
4. Ⓐ Ⓑ Ⓒ
5. Ⓐ Ⓑ Ⓒ
6. Ⓐ Ⓑ Ⓒ
7. Ⓐ Ⓑ Ⓒ
8. Ⓐ Ⓑ Ⓒ Ⓓ
9. Ⓐ Ⓑ Ⓒ
10. _____
11. _____
12. _____
13. Ⓐ Ⓑ Ⓒ
14. Ⓐ Ⓑ Ⓒ
15. Ⓐ Ⓑ Ⓒ
16. Ⓐ Ⓑ Ⓒ Ⓓ
17. Ⓐ Ⓑ Ⓒ
18. Ⓐ Ⓑ Ⓒ
19. Ⓐ Ⓑ Ⓒ
20. _____
21. Ⓐ Ⓑ Ⓒ
22. _____
23. Ⓐ Ⓑ Ⓒ Ⓓ
24. Ⓐ Ⓑ Ⓒ
25. Ⓐ Ⓑ Ⓒ
26. Ⓐ Ⓑ Ⓒ
27. Ⓐ Ⓑ Ⓒ
28. Ⓐ Ⓑ Ⓒ
29. Ⓐ Ⓑ Ⓒ Ⓓ
30. Ⓐ Ⓑ Ⓒ Ⓓ
31. Ⓐ Ⓑ Ⓒ Ⓓ
32. Ⓐ Ⓑ Ⓒ
33. _____
34. Ⓐ Ⓑ Ⓒ

35. _____
36. _____
37. _____
38. _____
39. _____
40. _____
41. _____
42. _____
43. _____
44. Ⓐ Ⓑ Ⓒ
45. _____
46. Ⓐ Ⓑ Ⓒ Ⓓ
47. Ⓐ Ⓑ Ⓒ
48. _____
49. Ⓐ Ⓑ Ⓒ
50. Ⓐ Ⓑ Ⓒ
51. Ⓐ Ⓑ Ⓒ
52. Ⓐ Ⓑ Ⓒ
53. Ⓐ Ⓑ Ⓒ
54. Ⓐ Ⓑ Ⓒ
55. _____
56. _____
57. Ⓐ Ⓑ Ⓒ Ⓓ
58. _____
59. _____
60. Ⓐ Ⓑ
61. Ⓐ Ⓑ Ⓒ Ⓓ
62. _____
63. Ⓐ Ⓑ Ⓒ
64. Ⓐ Ⓑ Ⓒ Ⓓ
65. Ⓐ Ⓑ Ⓒ Ⓓ
66. Ⓐ Ⓑ Ⓒ Ⓓ
67. Ⓐ Ⓑ Ⓒ Ⓓ
68. Ⓐ Ⓑ Ⓒ Ⓓ

69. Ⓐ Ⓑ Ⓒ Ⓓ
70. Ⓐ Ⓑ Ⓒ Ⓓ
71. Ⓐ Ⓑ Ⓒ Ⓓ
72. Ⓐ Ⓑ Ⓒ Ⓓ
73. Ⓐ Ⓑ Ⓒ Ⓓ
74. Ⓐ Ⓑ Ⓒ
75. Ⓐ Ⓑ Ⓒ Ⓓ
76. Ⓐ Ⓑ Ⓒ Ⓓ
77. Ⓐ Ⓑ Ⓒ Ⓓ
78. Ⓐ Ⓑ Ⓒ Ⓓ
79. Ⓐ Ⓑ Ⓒ Ⓓ
80. Ⓐ Ⓑ Ⓒ Ⓓ
81. Ⓐ Ⓑ Ⓒ Ⓓ
82. Ⓐ Ⓑ Ⓒ Ⓓ
83. Ⓐ Ⓑ Ⓒ Ⓓ
84. Ⓐ Ⓑ Ⓒ Ⓓ
85. Ⓐ Ⓑ Ⓒ
86. Ⓐ Ⓑ Ⓒ
87. Ⓐ Ⓑ Ⓒ
88. Ⓐ Ⓑ Ⓒ Ⓓ
89. Ⓐ Ⓑ Ⓒ Ⓓ
90. Ⓐ Ⓑ Ⓒ Ⓓ
91. Ⓐ Ⓑ Ⓒ Ⓓ
92. Ⓐ Ⓑ Ⓒ Ⓓ
93. Ⓐ Ⓑ Ⓒ Ⓓ
94. Ⓐ Ⓑ Ⓒ Ⓓ
95. Ⓐ Ⓑ Ⓒ Ⓓ
96. Ⓐ Ⓑ Ⓒ Ⓓ
97. _____
   _____
98. _____
   _____
99. Ⓐ Ⓑ Ⓒ Ⓓ
100. Ⓐ Ⓑ Ⓒ Ⓓ

answer sheet

Practice Test 1

1. Where is the FAA administrator's office located?

   (A) New York City, NY
   (B) Oklahoma City, OK
   (C) Washington, DC

2. Each primary office is managed by a/an

   (A) director.
   (B) administrator.
   (C) associate administrator.

3. The AFSS position that records meteorological data by documenting it accurately and promptly is the _____ position.

   (A) preflight
   (B) weather observer
   (C) maintenance

4. An airport identified by a flashing white and yellow rotating beacon is

   (A) lighted land.
   (B) lighted water.
   (C) military.

5. What runway marking consists of eight longitudinal white stripes of uniform dimensions arranged symmetrically on either side of the runway centerline?

   (A) Threshold
   (B) Displaced threshold
   (C) Relocated threshold

6. To apply the departure divergence rule, you must assign headings that diverge by at least _____ degrees.

   (A) 15
   (B) 30
   (C) 45

7. The minimum en route radar separation required for two aircraft between FL180 and FL600 is _____ miles.

   (A) 3
   (B) 5
   (C) 10

8. To clear aircraft to hold over different fixes at the same altitude, you must ensure that all

   (A) aircraft are cleared to make right turns.
   (B) holding pattern airspace areas do not overlap.
   (C) leg lengths are specified in minutes.
   (D) aircraft are using the same NAVAID to hold from.

9. The facility responsible for accepting, classifying, and disseminating Notices to Airmen (NOTAMs) is the

   (A) FSS.
   (B) Terminal.
   (C) Center.

10. Name the components of a primary radar system.

11. Name two types of radar.

12. What type of polarization would be used to reduce areas of heavy precipitation from the radar display?

13. Which document prescribes air traffic control procedures and phraseology used by the FAA?

   (A) Order 7110.65
   (B) Order 7210.3
   (C) *Aeronautical Information Manual*

14. Which document prescribes flight service procedures and phraseology used by the FAA?

   (A) *Flight Service Phraseology Guide*
   (B) Order 7210.3
   (C) Order 7110.10

15. Which document provides direction and guidance for operating and managing air traffic facilities and offices?

   (A) Order 7110.65
   (B) Order 7210.3
   (C) *Aeronautical Information Manual*

16. Temporary directions or one-time announcements are made through

   (A) changes.
   (B) notices.
   (C) supplements.
   (D) amendments.

17. Which of the following might be addressed in an LOA between two ARTCCs?

   (A) Approach control service
   (B) Radar handoff procedures
   (C) Authorization of separation service

18. Jet routes are included in what type of airspace?

   (A) Class A
   (B) Class B
   (C) Class C

19. The airspace that generally extends from the surface to 10,000 feet MSL and surrounds a busy airport is designated as Class _____ airspace.

   (A) A
   (B) B
   (C) C

20. Under whose authority is FAR issued?

21. Aircraft operating in the air or on airport surfaces are referred to as

   (A) air carriers.
   (B) air traffic.
   (C) air traffic control.

22. When should a pilot who deviates from an ATC clearance due to an emergency notify ATC of that deviation?

23. A pilot in command may deviate from FAR, Part 91 if

   (A) the aircraft is within Class G airspace.
   (B) there is an emergency requiring immediate action.
   (C) the aircraft is under visual conditions.
   (D) an ATC clearance is requested.

24. A VFR flight plan filing is

   (A) mandatory for all VFR flights.
   (B) recommended.
   (C) required for entering Class G airspace.

25. A VFR flight at 4,500 MSL within Class E airspace requires a flight visibility of _____ mile(s).

   (A) 1
   (B) 3
   (C) 5

26. The primary source of lift on an airfoil is created by a differential in

   (A) temperature.
   (B) pressure.
   (C) reaction.

27. The statement, "The internal pressure of a fluid decreases at points where the speed of the fluid increases" is a part of

    (A) Bernoulli's Principle.
    (B) Newton's Law of Motion.
    (C) Hindenberg's Theory.

28. What is created when an airfoil is moved through the air?

    (A) Drag
    (B) Lift
    (C) Relative wind

29. At approximately what angle of attack will air no longer flow smoothly over the wing's upper surface?

    (A) 5–10 degrees
    (B) 10–15 degrees
    (C) 13–18 degrees
    (D) 15–20 degrees

30. The most hazardous aspect of structural icing is

    (A) that it decreases weight.
    (B) that it increases drag.
    (C) that it creates reduced thrust.
    (D) airfoil distortion.

31. The pitch (angle of attack) of a helicopter rotor blade is controlled by the

    (A) cyclic.
    (B) throttle.
    (C) collective.
    (D) antitorque pedal.

32. The greatest wake turbulence is associated with which aircraft configuration?

    (A) Heavy, clean, fast
    (B) Heavy, dirty, slow
    (C) Heavy, clean, slow

33. Of an aircraft on approach to an airport or an aircraft cruising during en route, what condition will create the greatest wake turbulence effect?

34. Which has the greatest impact on wake turbulence?

    (A) Speed
    (B) Configuration
    (C) Weight

35. What is the name for the turbulent phenomenon created by aircraft passing through the atmosphere?

36. What category do helicopters fall under?

37. What category do turbojet engine aircraft fall under?

38. A small, twin-engine turboprop aircraft weighing 12,500 pounds or less will fall under which category?

39. An aircraft capable of 300,000 pounds of takeoff weight but that currently only has a takeoff weight of 225,000 pounds would fall into what weight class?

40. Who is responsible for identifying a mission as an active air defense scramble?

41. What is the name of the geographical point over which the receiver arrives in the observation/refueling position with respect to the assigned tanker?

42. When coordinates are used to define position, is latitude or longitude stated first?

43. How would these coordinates be read?

    29° 40' N, 35° 53' W

    45° 35' N, 82° 43' 22" E

44. The reference line for measuring north-south distances is the

    (A) great circle.
    (B) prime meridian.
    (C) equator.

45. How many minutes are there in 1 degree of latitude?

46. An aircraft flies for 2 hours at 275 knots. How many nautical miles has the aircraft covered?

    (A) 550
    (B) 600
    (C) 650
    (D) 700

47. A VOR antenna transmission pattern is

    (A) omni-directional.
    (B) nondirectional.
    (C) fan-shaped.

48. What are the four colors of colored airways?

49. What is the upper limit of a low-altitude VOR?

    (A) Up to and including 18,000 feet MSL
    (B) Up to but not including 18,000 MSL
    (C) Up to but not including 18,000 AGL

50. Maximum elevation figures (MEFs) depict the elevation of the highest

    (A) topographical feature on the chart.
    (B) known feature within each section of the chart.
    (C) elevation rounded up to the next 1,000 feet.

51. Airports with control towers are always depicted

    (A) in the color blue.
    (B) by a circle with runway configurations shown.
    (C) by the letter "T" next to the airport.

52. En route low-altitude charts are published every _____ days and are for use below _____ feet MSL.

    (A) 28; 24,000
    (B) 56; 18,000
    (C) 112; 10,000

53. The off route obstruction clearance altitude (OROCA) ensures an aircraft of _____ coverage.

    (A) obstruction clearance but no NAVAID/communications
    (B) NAVAID signal reception but no communications
    (C) communications coverage but no NAVAID signal

54. Airports with approved instrument approach procedures (IAPs) are depicted using the colors

    (A) green and brown.
    (B) brown and blue.
    (C) blue and green.

55. What is the primary reason Standard Instrument Departures (SID) have been developed?

56. Name the two types of SIDs.

57. Instrument Departure Procedure Routes have been established at certain airports to

    (A) facilitate transition between takeoff and en route operations.
    (B) eliminate the need for clearance delivery procedures.
    (C) ensure all aircraft depart on exactly the same route.
    (D) relieve airport congestion.

58. Identify the map symbol:

59. Identify the map symbol:

60. An aircraft must be in instrument flight conditions to execute an instrument approach procedure (IAP).

    (A) True
    (B) False

61. Runway visual range (RVR) is

    (A) the horizontal distance a pilot will see down the runway from the approach end.
    (B) given in nautical miles.
    (C) located in the airport diagram section of the IAP.
    (D) used only for military aircraft.

62. What instruments are affected by the pitot-static system?

63. What may be obtained from the attitude indicator?

(A) Rate of turn
(B) Degrees of bank
(C) Height above sea level

64. Communications search for missing aircraft, under the search and rescue (SAR) plan, is the primary responsibility of the

(A) FAA.
(B) rescue coordination center (RCC).
(C) U.S. military.
(D) Coast Guard.

65. An aircraft on an IFR flight plan that is estimated over the Will Rogers VORTAC at 2015 has failed to report. This aircraft is considered overdue at

(A) 2030.
(B) 2045.
(C) 2100.
(D) 2115.

66. When a VFR aircraft becomes overdue, who initiates the information request to departure station (QALQ) message?

(A) ARTCC
(B) FSS
(C) RCC
(D) ATCT

67. The alert notice (ALNOT) search area is generally described as

(A) 100 miles either side of the route of flight from departure point to destination.
(B) 50 miles either side of the route of flight from departure point to destination.
(C) 100 miles either side of the route of flight from the last reported position to destination.
(D) 50 miles either side of the route of flight from the last reported position to destination.

68. The transfer of search for an overdue aircraft to RCC is done after

(A) ALNOT search has been completed with negative results.
(B) the aircraft has not been located within 30 minutes after issuance of the ALNOT.
(C) 1 hour past estimated time of arrival (ETA).
(D) fuel exhaustion time plus 1 hour.

69. Decode the following: +TSRAGR.

(A) HEAVY THUNDERSTORM, SNOW, RAIN, AND SNOW GRAINS.
(B) THUNDERSTORM, HEAVY RAIN SHOWERS, AND HAIL.
(C) SEVERE THUNDERSTORM, RAIN, AND HAIL.
(D) THUNDERSTORM, HEAVY RAIN, HAIL.

70. Decode the following: SCT030 BKN080 OVC120.

(A) SCATTERED LAYER AT THREE HUNDRED, BROKEN LAYER AT EIGHT HUNDRED, OVERCAST LAYER AT ONE THOUSAND TWO HUNDRED FEET.
(B) THREE THOUSAND SCATTERED, EIGHT THOUSAND BROKEN, ONE TWO THOUSAND OVERCAST.
(C) THREE THOUSAND SCATTERED, CEILING EIGHT THOUSAND BROKEN, ONE TWO THOUSAND OVERCAST.
(D) THREE THOUSAND SCATTERED, CEILING AT EIGHT THOUSAND BROKEN, ONE TWO THOUSAND OVERCAST.

71. Decode the following: FEW025 SCT080.

   (A) TWO THOUSAND FIVE HUNDRED FEW, EIGHT THOUSAND SCATTERED.
   (B) FEW AT TWO THOUSAND FIVE HUNDRED, SCATTERED AT EIGHT THOUSAND.
   (C) FEW CLOUDS AT TWO THOUSAND FIVE HUNDRED, SCATTERED CLOUDS AT EIGHT THOUSAND.
   (D) FEW CLOUDS AT TWO THOUSAND FIVE HUNDRED, EIGHT THOUSAND SCATTERED.

72. Decode the following: TORNADO E30.

   (A) TORNADO EAST THREE ZERO MILES.
   (B) TORNADO EAST MOVING AT THREE ZERO MILES PER HOUR.
   (C) TORNADO EAST MOVING AT THREE ZERO.
   (D) TORNADO ENDED AT THREE ZERO PAST THE HOUR.

73. Decode the following: CIG 005V008.

   (A) CEILING VARIABLE BETWEEN FIVE HUNDRED AND EIGHT HUNDRED.
   (B) CEILING FIVE HUNDRED VARIABLE TO EIGHT HUNDRED.
   (C) CEILING FIVE HUNDRED VARYING TO EIGHT HUNDRED.
   (D) CEILING VARIABLE AT FIVE HUNDRED AT EIGHT HUNDRED.

74. Pilot weather reports (PIREPs) are used by FSSs to

   (A) brief pilots on weather conditions.
   (B) determine most favorable altitudes.
   (C) amend/revise forecasts and advisories.

75. The purpose of a PIREP is to

   (A) report a pilot's position.
   (B) report meteorological conditions in flight.
   (C) report a pilot incident.
   (D) present a pilot's report of an accident.

76. PIREPs are used by _____ to expedite the traffic flow in the vicinity of an airport.

   (A) the National Weather Service
   (B) Flight Service Stations (FSSs)
   (C) centers
   (D) towers

77. Controllers solicit PIREPs when _____ is reported.

   (A) a ceiling of 10,000 feet overcast
   (B) moderate turbulence
   (C) trace icing
   (D) in-flight visibility of 7 miles

78. Each PIREP must include the type of aircraft, altitude, location, and _____.

   (A) time
   (B) sky conditions
   (C) temperature
   (D) remarks

REFER TO THE FOLLOWING PIREP TO ANSWER QUESTIONS 79 THROUGH 85.

```
OKC UA /OV OKC180010/TM 1516/FL120/
TP C500/SK BKN035-TOP075/OVC095 /WX
FV01SM RA/TA M04/TB MOD 050-070/RM
TCU W DURC
```

79. At what altitude(s) did the aircraft first encounter turbulence?

   (A) Unknown
   (B) 3,500–7,500 feet
   (C) 5,000–7,000 feet
   (D) 12,000 feet

80. What is the type of aircraft that made this report?

   (A) FV01
   (B) C500
   (C) TA04
   (D) TM1516

81. What is the height of the base of the second layer?

   (A) Not reported
   (B) 3,500 feet
   (C) 7,500 feet
   (D) 9,500 feet

82. What was the weather element that caused the reduction in visibility?

   (A) Snow
   (B) Rain showers
   (C) Rain
   (D) Hail

83. What was the intensity of the turbulence?

   (A) Severe
   (B) Extreme
   (C) Light
   (D) Moderate

84. What is included in the remarks?

   (A) West of Tecumseh
   (B) Towering cumulus clouds of unknown intensity
   (C) Towering cumulus clouds west of aircraft
   (D) No remarks

85. The two TAF report types are routine and

   (A) delayed.
   (B) special.
   (C) amended.

86. How often are TAFs scheduled for issuance per day?

   (A) Twice
   (B) Three times
   (C) Four times

87. TAFs are normally valid for how many hours?

   (A) 12
   (B) 18
   (C) 24

88. What information is found in Block 5 of an en route strip?

   (A) Revision number
   (B) Aircraft type
   (C) Filed true airspeed
   (D) Strip number

89. Which block is used to record the aircraft ID on a flight service strip?

   (A) 1
   (B) 3
   (C) 5
   (D) 7

90. What needs to be added to the letter "S" when hand printed to prevent misreading it as a "5"?

   (A) A box around the letter
   (B) A circle around the letter
   (C) A horizontal line above the letter
   (D) A horizontal line below the letter

91. The letters "OTP" on a strip stand for

   (A) VFR conditions-on-top.
   (B) oceanic transfer point.
   (C) vectors above.
   (D) vectors around.

92. What is the symbol to indicate that an aircraft's clearance is void if NOT airborne by a specific time?

   (A) V~
   (B) ~∧
   (C) v<
   (D) |V|

93. What symbol should be used to delete any unwanted or unused altitude information?

   (A) X
   (B) −
   (C) +
   (D) /

94. Which control symbol indicates that flight information has been forwarded?

    (A) Slash
    (B) Red circle
    (C) Check mark
    (D) B and C

95. When stripmarking, do NOT draw a horizontal line through

    (A) unused symbols.
    (B) a past frequency the aircraft used.
    (C) a call sign.
    (D) an altitude until the aircraft has reported leaving the altitude.

96. Flight progress strips are used for

    (A) traffic count only.
    (B) traffic sequencing only.
    (C) posting current data on air traffic.
    (D) traffic metering.

97. In any option, strips are produced on either special _____ or they are _____.

98. Compared to the terminal strip, the en route strip is _____ and has 12 more _____.

99. The type of clearance that provides for intermediate stops while en route is a/an _____ Clearance.

    (A) Approach
    (B) Through
    (C) Composite
    (D) Cruise

100. An authorization for a pilot to conduct flight at any altitude from the minimum IFR altitude up to and including the altitude specified in the clearance is a/an _____ Clearance.

    (A) Cruise
    (B) Landing
    (C) Approach
    (D) Composite

ANSWER KEY

1. C
2. C
3. B
4. B
5. A
6. C
7. B
8. B
9. A
10. transmitter, antenna, receiver, and radar display
11. primary and secondary
12. circular polarization
13. A
14. C
15. B
16. B
17. B
18. A
19. B
20. FAA administrator
21. B
22. as soon as possible
23. B
24. B
25. B
26. B
27. A
28. B
29. D
30. D
31. C
32. C
33. an aircraft on approach to an airport
34. C
35. wake turbulence
36. CAT I
37. CAT III
38. CAT II
39. heavy
40. the airborne data converter/formatter (ADCF) initiating the scramble
41. air refueling control point (ARCP)

42. latitude
43. 29 degrees, 40 minutes, north (latitude), 35 degrees, 53 minutes, west (longitude), AND 45 degrees, 35 minutes, north (latitude), 82 degrees, 43 minutes, 22 seconds, east (longitude)
44. C
45. 60
46. A
47. A
48. amber, blue, green, and red
49. B
50. B
51. A
52. B
53. A
54. C
55. to expedite clearance delivery and to facilitate transition between takeoff and en route operations
56. Pilot Navigational and Vector
57. A
58. holding pattern
59. DME mileage
60. B
61. A
62. airspeed indicator, vertical speed indicator, and altimeter
63. B
64. A
65. B
66. B
67. D
68. A
69. D
70. C
71. D
72. D
73. A
74. A
75. B
76. D

answers practice test 1

77. B	89. A
78. A	90. D
79. C	91. A
80. B	92. C
81. D	93. A
82. C	94. D
83. D	95. D
84. C	96. C
85. C	97. printers; handwritten
86. C	98. larger blocks
87. C	99. B
88. C	100. A

ANSWER SHEET PRACTICE TEST 2

1. Ⓐ Ⓑ Ⓒ
2. Ⓐ Ⓑ Ⓒ
3. Ⓐ Ⓑ Ⓒ Ⓓ
4. Ⓐ Ⓑ Ⓒ
5. Ⓐ Ⓑ Ⓒ
6. Ⓐ Ⓑ Ⓒ
7. _____
8. _____
_____
9. Ⓐ Ⓑ Ⓒ Ⓓ
10. _____
11. _____
12. Ⓐ Ⓑ Ⓒ Ⓓ
13. Ⓐ Ⓑ Ⓒ
14. Ⓐ Ⓑ Ⓒ
15. Ⓐ Ⓑ Ⓒ
16. Ⓐ Ⓑ Ⓒ Ⓓ
17. Ⓐ Ⓑ Ⓒ
18. Ⓐ Ⓑ Ⓒ
19. Ⓐ Ⓑ Ⓒ
20. Ⓐ Ⓑ Ⓒ
21. Ⓐ Ⓑ Ⓒ
22. Ⓐ Ⓑ Ⓒ Ⓓ
23. Ⓐ Ⓑ Ⓒ Ⓓ
24. Ⓐ Ⓑ Ⓒ
25. Ⓐ Ⓑ Ⓒ
26. Ⓐ Ⓑ Ⓒ
27. _____
28. Ⓐ Ⓑ Ⓒ
29. Ⓐ Ⓑ Ⓒ
30. Ⓐ Ⓑ Ⓒ Ⓓ
31. _____
32. _____
33. _____
34. _____
_____

35. _____
36. _____
37. Ⓐ Ⓑ Ⓒ
38. _____
39. _____
40. _____
41. Ⓐ Ⓑ Ⓒ Ⓓ
42. Ⓐ Ⓑ Ⓒ
43. Ⓐ Ⓑ Ⓒ Ⓓ
44. Ⓐ Ⓑ Ⓒ
45. _____
46. Ⓐ Ⓑ Ⓒ
47. Ⓐ Ⓑ Ⓒ
48. Ⓐ Ⓑ Ⓒ
49. Ⓐ Ⓑ Ⓒ Ⓓ
50. Ⓐ Ⓑ Ⓒ
51. Ⓐ Ⓑ Ⓒ
52. Ⓐ Ⓑ Ⓒ
53. Ⓐ Ⓑ Ⓒ
54. Ⓐ Ⓑ Ⓒ
55. Ⓐ Ⓑ Ⓒ Ⓓ
56. Ⓐ Ⓑ
57. Ⓐ Ⓑ Ⓒ Ⓓ
58. Ⓐ Ⓑ Ⓒ
59. Ⓐ Ⓑ Ⓒ
60. Ⓐ Ⓑ
61. Ⓐ Ⓑ Ⓒ
62. Ⓐ Ⓑ Ⓒ
63. Ⓐ Ⓑ Ⓒ Ⓓ
64. Ⓐ Ⓑ Ⓒ
65. Ⓐ Ⓑ Ⓒ
66. Ⓐ Ⓑ Ⓒ
67. Ⓐ Ⓑ Ⓒ
68. Ⓐ Ⓑ Ⓒ

69. _____
70. _____
71. Ⓐ Ⓑ Ⓒ
72. _____
73. _____
74. _____
75. _____
76. _____
77. _____
78. _____
79. _____
80. Ⓐ Ⓑ Ⓒ Ⓓ
81. Ⓐ Ⓑ Ⓒ Ⓓ
82. Ⓐ Ⓑ Ⓒ Ⓓ
83. Ⓐ Ⓑ Ⓒ Ⓓ
84. Ⓐ Ⓑ Ⓒ Ⓓ
85. Ⓐ Ⓑ Ⓒ Ⓓ
86. Ⓐ Ⓑ Ⓒ Ⓓ
87. _____
88. _____
89. _____
90. _____
91. _____
92. _____
93. _____
94. _____
95. _____
96. _____
97. Ⓐ Ⓑ Ⓒ
98. Ⓐ Ⓑ Ⓒ Ⓓ Ⓔ Ⓕ
Ⓖ Ⓗ Ⓘ Ⓙ Ⓚ
99. Ⓐ Ⓑ Ⓒ Ⓓ Ⓔ Ⓕ
Ⓖ Ⓗ Ⓘ Ⓙ Ⓚ
100. Ⓐ Ⓑ Ⓒ Ⓓ

Practice Test 2

1. Which Automated Flight Service Station (AFSS) position initiates required search and rescue situations?

   (A) Preflight
   (B) Weather Observer
   (C) Flight Data/Notice to Airmen (NOTAM)/ Coordinator

2. Which AFSS position provides local airport advisories?

   (A) In-flight
   (B) Preflight
   (C) Weather Observer

3. Which control facility has NO direct authority over IFR or VFR traffic?

   (A) Tower
   (B) TRACON
   (C) AFSS
   (D) ARTCC

4. An unusable portion of runway that appears usable and is marked with large yellow chevrons identifies a

   (A) blast pad.
   (B) closed runway.
   (C) displaced threshold.

5. The centerline of a taxiway is marked with a _____ line.

   (A) dashed yellow
   (B) continuous yellow
   (C) continuous white

6. For a terminal facility to provide visual separation between two arriving IFR aircraft, the following condition must exist:

   (A) One of the aircraft must be visually observed by the tower.
   (B) Both aircraft must be visually observed by the tower.
   (C) The pilots of both aircraft must see each other.

7. If you had two aircraft AT FL310, would you be correct in assigning one of the aircraft an altitude of FL320?

8. The standard minimum longitudinal separation between two aircraft using DME is _____ minutes or _____ miles.

9. Airmen's information is disseminated via aeronautical charts and

   (A) satellite communications.
   (B) facility directives.
   (C) flight information publications.
   (D) FAA orders.

10. Where is the transponder located?

11. What are the five major components of the secondary radar system?

12. Which radar-based system uses both a ground-based interrogator and an aircraft-based transponder?

    (A) Primary radar
    (B) Airport radar
    (C) Secondary radar
    (D) Global position radar

13. Which document contains the approved words and phrase contractions used by personnel in the FAA?

    (A) Order 7350.7
    (B) *Aeronautical Information Manual*
    (C) Order 7340.1

14. Which document lists the location identifiers authorized by the FAA, the Department of the Navy, and Transport Canada?

    (A) Order 7350.7
    (B) Order 7340.1
    (C) *Aeronautical Information Manual*

15. Which document provides the aviation community with basic flight information and ATC procedures for use in the U.S. National Airspace System (NAS)?

    (A) Order 7350.7
    (B) Order 7340.1
    (C) *Aeronautical Information Manual*

16. When used in Orders 7110.10, 7110.65, and 7210.3, the word "will" means

    (A) recommended.
    (B) not a requirement for application of a procedure.
    (C) optional.
    (D) mandatory.

17. Responsibility for approval of a Letter of Agreement rests with the

    (A) Regional Service Area Office.
    (B) Flight Inspection Field Office.
    (C) General Aviation District Office.

18. The authority and responsibility for flying in Class G airspace belongs to the

    (A) pilot.
    (B) military.
    (C) air traffic controller.

19. The special-use airspace that overlies an aerial gunnery range is called a _____ area.

    (A) prohibited
    (B) restricted
    (C) warning

20. Authorization by ATC for the purpose of preventing collisions between known aircraft for an aircraft to proceed under specified traffic conditions within controlled airspace is called an ATC

    (A) approval.
    (B) direction.
    (C) clearance.

21. A level of constant atmospheric pressure related to a reference datum of 29.92 inches of mercury stated in three digits is referred to as

    (A) flight level.
    (B) aircraft altitude.
    (C) mean sea level (MSL) altitude.

22. What pre-flight action does FAR, Part 91 require pilots to take before beginning a flight?

    (A) File a flight plan
    (B) Receive ATC authorization for the flight
    (C) Advise ATC of intentions
    (D) Become familiar with all available information concerning the flight

23. Pilots of two aircraft may operate as a formation flight when

   (A) authorization is obtained from ATC.

   (B) flight visibility is at least 3 miles.

   (C) prior arrangements are made and no paying passengers are aboard.

   (D) flight is conducted at or above 1,500 feet MSL.

24. The distance from clouds for VFR flights in Class B airspace is

   (A) 2,000 feet horizontally.

   (B) clear of clouds.

   (C) 1 mile horizontally.

25. The distance from clouds for VFR flights in Class C and D airspace is

   (A) 500 feet above, 1,000 feet below, and 2,000 feet horizontal.

   (B) 500 feet below, 2,000 feet above, and 1,000 feet horizontal.

   (C) 500 feet below, 1,000 feet above, and 2,000 feet horizontal.

26. An appropriate VFR altitude on a magnetic course of 250 degrees and more than 3,000 feet above the surface would be _____ feet.

   (A) 7,000

   (B) 7,500

   (C) 8,500

27. Which two movements are controlled by the control yoke?

28. Which of the following is a primary control surface?

   (A) Variable-pitch propeller

   (B) Flap

   (C) Rudder

29. The extension of flaps causes an increase in

   (A) stall speed.

   (B) airspeed.

   (C) drag.

30. What type of icing is an aircraft likely to encounter when flying in temperatures above freezing?

   (A) Pitot tube icing

   (B) Wing icing

   (C) Carburetor icing

   (D) Windshield icing

31. What are the circular patterns created by wake turbulence often known as?

32. For fixed-winged aircraft, vortices begin at which stage of flight?

33. For fixed-winged aircraft, vortices end at which stage of flight?

34. When observing an aircraft from behind, the circulation of vortices off the right wingtip is _____ and is _____ off the left wingtip.

35. An aircraft in the small weight class has a maximum certified takeoff weight of _____ pounds or less.

36. If an aircraft has a 250,000-pound maximum certified takeoff weight, what is its weight class?

37. What is the general speed range for CAT II aircraft?

   (A) 100–160 knots

   (B) 160–250 knots

   (C) 250–500 knots

38. Name two types of engines that use propellers.

39. What kind of aircraft movement is expedited when the term "NAOC" appears in the remarks section of a flight plan?

40. A U.S. Air Force (USAF) aircraft on an atmospheric sampling mission will use which call sign?

practice test

41. A moving altitude reservation (ALTRV) includes what phases?

- **(A)** The en route and arrival phase
- **(B)** Departure and cruise phase
- **(C)** The fixed airspace and time phase
- **(D)** Standard and nonstandard

42. At 1 p.m. daylight saving time (DST) in New York City, the time is _____ UTC. (Note: conversion factor is +5)

- **(A)** 1600
- **(B)** 1700
- **(C)** 1800

43. An aircraft travels at 300 knots for 1 hour, 30 minutes. How many nautical miles has the aircraft traveled?

- **(A)** 400
- **(B)** 450
- **(C)** 500
- **(D)** 600

44. The angular difference between true north and magnetic north at any given place is called

- **(A)** variation.
- **(B)** deviation.
- **(C)** isogonic line.

45. What term denotes a magnetic compass error that is caused by materials within the aircraft that possess magnetic properties?

46. True heading is true course corrected for effects of

- **(A)** magnetic variation.
- **(B)** compass error.
- **(C)** wind.

47. A VOR station projects

- **(A)** 360 usable true radials.
- **(B)** 360 usable magnetic radials.
- **(C)** an infinite number of bearings.

48. The base of the Jet Route System is _____ feet MSL.

- **(A)** 16,000
- **(B)** 18,000
- **(C)** 45,000

49. The different classes of VORs are

- **(A)** high, low, terminal.
- **(B)** high, medium, low.
- **(C)** high, low, compass locator.
- **(D)** high, medium, terminal.

50. In the airport data "450 L 51 122.7," the letter "L" indicates

- **(A)** the category of NAVAID located at the airport.
- **(B)** a left-hand traffic pattern is used at that airport.
- **(C)** the airport has runway lighting.

51. In the airport data "4500 L 72 122.95," "4500" is the

- **(A)** airport elevation above sea level.
- **(B)** length of the longest runway.
- **(C)** height above sea level of the tallest obstruction within 5 NM.

52. When included in the airport data, (A) means

- **(A)** the airport is surrounded by Class A airspace.
- **(B)** alternate approach minimums are applicable at that airport.
- **(C)** Automatic Terminal Information Service (ATIS) is available.

53. An asterisk (*) in the airport data could be used to indicate

- **(A)** part-time status of surrounding airspace.
- **(B)** pilot-controlled lighting.
- **(C)** presence of a rotating beacon on the field.

54. A frequency value that is underlined within a communication box indicates that

- **(A)** no HIWAS broadcast is available through that facility.
- **(B)** no voice is transmitted on that frequency.
- **(C)** a NOTAM is issued pertaining to an abnormal status situation.

55. SIDs and STARs are listed alphabetically in the U.S. Terminal Procedures Publication—first under _____ and then under _____.

(A) SIDs; STARs
(B) airport name; city
(C) index; legend
(D) city; airport name

56. Pilots are required to include the phrase "No SID" on their flight plans if they do NOT want ATC to assign a SID to their flights.

(A) True
(B) False

57. The purpose of a STAR is to

(A) expedite ATC arrival procedures.
(B) reduce coordination between ATC facilities.
(C) codify clearances to pilots.
(D) establish "one-way streets."

58. An approach is termed "precision" because it

(A) lines up the aircraft with the active runway.
(B) provides electronic glideslope information.
(C) allows the aircraft to descend safely through the overcast.

59. An instrument approach procedure (IAP) is designed to provide

(A) an IFR descent to a point where the active runway is in sight.
(B) an IFR descent to a point where a safe landing can be made.
(C) altitude guidance to a descending aircraft.

60. A localizer approach is less accurate than an ILS approach because no electronic altitude guidance is provided.

(A) True
(B) False

61. The VOR course deviation needle will indicate the aircraft's position in relation to the selected

(A) heading.
(B) radial.
(C) bearing.

62. The range displayed on the DME indicator is called _____ range.

(A) omni
(B) straight
(C) slant

63. The purpose of TCAS is to

(A) assist the controller in maintaining separation.
(B) prevent mid-air collisions.
(C) document unsafe situations.
(D) allow a pilot deviation from an ATC clearance.

64. In which emergency condition would a pilot transmit "PAN-PAN, PAN-PAN, PAN-PAN?"

(A) Help
(B) Distress
(C) Urgency

65. The minimum information required for handling an emergency is

(A) aircraft identification and type, nature of the emergency, and pilot's desires.
(B) aircraft identification, altitude, fuel remaining in time.
(C) aircraft identification and type, altitude, color of aircraft.

66. If an aircraft declares an emergency while you are working it on your frequency, you should normally

(A) assign the emergency frequency.
(B) leave the aircraft on your frequency.
(C) instruct the aircraft to change to an alternate frequency.

practice test

67. When a bomb threat has been received involving an aircraft you are working, you should inform the pilot of the threat and

    (A) instruct the pilot to land as soon as possible.
    (B) assign Code 7700.
    (C) comply with any pilot requests.

68. The temperature to which air must be cooled to become saturated by water vapor already in the air is

    (A) relative humidity.
    (B) dew point.
    (C) lapse rate.

69. The standard lapse rate in the troposphere is how many degrees per thousand feet?

70. What force deflects air to the right in the Northern Hemisphere and to the left in the Southern Hemisphere?

71. The temperature increasing with an increase in altitude is known as a/an

    (A) lapse rate.
    (B) isothermal layer.
    (C) temperature inversion.

72. Most weather occurs in which layer of the atmosphere?

73. What is the standard barometric pressure?

74. What is a trough?

75. Which pressure system is likely to produce the most severe weather? Why?

76. The area where two different air masses meet is called a _____.

77. Clouds can indicate what three things concerning the air around them?

78. Name two types of clouds with extensive vertical development.

79. What must air become before condensation or sublimation can occur?

80. Which agency/office collects and analyzes meteorological and hydrological data and subsequently prepares weather forecasts?

    (A) National Weather Service
    (B) National Center of Environmental Prediction
    (C) U.S. Weather Bureau
    (D) Aviation Weather Center (AWC)

81. The center responsible for issuing area forecasts, AIRMETs, and SIGMETs is the

    (A) Storm Prediction Center.
    (B) Tropical Prediction Center.
    (C) National Center Operation.
    (D) Aviation Weather Center.

82. Providing forecast, weather consultation, and advice to managers is the role of the

    (A) Traffic Management Unit.
    (B) Weather Forecast Office.
    (C) Center Weather Service Unit.
    (D) Storm Prediction Center.

83. Terminal aerodrome forecast (TAF) and Transcribed Weather En Route Broadcast (TWEB) are products of the

    (A) Aviation Weather Center.
    (B) Weather Forecast Office.
    (C) Storm Prediction Center.
    (D) National Center of Operations.

84. Center Weather Service Units are located

    (A) at the Weather Forecast Office.
    (B) adjacent to all Level 5 control towers.
    (C) within all ARTCCs.
    (D) within all Automated Flight Service Stations (AFSSs).

85. Center Weather Service Units are a joint agency aviation weather support team composed of personnel from the NWS and

    (A) the DOD.
    (B) the FAA Traffic Management Unit.
    (C) Flight Service Option.
    (D) National Oceanic and Atmospheric Administration (NOAA).

86. The temperature to which air must be cooled to become saturated is called

    (A) lapse rate.
    (B) dew point.
    (C) standard saturation.
    (D) inversion.

87. How do you identify an airport traffic control tower?

88. How are AFSSs identified?

89. How is Oakland, CA ARTCC identified?

90. What is the prefix for a domestic general aviation aircraft when the aircraft type, model name, and/or manufacturer's name are unknown?

91. What is the phraseology for American Airlines Flight 52?

92. What is the prefix for a civilian airborne ambulance flight?

93. Name the letter prefixes for the following military services: Air Force, Army, and Navy.

94. What letter precedes the airway number for a VOR airway? How is it pronounced?

95. Name the seven types of coordination.

96. What is the action in which the responsibility for separation of an aircraft is changed from one controller to another?

97. After the relieving specialist has assumed responsibility for the sector, the relieved specialist

    (A) immediately leaves the area.
    (B) reviews all information for omissions or inaccuracies.
    (C) signs off the position and remains at the sector for 10 minutes.

98. Authorization for pilots to proceed from point of origin to point of destination is called

    (A) taxi clearance.
    (B) approach clearance.
    (C) composite flight plan clearance.
    (D) landing clearance.
    (E) takeoff clearance.
    (F) amended clearance.
    (G) departure clearance.
    (H) cruise clearance.
    (I) holding clearance.
    (J) altitude reservation clearance.
    (K) through clearance.

99. Authorization for pilots to conduct flight at any altitude from the minimum IFR altitude up to and including the altitude specified in the clearance is called

    (A) taxi clearance.
    (B) approach clearance.
    (C) composite flight plan clearance.
    (D) landing clearance.
    (E) takeoff clearance.
    (F) amended clearance.
    (G) departure clearance.
    (H) cruise clearance.
    (I) holding clearance.
    (J) altitude reservation clearance.
    (K) through clearance.

100. The purpose of an ATC clearance is to

    (A) relieve controller stress.
    (B) provide classified instructions to pilots.
    (C) prevent collision between known aircraft.
    (D) provide for emergency situations.

practice test

ANSWER KEY

1. C
2. A
3. C
4. A
5. B
6. B
7. Yes, if both aircraft are Reduced Vertical Separation Minimum (RVSM) equipped. Otherwise, you would need 2,000 feet vertical separation.
8. 10 minutes; 20 miles.
9. C
10. in the aircraft
11. interrogator, transponder, antenna, decoder, radar display
12. C
13. C
14. A
15. C
16. B
17. A
18. A
19. B
20. C
21. A
22. D
23. C
24. B
25. C
26. C
27. roll and pitch
28. C
29. C
30. C
31. "wake vortex" or "wingtip vortices"
32. at rotation or when lift begins
33. at touchdown or when lift ends
34. counterclockwise; clockwise
35. 41,000
36. large
37. B
38. reciprocating and turboprop
39. NIGHT WATCH

40. SAMP
41. A
42. B
43. B
44. A
45. deviation
46. C
47. B
48. B
49. A
50. C
51. A
52. C
53. A
54. B
55. D
56. B
57. A
58. B
59. B
60. A
61. B
62. C
63. B
64. C
65. A
66. B
67. C
68. B
69. 2° Celsius
70. Coriolis Force
71. C
72. troposphere
73. 29.92 inches of mercury
74. an elongated area of low pressure
75. Low. Rising air is conducive to cloudiness, restricted visibilities, turbulence, and precipitation.
76. front
77. upward motion, stability, and moisture
78. towering cumulus and cumulonimbus
79. saturated

80. A
81. D
82. C
83. B
84. C
85. B
86. B
87. name of facility followed by the word "TOWER"
88. name of station followed by the word "RADIO"
89. OAKLAND CENTER
90. NOVEMBER
91. AMERICAN FIFTY-TWO
92. LIFEGUARD
93. A, R, and VV
94. V; "VICTOR"
95. radar handoffs, radar point outs, transfer of control, runway crossings, forwarding flight plan information, arrival information (i.e., inbounds), clearance and instructions
96. transfer of control
97. B
98. G
99. H
100. C

answers

practice test 2

ANSWER SHEET PRACTICE TEST 3

1. Ⓐ Ⓑ Ⓒ Ⓓ
2. Ⓐ Ⓑ Ⓒ Ⓓ
3. Ⓐ Ⓑ Ⓒ Ⓓ
4. Ⓐ Ⓑ Ⓒ
5. Ⓐ Ⓑ Ⓒ Ⓓ
6. _____
7. _____
8. Ⓐ Ⓑ Ⓒ Ⓓ
9. Ⓐ Ⓑ Ⓒ Ⓓ
10. Ⓐ Ⓑ Ⓒ Ⓓ
11. Ⓐ Ⓑ Ⓒ Ⓓ
12. Ⓐ Ⓑ Ⓒ Ⓓ
13. Ⓐ Ⓑ Ⓒ Ⓓ
14. Ⓐ Ⓑ Ⓒ Ⓓ
15. Ⓐ Ⓑ Ⓒ Ⓓ
16. _____
17. Ⓐ Ⓑ Ⓒ
18. Ⓐ Ⓑ Ⓒ
19. Ⓐ Ⓑ Ⓒ Ⓓ
20. Ⓐ Ⓑ Ⓒ
21. Ⓐ Ⓑ Ⓒ
22. Ⓐ Ⓑ Ⓒ Ⓓ
23. Ⓐ Ⓑ Ⓒ Ⓓ
24. Ⓐ Ⓑ Ⓒ
25. Ⓐ Ⓑ Ⓒ
26. _____
27. Ⓐ Ⓑ Ⓒ Ⓓ
28. Ⓐ Ⓑ Ⓒ Ⓓ
29. Ⓐ Ⓑ Ⓒ Ⓓ
30. Ⓐ Ⓑ Ⓒ Ⓓ
31. Ⓐ Ⓑ Ⓒ
32. _____
   _____
33. _____
   _____

34. _____
   _____
35. _____
36. _____
37. _____
38. _____
39. _____
40. Ⓐ Ⓑ Ⓒ Ⓓ
41. Ⓐ Ⓑ Ⓒ Ⓓ
42. Ⓐ Ⓑ Ⓒ
43. _____
44. Ⓐ Ⓑ Ⓒ Ⓓ
45. Ⓐ Ⓑ Ⓒ Ⓓ
46. Ⓐ Ⓑ Ⓒ Ⓓ
47. Ⓐ Ⓑ Ⓒ
48. Ⓐ Ⓑ Ⓒ Ⓓ
49. Ⓐ Ⓑ Ⓒ Ⓓ
50. Ⓐ Ⓑ Ⓒ
51. Ⓐ Ⓑ Ⓒ
52. Ⓐ Ⓑ Ⓒ Ⓓ
53. Ⓐ Ⓑ Ⓒ
54. Ⓐ Ⓑ Ⓒ
55. Ⓐ Ⓑ Ⓒ
56. Ⓐ Ⓑ Ⓒ Ⓓ
57. Ⓐ Ⓑ Ⓒ Ⓓ
58. Ⓐ Ⓑ
59. Ⓐ Ⓑ
60. _____
61. Ⓐ Ⓑ
62. Ⓐ Ⓑ Ⓒ Ⓓ
63. Ⓐ Ⓑ Ⓒ Ⓓ
64. _____
65. Ⓐ Ⓑ Ⓒ
66. Ⓐ Ⓑ Ⓒ

67. Ⓐ Ⓑ Ⓒ Ⓓ
68. Ⓐ Ⓑ Ⓒ Ⓓ
69. Ⓐ Ⓑ Ⓒ
70. Ⓐ Ⓑ Ⓒ Ⓓ
71. Ⓐ Ⓑ Ⓒ Ⓓ
72. Ⓐ Ⓑ Ⓒ Ⓓ
73. Ⓐ Ⓑ Ⓒ Ⓓ
74. Ⓐ Ⓑ Ⓒ
75. Ⓐ Ⓑ Ⓒ Ⓓ
76. Ⓐ Ⓑ Ⓒ Ⓓ
77. Ⓐ Ⓑ Ⓒ Ⓓ
78. Ⓐ Ⓑ Ⓒ Ⓓ
79. Ⓐ Ⓑ Ⓒ Ⓓ
80. Ⓐ Ⓑ Ⓒ Ⓓ
81. Ⓐ Ⓑ Ⓒ Ⓓ
82. Ⓐ Ⓑ Ⓒ Ⓓ
83. Ⓐ Ⓑ Ⓒ Ⓓ
84. Ⓐ Ⓑ Ⓒ Ⓓ
85. Ⓐ Ⓑ Ⓒ Ⓓ
86. Ⓐ Ⓑ Ⓒ Ⓓ
87. Ⓐ Ⓑ Ⓒ Ⓓ
88. Ⓐ Ⓑ Ⓒ
89. _____
90. Ⓐ Ⓑ
91. Ⓐ Ⓑ Ⓒ Ⓓ
92. Ⓐ Ⓑ Ⓒ Ⓓ
93. Ⓐ Ⓑ Ⓒ Ⓓ
94. Ⓐ Ⓑ Ⓒ Ⓓ
95. Ⓐ Ⓑ Ⓒ Ⓓ
96. Ⓐ Ⓑ Ⓒ Ⓓ
97. Ⓐ Ⓑ Ⓒ Ⓓ
98. Ⓐ Ⓑ Ⓒ Ⓓ
99. Ⓐ Ⓑ Ⓒ Ⓓ
100. Ⓐ Ⓑ Ⓒ Ⓓ

answer sheet

Practice Test 3

1. The primary NAVAIDs for the nation's airways in the National Airspace System are

   (A) marker beacons.
   (B) VORs/VORTACs.
   (C) NDBs.
   (D) ILSs.

2. The mission of the Traffic Management System is to

   (A) regulate air traffic procedures.
   (B) balance air traffic demand with system capacity.
   (C) implement the use of state-of-the-art equipment.
   (D) ascertain controller stress and workload.

3. The operation of the Traffic Management System is the responsibility of the

   (A) Central Altitude Reservation.
   (B) ARTCC Traffic Management Unit (TMU) for each area.
   (C) Air Traffic Manager.
   (D) Air Traffic Control System Command Center (ATCSCC).

4. An "H" inside a large cross is the recommended marking for a _____ heliport.

   (A) hospital
   (B) civil
   (C) military

5. A runway with a magnetic heading of 003 degrees should be designated Runway

   (A) 0.
   (B) 1.
   (C) 3.
   (D) 36.

6. If you were holding two aircraft at different fixes, one at 6,000 feet and one at 7,000 feet, but the holding pattern airspace(s) overlapped, would you have separation? If so, what kind?

7. Which type of separation in the en route environment, other than visual, would allow you to place two aircraft with the least distance between aircraft?

8. Who is responsible for originating Notices to Airmen (NOTAMs)?

   (A) Facility responsible for monitoring or controlling the navigational aid
   (B) Center in whose area the outage occurs
   (C) Terminal in whose area the outage occurs
   (D) Flight Service Station

9. Classification and dissemination of NOTAMs is the responsibility of

   (A) the National Flight Data Center.
   (B) ARTCCs.
   (C) FSSs.
   (D) the originating facility.

10. What is the name of a radio detection device that provides range, azimuth, and/or elevation information?

    (A) Transponder
    (B) Radar
    (C) Nondirectional beacon
    (D) VORTAC

11. Which radar system relies on reflected radio signals and does NOT require cooperative equipment in aircraft?

    (A) Primary radar
    (B) Secondary radar
    (C) Airport radar
    (D) Positive radar

12. What are two types of radar jamming?

    (A) Position and passive
    (B) Action and active
    (C) Precise and passive
    (D) Passive and active

13. When used in Orders 7110.10, 7110.65, and 7210.3, the word "shall" means that the procedure is

    (A) recommended.
    (B) optional.
    (C) approved.
    (D) mandatory.

14. When used in Orders 7110.10, 7110.65, and 7210.3, the word "should" means that the procedure is

    (A) recommended.
    (B) optional.
    (C) approved.
    (D) mandatory.

15. Revised, reprinted, or new pages in Orders 7110.10, 7110.65, and 7210.3 are indicated by bold

    (A) asterisks.
    (B) horizontal lines.
    (C) vertical lines.
    (D) stars.

16. Who may be delegated the authority to approve a Letter of Agreement?

17. What type of special-use airspace is found over international waters?

    (A) Prohibited area
    (B) Controlled firing area
    (C) Warning area

18. Prohibited area vertical airspace begins at

    (A) 3,000 feet.
    (B) the surface of the earth.
    (C) 1,500 feet.

19. What airspace is generally established from the surface to 4,000 feet above the airport elevation and has an operational control tower?

    (A) Class B
    (B) Class C
    (C) Class D
    (D) Class E

20. Control of all air traffic within designated airspace by air traffic control is called _____ control.

    (A) restricted
    (B) precision
    (C) positive

21. What aircraft operating within the United States are subject to FAR, Part 91?

    (A) Military only
    (B) Civilian
    (C) All aircraft

22. An aircraft has the right-of-way over all other aircraft when it is in

(A) VFR conditions.
(B) distress.
(C) IFR conditions.
(D) controlled airspace.

23. The maximum speed authorized by FAR for aircraft below 10,000 feet MSL is _____ knots.

(A) 250
(B) 200
(C) 180
(D) 150

24. No person may operate aircraft in controlled airspace under IFR unless they have filed a

(A) flight plan.
(B) flight plan and received an ATC clearance.
(C) flight plan and requested a clearance.

25. If the takeoff minimum at a civil airport is NOT prescribed for a twin-engine aircraft, the minimum visibility for an IFR departure is _____ mile(s).

(A) .5
(B) 1
(C) 1.5

26. An aircraft is cleared from Alfa to Kilo airport by other than the filed routing. How will the pilot proceed if radio failure occurs?

27. "The internal pressure of a fluid decreases at points where the speed of the fluid increases" is a part of

(A) Einstein's Theory.
(B) Bernoulli's Principle.
(C) Newton's Law.
(D) Federal Aviation Regulations (FAR).

28. When air is forced to travel at a faster speed across the top of a wing than across the bottom, it results in _____ the wing.

(A) lower pressure above
(B) lower pressure below
(C) higher pressure above
(D) atmospheric pressure above

29. Which statement best expresses Newton's Third Law of Motion?

(A) The greater the angle of attack, the greater the lift produced.
(B) Increased speed of a fluid results in decreased pressure.
(C) For every action, there is an equal and opposite reaction.
(D) In straight and level flight, thrust equals drag.

30. Hypoxia is a condition of the body that occurs with

(A) a lack of oxygen in the body tissue.
(B) a lack of oxygen in the air.
(C) excessively fast breathing.
(D) a lack of carbon dioxide in the body.

31. Vortices from large aircraft will sink approximately 300 to 500 feet per minute and level off below the flight path at approximately

(A) 90 feet.
(B) 900 feet.
(C) 9,000 feet.

32. With no wind, vortices within 100 to 200 feet of the ground will move _____ to _____ knots laterally across the ground.

33. For landing aircraft, crosswinds of 1 to 5 knots tend to _____ the lateral movement of one vortex, while _____ the movement of the other.

34. Hazardous conditions occur when the induced roll exceeds what level?

35. Turbojet engines are limited to what weight class of aircraft?

36. What are the three basic wing placement positions?

37. What are the three basic wing shapes or configurations?

38. Name all the basic tail configurations.

39. What are two types of formation flights?

40. Who shall identify a scramble as an active air defense mission?

    (A) The en route controller providing service to the interceptors
    (B) The pilot commanding the interceptor flight
    (C) The Air Defense Control Facility initiating the scramble
    (D) The terminal launching interceptors

41. During aerial refueling, which of the following is an ATC responsibility?

    (A) Coordinate altitude and route clearances at least 5 minutes before completing air refueling.
    (B) Position aircraft vertically before reaching the planned exit point.
    (C) Ensure receiver aircraft are released to tanker frequency departing air refueling initiation point (ARIP).
    (D) Navigate for receiver and tanker after ARIP.

42. Navigation by reference to visible landmarks is called

    (A) dead reckoning.
    (B) pilotage.
    (C) radio navigation.

43. What method of navigation requires flying a predetermined course, taking into account the effects of wind?

44. An aircraft travels at 360 knots for 1 hour, 30 minutes. How many nautical miles has the aircraft traveled?

    (A) 360
    (B) 450
    (C) 540
    (D) 720

45. Circles parallel to the equator are called

    (A) great circles.
    (B) parallels of longitude.
    (C) meridians.
    (D) parallels of latitude.

46. The Prime Meridian is the

    (A) great circle passing through the north and south poles.
    (B) line located at 0° latitude.
    (C) great circle running east and west around the earth.
    (D) line located at 0° longitude.

47. A TACAN station projects

    (A) 360 usable true radials.
    (B) 360 usable magnetic radials.
    (C) an infinite number of bearings.

48. An NDB used in conjunction with the Instrument Landing System (ILS) is called a/an

    (A) compass locator.
    (B) marker beacon.
    (C) Outer Marker (OM).
    (D) automatic direction finder (ADF).

49. The component of the ILS that provides the descent angle is the

    (A) marker beacon.
    (B) localizer.
    (C) glideslope.
    (D) back course marker.

50. A pilot can receive Hazardous In-flight Weather Advisory Service (HIWAS) broadcasts via the voice portion of a navigational aid if its communications box has a/an

(A) frequency written above the box.

(B) asterisk preceding the NAVAID frequency number.

(C) blue solid circle with a white H.

51. The boundary of Class B airspace is always depicted in what color?

(A) Magenta

(B) Blue

(C) Dark gray

52. What chart(s) or publication(s) would you use to find out whether an airport has a control tower, and what the tower frequency is?

(A) Sectional aeronautical chart

(B) Terminal area chart

(C) Airport/facility directory

(D) All of the above

53. A "(T)" next to a facility's name means

(A) the facility is temporarily unmonitored.

(B) Transcribed Weather Broadcasts are available.

(C) the facility is a terminal class NAVAID.

54. Which of the following is NOT found in a communication box?

(A) NAVAID frequency

(B) Symbol indicating the availability of Automatic Terminal Information Service (ATIS) broadcasts

(C) Morse code identification of the NAVAID

55. Light brown shading indicates the presence of

(A) uncontrolled airspace.

(B) controlled airspace.

(C) a warning area.

56. A pilot would most likely be issued a STAR from a/an _____ controller.

(A) tower

(B) approach

(C) ground

(D) en route

57. To accept a clearance for the DANDD 1 arrival to Denver, the pilot must be in possession of the _____ for that STAR.

(A) altitude restrictions

(B) textual description

(C) pertinent frequencies

(D) plan view

58. A specific STAR may serve several different airports.

(A) True

(B) False

59. There are three types of precision approaches: ILS, MLS, and precision approach radar (PAR).

(A) True

(B) False

60. Name the five sections of the IAP chart.

61. Marker beacons are depicted in the plan view section of an instrument approach chart.

(A) True

(B) False

62. To fly a desired course toward a VOR station, a pilot must ensure that the aircraft's heading agrees with the course set on the VOR course selector, that the instrument displays a "TO" indication, and that the

(A) VOR needle is centered.

(B) aircraft is not climbing or descending.

(C) magnetic compass is not precessed.

(D) airspeed is constant.

63. The Horizontal Situation Indicator is a combination of three instruments: the glideslope indicator, the VHF Omni-directional Range/range localizer (VOR/LOC) indicator, and the

    (A) magnetic compass.
    (B) attitude indicator.
    (C) automatic direction finder.
    (D) heading indicator.

64. When is an aircraft on an IFR flight plan considered overdue?

65. At the QALQ stage, between what two points would a search area be established when attempting to locate an overdue aircraft?

    (A) Point of departure and last reported position
    (B) Last reported position and destination
    (C) Point of departure and destination

66. An information request (INREQ) message is sent

    (A) 30 minutes after the ETA.
    (B) 1 hour after an aircraft becomes overdue.
    (C) if the reply to the QALQ is negative.

67. An interagency agreement that provides for the effective use of all facilities during search and rescue missions is called a/an

    (A) Search and Rescue Mission.
    (B) Rescue Coordination Center.
    (C) National Search and Rescue Plan.
    (D) Alert Notice.

68. The Rescue Coordination Center is operated by the

    (A) FCC.
    (B) ARTCC.
    (C) ATCT.
    (D) military.

69. Prevailing visibility is the _____ distance that can be seen throughout at least half of the horizon circle.

    (A) least
    (B) farthest
    (C) greatest

70. A routine hourly observation that meets special criteria will be reported as

    (A) METAR.
    (B) SPECI.
    (C) SP METAR.
    (D) statute miles (SM).

71. Station identifiers for all weather reporting stations in the contiguous United States begin with a/an

    (A) "A."
    (B) "K."
    (C) "P."
    (D) "AP."

72. Station identifiers for all weather reporting stations in Alaska begin with a

    (A) "P."
    (B) "PA."
    (C) "K."
    (D) "PH."

73. In a METAR report, the visibility element follows the _____ element.

    (A) sky conditions
    (B) wind
    (C) location identifier
    (D) weather

74. Variable visibility is indicated by

   (A) a "V" between the visibility value and "SM" and the minimum and maximum visibility entered in remarks separated by "V."

   (B) "V" following the "SM" and the minimum and maximum visibility entered in remarks separated by "V."

   (C) entering the minimum and maximum visibility in remarks preceded by VIS and separated by "V."

75. Where is the RVR value reported in a METAR or SPECI report?

   (A) After the wind element
   (B) After the visibility element
   (C) After the weather element
   (D) In Remarks

76. What is the difference between SKC and CLR?

   (A) SKC is reported at manual stations when the sky is clear; CLR is reported at automated stations when the sky is clear.

   (B) CLR is reported at manual stations when the sky is clear; SKC is reported at automated stations when the sky is clear below 12,000 feet.

   (C) SKC is reported at manual stations when the sky is clear; CLR is reported at automated stations when no clouds below 12,000 feet are reported.

   (D) SKC and CLR are interchangeable.

77. Cloud heights are reported in

   (A) hundreds of feet.
   (B) meters.
   (C) oktas.
   (D) kilometers.

78. Reportable cloud layer types are

   (A) X, SCT, BKN, OVC.
   (B) VV, FEW, SCT, BKN, OVC.
   (C) –X, SCT, BKN, OVC.
   (D) X, FEW, SCT, BKN, OVC.

79. In a METAR report, the temperature/dew point group follows the _____ element.

   (A) altimeter
   (B) visibility
   (C) sky condition
   (D) weather

80. If the temperature element is missing, the element in the METAR report is

   (A) omitted.
   (B) replaced with "M."
   (C) replaced with "MM."
   (D) replaced with "//."

81. In a METAR report, the altimeter element follows the

   (A) temperature/dew point group.
   (B) visibility element.
   (C) sky condition element.
   (D) present weather element.

82. VC indicates that the location of a weather phenomena is

   (A) within 5 miles of the observation point.
   (B) between 5 and 10 miles of the observation point.
   (C) between 10 and 30 miles of the observation point.
   (D) within 10 miles of the airport.

83. "00000KT" is decoded as

   (A) "WIND LIGHT AND VARIABLE."
   (B) "WIND CALM."
   (C) "WIND LESS THAN THREE KNOTS."
   (D) "WIND LIGHT."

84. Decode "32012G22KT 280V350."

   (A) "WIND THREE TWO ZERO AT
       ONE TWO PEAK GUST TWO
       TWO, WIND VARIABLE
       BETWEEN TWO EIGHT ZERO
       AND THREE FIVE ZERO."
   (B) "WIND ZERO THREE TWO AT
       ONE TWO GUSTS TWO TWO,
       WIND VARIABLE BETWEEN
       TWO EIGHT ZERO AND
       THREE FIVE ZERO."
   (C) "WIND THREE TWO ZERO AT
       ONE TWO, GUSTS TWO TWO,
       WIND VARIABLE BETWEEN
       TWO EIGHT ZERO AND
       THREE FIVE ZERO."
   (D) "WIND ZERO THREE TWO AT
       ONE TWO PEAK GUSTS TWO
       TWO, WIND VARIABLE
       BETWEEN TWO EIGHT ZERO
       AND THREE FIVE ZERO."

85. Decode "10SM."

   (A) "VISIBILITY TEN MILES."
   (B) "VISIBILITY TEN STATUTE
       MILES."
   (C) "VISIBILITY TEN."
   (D) "VISIBILITY ONE ZERO."

86. Decode "M1/4SM."

   (A) "VISIBILITY MINUS ONE-
       QUARTER MILE."
   (B) "VISIBILITY LESS THAN
       ONE-QUARTER STATUTE
       MILE."
   (C) "VISIBILITY LESS THAN
       ONE-QUARTER."
   (D) "VISIBILITY BELOW ONE-
       QUARTER."

87. Decode "R17/M0600FT."

   (A) "RVR FOR RUNWAY ONE
       SEVEN IS BELOW SIX
       HUNDRED FEET."
   (B) "RUNWAY ONE SEVEN
       MIDDLE VISUAL RANGE SIX
       HUNDRED FEET."
   (C) "RUNWAY ONE SEVEN RVR
       LESS THAN SIX HUNDRED."
   (D) "RUNWAY ONE SEVEN
       VISUAL RANGE MORE THAN
       SIX HUNDRED."

88. When you have run out of writing
    space on a strip for a particular
    flight, you should

   (A) use a note pad to record any
       additional information on that
       flight.
   (B) use additional strips to record
       information and consider all
       strips as one.
   (C) erase the least important
       information and continue to
       record the most current infor-
       mation on the same strip.

89. On a flight service flight progress
    strip, in which block is the departure
    point information recorded?

90. Strips are considered legal documents.

   (A) True
   (B) False

91. Which of the items listed below is
    NOT one of the three designations
    for a terminal strip?

   (A) Preflight
   (B) Departure
   (C) Overflight
   (D) Arrival

92. On all terminal strips, Block 5 is
    used for what purpose?

   (A) Aircraft ID
   (B) Aircraft type
   (C) Computer ID
   (D) Beacon code

93. For terminal arrival strips, altitude
    information is found in which block?

   (A) 6
   (B) 7
   (C) 8
   (D) 9

94. In which block would you find the
    destination airport on a terminal
    arrival strip?

   (A) 2A
   (B) 8A
   (C) 9A
   (D) 18

95. The proposed departure time on a terminal departure strip can be found in which block?

(A) 4
(B) 6
(C) 8
(D) 9

96. For the terminal departure strip, Block 7 is used for what?

(A) Computer ID
(B) Requested altitude
(C) Departure airport
(D) Filed flight plan route

97. On a terminal overflight strip, altitude and route of flight can be found in which block?

(A) 3
(B) 5
(C) 7
(D) 9

98. In which block can the aircraft ID be found on an en route strip?

(A) 1
(B) 3
(C) 11
(D) 13

99. The first three items in an ATC departure clearance are aircraft identification,

(A) clearance limit, and departure procedure.
(B) clearance limit, and altitude.
(C) altitude, and route of flight.
(D) clearance limit, and holding instructions.

100. The term "ATC" should be included in clearances relayed through a/an

(A) VFR tower.
(B) ARTCC.
(C) approach control.
(D) dispatcher.

practice test

ANSWER KEY

1. B
2. B
3. D
4. A
5. D
6. yes, vertical separation
7. vertical separation; 1,000 feet
8. A
9. C
10. B
11. A
12. D
13. D
14. A
15. C
16. ATREPs, RADLOs, and air traffic managers
17. C
18. B
19. B
20. C
21. C
22. B
23. A
24. B
25. B
26. via routing received in last ATC clearance
27. B
28. A
29. C
30. A
31. B
32. 2; 3
33. stall; increasing
34. roll control of the aircraft
35. Turbojet engines are in all weight classes of aircraft.
36. high-wing, low-wing, and mid-wing
37. straight-wing, swept-wing, and delta-wing

38. There are six basic tail configurations: conventional tail, forward slant vertical stabilizer, horizontal stabilizer above the fuselage, "T" tail (swept or straight), "V" tail, and twin boom tail.
39. standard and nonstandard
40. C
41. C
42. B
43. dead reckoning
44. C
45. D
46. D
47. B
48. A
49. C
50. C
51. B
52. D
53. C
54. B
55. A
56. D
57. B
58. A
59. A
60. margin identification, plan view, profile view, airport diagram, and minimums section
61. A
62. A
63. D
64. An aircraft is considered overdue when neither communications nor radar contact can be established and 30 minutes have passed since (1) ETA over a specified or compulsory reporting point or (2) at a clearance limit or clearance void time.
65. C
66. C
67. C

68. D
69. C
70. B
71. B
72. B
73. B
74. C
75. B
76. C
77. A
78. B
79. C
80. A
81. A
82. B
83. B
84. C

85. D
86. C
87. C
88. B
89. Block 4
90. A
91. A
92. D
93. D
94. C
95. B
96. B
97. D
98. B
99. A
100. D

answers

practice test 3

ANSWER SHEET PRACTICE TEST 4

1. Ⓐ Ⓑ Ⓒ Ⓓ
2. Ⓐ Ⓑ Ⓒ Ⓓ
3. Ⓐ Ⓑ
4. Ⓐ Ⓑ Ⓒ Ⓓ
5. Ⓐ Ⓑ Ⓒ Ⓓ
6. Ⓐ Ⓑ Ⓒ Ⓓ
7. Ⓐ Ⓑ Ⓒ Ⓓ
8. Ⓐ Ⓑ Ⓒ Ⓓ
9. Ⓐ Ⓑ Ⓒ Ⓓ
10. Ⓐ Ⓑ Ⓒ Ⓓ
11. Ⓐ Ⓑ Ⓒ Ⓓ
12. Ⓐ Ⓑ Ⓒ Ⓓ
13. Ⓐ Ⓑ Ⓒ Ⓓ
14. Ⓐ Ⓑ Ⓒ Ⓓ
15. Ⓐ Ⓑ Ⓒ
16. Ⓐ Ⓑ Ⓒ
17. Ⓐ Ⓑ Ⓒ Ⓓ
18. Ⓐ Ⓑ Ⓒ Ⓓ
19. Ⓐ Ⓑ Ⓒ
20. _____
21. Ⓐ Ⓑ Ⓒ Ⓓ
22. Ⓐ Ⓑ Ⓒ Ⓓ
23. _____
24. _____
25. Ⓐ Ⓑ Ⓒ Ⓓ
26. Ⓐ Ⓑ Ⓒ Ⓓ
27. Ⓐ Ⓑ Ⓒ Ⓓ
28. Ⓐ Ⓑ Ⓒ Ⓓ
29. Ⓐ Ⓑ
30. _____
31. _____
32. _____
33. _____
34. _____

35. _____
36. _____
37. Ⓐ Ⓑ Ⓒ Ⓓ
38. Ⓐ Ⓑ Ⓒ Ⓓ
39. Ⓐ Ⓑ Ⓒ Ⓓ
40. Ⓐ Ⓑ Ⓒ Ⓓ
41. Ⓐ Ⓑ Ⓒ Ⓓ
42. Ⓐ Ⓑ Ⓒ Ⓓ
43. Ⓐ Ⓑ Ⓒ Ⓓ
44. Ⓐ Ⓑ Ⓒ Ⓓ
45. Ⓐ Ⓑ Ⓒ Ⓓ
46. Ⓐ Ⓑ Ⓒ
47. Ⓐ Ⓑ Ⓒ
48. Ⓐ Ⓑ Ⓒ Ⓓ
49. Ⓐ Ⓑ Ⓒ Ⓓ
50. Ⓐ Ⓑ Ⓒ
51. Ⓐ Ⓑ Ⓒ
52. Ⓐ Ⓑ Ⓒ Ⓓ
53. Ⓐ Ⓑ Ⓒ
54. Ⓐ Ⓑ Ⓒ
55. Ⓐ Ⓑ Ⓒ
56. Ⓐ Ⓑ Ⓒ Ⓓ
57. _____
58. _____
59. _____
60. Ⓐ Ⓑ
61. Ⓐ Ⓑ
62. Ⓐ Ⓑ Ⓒ Ⓓ
63. Ⓐ Ⓑ Ⓒ Ⓓ
64. Ⓐ Ⓑ Ⓒ
65. Ⓐ Ⓑ Ⓒ
66. Ⓐ Ⓑ Ⓒ
67. Ⓐ Ⓑ Ⓒ
68. _____

69. Ⓐ Ⓑ Ⓒ Ⓓ
70. Ⓐ Ⓑ Ⓒ Ⓓ
71. Ⓐ Ⓑ Ⓒ Ⓓ
72. Ⓐ Ⓑ Ⓒ Ⓓ
73. Ⓐ Ⓑ Ⓒ Ⓓ
74. Ⓐ Ⓑ Ⓒ
75. Ⓐ Ⓑ Ⓒ
76. _____
77. Ⓐ Ⓑ Ⓒ Ⓓ Ⓔ Ⓕ
78. Ⓐ Ⓑ Ⓒ Ⓓ Ⓔ Ⓕ
79. Ⓐ Ⓑ Ⓒ Ⓓ Ⓔ Ⓕ
80. Ⓐ Ⓑ Ⓒ Ⓓ Ⓔ Ⓕ
81. Ⓐ Ⓑ Ⓒ Ⓓ Ⓔ Ⓕ
82. Ⓐ Ⓑ Ⓒ Ⓓ Ⓔ Ⓕ
83. Ⓐ Ⓑ Ⓒ Ⓓ Ⓔ Ⓕ
84. Ⓐ Ⓑ Ⓒ Ⓓ Ⓔ Ⓕ
85. Ⓐ Ⓑ Ⓒ Ⓓ Ⓔ Ⓕ
86. _____
87. _____
88. _____
89. _____
90. _____
91. _____
92. Ⓐ Ⓑ Ⓒ
93. Ⓐ Ⓑ Ⓒ
94. Ⓐ Ⓑ
95. _____
_____
96. Ⓐ Ⓑ Ⓒ
97. Ⓐ Ⓑ Ⓒ
98. _____
99. Ⓐ Ⓑ Ⓒ Ⓓ
100. Ⓐ Ⓑ Ⓒ Ⓓ

answer sheet

Practice Test 4

1. The primary function of the Traffic Management Unit (TMU) is to

   (A) monitor and balance traffic flows within its area of responsibility in accordance with traffic management directives.
   (B) ensure maximum efficiency in the use of the total National Airspace System, thereby producing a safe, orderly, and expeditious flow of traffic.
   (C) manage the flow of air traffic throughout the National Airspace System to achieve optimum use of the navigable airspace and minimize the effect of air traffic delays.
   (D) manage the flow of tower traffic by ensuring that traffic demand does not exceed operationally minimal levels of traffic.

2. The primary purpose of the Air Traffic Control System is to

   (A) prevent collision.
   (B) organize the flow of traffic.
   (C) expedite the flow of traffic.
   (D) do all of the above.

3. Additional services are optional on the part of the controller.

   (A) True
   (B) False

4. A _____ consists of markings of pairs of three, then two, and then one rectangular bar on each side of the runway centerline, 500 feet apart.

   (A) threshold
   (B) fixed distance
   (C) touchdown zone
   (D) touchdown aim point

5. What runway marking identifies the full-length runway pavement area?

   (A) Continuous side stripes
   (B) Dashed side stripes
   (C) Continuous centerlines
   (D) Dashed centerlines

6. The minimum vertical separation required for non-RVSM aircraft between FL290 and FL410 is _____ feet.

   (A) 1,000
   (B) 2,000
   (C) 3,000
   (D) 4,000

7. The minimum vertical separation for IFR flight at and below FL280 is _____ feet.

(A) 5,000
(B) 2,000
(C) 1,000
(D) 4,000

8. Supervising the regional collection and dissemination of NOTAMs is the responsibility of

(A) Flight Service Specialists.
(B) the National Flight Data Center.
(C) the center in whose area the outage occurs.
(D) the Service Area Office.

9. Name the electronic device that permits radar presentations only from targets in motion.

(A) Anomalous propagation
(B) Moving target indicator
(C) Primary radar
(D) Linear polarization

10. Which radar feature reduces or eliminates echoes from precipitation?

(A) Circular polarization
(B) Linear polarization
(C) Passive radar
(D) Inversion

11. What causes anomalous propagation clutter on primary radar systems?

(A) Particles in the air slowing the radar signal
(B) Moisture in the air bending the radar signal
(C) Warm air over cold air deflecting the radar signal
(D) Cold air over warm air reflecting the radar signal

12. Which document prescribes air traffic procedures and phraseology used by air traffic controllers?

(A) Order 7210.3
(B) Order 7110.65
(C) *Aeronautical Information Manual*
(D) *Terminal Phraseology Guide*

13. When used in Orders 7110.10, 7110.65, and 7210.3, the word "may" means that the procedure is

(A) recommended.
(B) approved.
(C) optional.
(D) mandatory.

14. Which document provides direction and guidance for operating and managing air traffic facilities?

(A) Order 7110.10
(B) Order 7210.3
(C) *Aeronautical Information Manual*
(D) *Terminal Phraseology Guide*

15. Which of the following would NOT require the development of a Letter of Agreement?

(A) Inter-facility coordination
(B) Intra-facility coordination
(C) Airport emergency services

16. In what type of airspace would a high volume of pilot training take place?

(A) Restricted area
(B) Controlled firing area
(C) Alert area

17. The lower limit of Class B airspace is

(A) 1,200 feet AGL.
(B) 1,200 feet MSL.
(C) 1,500 feet AGL.
(D) the surface.

18. Airspace of defined dimensions, confined activities, and limitations imposed on nonusers is identified as

    (A) uncontrolled.
    (B) Class E.
    (C) special-use.
    (D) Class G.

19. When may pilots of two different aircraft operate as a formation flight?

    (A) When authorization is obtained from air traffic control
    (B) When light visibility is at least 3 miles
    (C) When prior arrangements have been made and no paying passengers are aboard

20. What is the maximum speed of VFR aircraft below Class B airspace?

21. Airspeed in a VFR corridor through Class B airspace shall NOT be more than _____ knots.

    (A) 150
    (B) 180
    (C) 200
    (D) 250

22. When may a pilot deviate from an ATC clearance?

    (A) To expedite the flight
    (B) For passenger convenience
    (C) In an emergency
    (D) In VFR weather conditions

23. If a route has NOT been assigned, or if ATC has NOT advised that a route may be expected, what action will the pilot take in the event of radio failure?

24. When a two-way radio failure occurs, what is a pilot expected to do when the aircraft arrives at a clearance limit from which an approach begins?

25. No person may operate an aircraft under VFR in Class C airspace with a flight visibility of less than

    (A) 1 NM.
    (B) 2 SM.
    (C) 3 NM.
    (D) 3 SM.

26. The three principal airfoils on an aircraft that produce lift are the

    (A) wing, fuselage, and propeller.
    (B) wing, propeller, and vertical tail surfaces.
    (C) wing, propeller, and horizontal tail surfaces.
    (D) wing, vertical, and horizontal tail surfaces.

27. An imaginary straight line drawn from the leading edge to the trailing edge of a cross-section of an airfoil is called the

    (A) chord.
    (B) camber.
    (C) relative wind.
    (D) angle of attack.

28. The direction of the relative wind is determined by the

    (A) chord line of the wing.
    (B) flight path of the aircraft.
    (C) direction of the prevailing wind.
    (D) angle of attack.

29. Hyperventilation results from anxiety or tension.

    (A) True
    (B) False

30. Counter control is most effective and roll is minimal when the wingspan and the ailerons extend beyond the _____ of the vortex.

31. A hovering helicopter creates a downwash from its main rotors that can travel up to how far?

32. What must a helicopter be doing to generate wingtip vortices?

33. What is another name for jet blast?

34. Teardrop, oval, round, and square are what types of identifying features of an aircraft?

35. Aircraft designed function, type of engine power plant used, and type of materials used affect what type of aircraft feature?

36. What are the three basic types of landing gear?

37. What are the three categories of aircraft?

    (A) Category A, Category B, Category C
    (B) Category S, Category L, Category H
    (C) Category I, Category II, Category III
    (D) Single, twin, multi

38. For aerial refueling, when does Military Assumes Responsibility for Separation of Aircraft (MARSA) procedures begin?

    (A) When the tanker advises ATC of the acceptance of MARSA
    (B) When the receiver advises ATC of the acceptance of MARSA
    (C) When ATC accepts MARSA from the tanker
    (D) When the tanker and receiver are vertically positioned within the airspace

39. What are two types of ALTRV classifications?

    (A) Moving and nonstandard
    (B) Moving and stationary
    (C) Standard and nonstandard
    (D) Standard and moving

40. The geographic point over which the receiver arrives in the observation/refueling position with respect to the assigned tanker is the definition of

    (A) ARIP.
    (B) AREX.
    (C) MARSA.
    (D) ARCP.

41. Positions on the earth's surface are described in terms of

    (A) latitude and longitude.
    (B) latitude and parallels.
    (C) degrees and arcs.
    (D) longitude and meridians.

42. A nautical mile equals _____ statute miles (SM).

    (A) 1.05
    (B) 1.15
    (C) 1.5
    (D) 1.76

43. An aircraft flies for 3 hours at 150 knots. How many nautical miles has the aircraft covered?

    (A) 450
    (B) 500
    (C) 550
    (D) 600

44. Coordinated Universal Time is also referred to as _____ time.

    (A) Alfa
    (B) Charlie
    (C) X-ray
    (D) Zulu

45. Time zones are established for every

    (A) 7.5° of longitude.
    (B) 15° of latitude.
    (C) 15° of longitude.
    (D) 20° of latitude.

46. TACAN frequencies are in the _____ band.

    (A) low or median frequency (L/MF)
    (B) VHF
    (C) UHF

47. DME distance is displayed

    (A) as slant range distance.
    (B) as horizontal distance.
    (C) in time to station.

48. The vertical dimensions of a low-altitude VOR airway are from

   (A) the surface up to 18,000 feet.
   (B) the surface up to 17,999 feet.
   (C) 12,000 feet MSL up to but not including 18,000 feet.
   (D) 1,200 feet AGL up to but not including 18,000 feet.

49. One of the characteristics of the MLS is

   (A) 360° radials.
   (B) curved approach paths.
   (C) UHF frequency range.
   (D) high frequency.

50. The height of an obstruction is indicated on the chart in feet above

   (A) ground level (AGL).
   (B) mean sea level (MSL).
   (C) AGL and MSL.

51. A major difference between a sectional chart and a terminal area chart is that the terminal area chart

   (A) provides greater detail and a larger scale.
   (B) is used primarily for IFR flight in the terminal area.
   (C) uses a different set of symbols for man-made and topographical features.

52. The airport/facility directory is designed primarily as a

   (A) source of definitions and airport terms.
   (B) compilation of airline and airport flight connections.
   (C) guidebook of things to do and see at your destination.
   (D) pilot's operational manual.

53. A Mode C area, which requires an aircraft to have Mode C equipment onboard, is depicted by

   (A) solid blue shading inside of a solid blue outline.
   (B) a hatched blue line around the boundary.
   (C) an unshaded area outlined by a solid blue line.

54. An appropriate IFR altitude for an aircraft on a true heading of 178° is

   (A) not able to be determined.
   (B) 15,000 feet.
   (C) 8,000 feet.

55. The primary purpose of an IFR area chart is to furnish

   (A) visual landmarks for use in congested areas.
   (B) terminal data for IFR flights.
   (C) navigation information using a smaller scale than the en route low-altitude charts.

56. To locate a SID or STAR, select the correct U.S. Terminal Procedures Volume, then before using it,

   (A) look in the index under airport name.
   (B) look in the index under city name.
   (C) find the appropriate section.
   (D) check for currency.

57. Identify this map symbol: △

58. Identify this map symbol:

   ◀ ·····················

59. What is the purpose of the IAP chart?

60. Controllers are responsible for providing current prevailing visibility/RVR appropriate to the runway in use; however, they are NOT responsible for determining that landing minimums do or do NOT exist.

   (A) True
   (B) False

61. A localizer approach is a precision approach.

    (A) True
    (B) False

62. Which of the following instruments is a self-contained direction-seeking instrument?

    (A) Heading indicator/directional gyroscope (DG)
    (B) Magnetic compass
    (C) Altitude indicator
    (D) VOR indicator

63. Because of precession, the heading indicator is periodically set by the pilot to agree with the

    (A) attitude indicator.
    (B) altimeter.
    (C) magnetic compass.
    (D) directional gyroscope (DG).

64. Which facility has initial search-and-rescue responsibility for aircraft on a VFR flight plan?

    (A) ARTCC
    (B) RCC
    (C) FSS

65. Which facility has search-and-rescue responsibility for aircraft on a Special VFR flight plan?

    (A) ARTCC
    (B) RCC
    (C) FSS

66. Which air force base is responsible for search-and-rescue coordination for the inland region of the contiguous states?

    (A) Elmendorf AFB
    (B) Scott AFB
    (C) Langley AFB

67. Which facility is equipped and manned to coordinate and conduct search-and-rescue operations in an area designated by the National Search and Rescue Plan?

    (A) ARTCC
    (B) RCC
    (C) FSS

68. When is an aircraft on a VFR flight plan considered overdue?

69. A tropical cyclone in the Atlantic or eastern Pacific Ocean is called a

    (A) typhoon.
    (B) hurricane.
    (C) disturbance.
    (D) willy-willy.

70. Turbulence that causes changes in altitude and/or attitude, but allows the aircraft to remain in positive control at all times should be identified as

    (A) extreme.
    (B) severe.
    (C) moderate.
    (D) light.

71. A wind shear produces the greatest hazards to aircraft

    (A) on the ground.
    (B) in middle altitudes.
    (C) in high altitudes.
    (D) when taking off, approaching, and landing.

72. The weather-related hazard to aircraft that can accelerate forward and downward speeds, causing aircraft to crash on departure or landing is called a

    (A) wind shear.
    (B) tailwind.
    (C) crosswind.
    (D) microburst.

73. A large downburst producing an outflow of wind in excess of 2.5 miles horizontally, lasting 5 to 30 minutes at speeds up to 134 mph is called

(A) wind shear.
(B) macroburst.
(C) cyclonic wind.
(D) wake turbulence.

74. A SPECI is issued when the visibility decreases to _____ miles.

(A) less than 3
(B) 3
(C) more than 3

75. A METAR contains a report on wind, visibility, RVR, weather, sky condition, temperature, dew point, and

(A) barometric pressure.
(B) visibility aloft.
(C) altimeter setting.

76. What is an aviation routine weather report called?

77. Which country/state/region designator is assigned to the United Kingdom?

(A) E
(B) PH
(C) PA
(D) M
(E) T
(F) C

78. Which country/state/region designator is assigned to the contiguous 48 states?

(A) K
(B) PH
(C) PA
(D) M
(E) T
(F) C

79. Which country/state/region designator is assigned to the eastern Caribbean?

(A) K
(B) PH
(C) PA
(D) M
(E) T
(F) C

80. Which country/state/region designator is assigned to Hawaii?

(A) K
(B) PH
(C) PA
(D) M
(E) T
(F) C

81. Which country/state/region designator is assigned to Mexico and the western Caribbean?

(A) K
(B) PH
(C) PA
(D) M
(E) T
(F) C

82. Which country/state/region designator is assigned to Canada?

(A) K
(B) PH
(C) PA
(D) M
(E) T
(F) C

83. Which country/state/region designator is assigned to central Greenland?

(A) K
(B) PH
(C) PA
(D) T
(E) C
(F) B

84. Which country/state/region designator is assigned to Alaska?

    (A) K
    (B) PH
    (C) PA
    (D) M
    (E) T
    (F) C

85. Which country/state/region designator is assigned to the western Pacific?

    (A) K
    (B) PH
    (C) PA
    (D) M
    (E) C
    (F) PG

86. Decode the date/time group "012350."

87. When the modifier "AUTO" appears in the body of a report, where would the type of sensor be found?

88. The first priority during coordination or during the transfer of information is _____.

89. You should use authorized symbols or abbreviations to record what three items?

90. What is the meaning of "Z"?

91. What does the abbreviation "RX" stand for?

92. What does this symbol stand for?

    M→

    (A) Maintain
    (B) Moving eastbound
    (C) Maximum forward speed

93. To delete any unused or unwanted symbols or items, use a/an

    _____.

    (A) / or O
    (B) X or ?
    (C) 0 or X

94. Flight progress strips are used only as aids and are NOT legal documents.

    (A) True
    (B) False

95. Strips are _____ and _____ differently for each air traffic option.

96. The terminal strip has three different uses, including

    (A) preflight, overflight, and arrival.
    (B) departure, arrival, and overflight.
    (C) departure, arrival, and approach.

97. In comparison to the terminal strip, the en route strip is

    (A) larger with more blocks.
    (B) smaller with fewer blocks.
    (C) no different in size.

98. In which block of an en route strip does the aircraft type appear?

99. The pilot-in-command of an aircraft shall comply with all provisions of an ATC clearance unless an amended clearance has been obtained or

    (A) the pilot is conducting military operations.
    (B) the pilot is participating in a speed run.
    (C) the pilot is operating aircraft in IFR conditions.
    (D) an emergency exists.

100. A controller shall use the prefix phrases "ATC CLEARS," "ATC ADVISES," or "ATC REQUESTS" when a clearance, advisory, or request is relayed

    (A) through a tower.
    (B) through a non-ATC facility.
    (C) through a Flight Service Station.
    (D) to a general aviation aircraft.

ANSWER KEY

1. A
2. D
3. B
4. C
5. A
6. B
7. C
8. D
9. B
10. A
11. B
12. B
13. C
14. B
15. B
16. C
17. D
18. C
19. C
20. 200 knots
21. C
22. C
23. proceed using the route filed in the flight plan
24. Commence descent and approach as closely as possible to the expect further clearance (EFC) point, if one has been received. Without an EFC point, begin descent and approach as closely as possible to the calculated/ amended ETA.
25. C
26. C
27. A
28. B
29. A
30. outer edges
31. up to 3 times the diameter of its rotors
32. It must be in a forward flight.
33. thrust stream turbulence
34. windows
35. the fuselage

36. tricycle, conventional (a.k.a., "tail dragger"), and tandem
37. C
38. A
39. B
40. D
41. A
42. B
43. A
44. D
45. C
46. C
47. A
48. C
49. B
50. C
51. A
52. D
53. C
54. A
55. B
56. D
57. non-compulsory reporting point
58. lost communications track
59. to portray the aeronautical data required to execute instrument approach procedures (IAP) to airports
60. A
61. B
62. B
63. C
64. C
65. A
66. C
67. B
68. ETA + 30 minutes
69. B
70. C
71. D
72. D
73. B
74. A
75. C

76. METAR
77. A
78. A
79. E
80. B
81. D
82. F
83. B
84. C
85. F
86. "TWO THREE FIVE ZERO OBSERVATION."
87. remarks section
88. emergencies
89. clearances, reports, instructions
90. Zulu time: Greenwich mean time or Consolidated Universal Time
91. report crossing
92. A
93. B
94. B
95. sized; formatted
96. B
97. A
98. Block 4
99. D
100. B

ANSWER SHEET PRACTICE TEST 5

1. Ⓐ Ⓑ Ⓒ Ⓓ
2. Ⓐ Ⓑ Ⓒ Ⓓ
3. Ⓐ Ⓑ
4. Ⓐ Ⓑ Ⓒ Ⓓ
5. Ⓐ Ⓑ Ⓒ Ⓓ
6. Ⓐ Ⓑ Ⓒ Ⓓ
7. Ⓐ Ⓑ Ⓒ Ⓓ
8. Ⓐ Ⓑ Ⓒ Ⓓ
9. Ⓐ Ⓑ Ⓒ Ⓓ
10. Ⓐ Ⓑ Ⓒ Ⓓ
11. Ⓐ Ⓑ Ⓒ Ⓓ
12. Ⓐ Ⓑ Ⓒ Ⓓ
13. Ⓐ Ⓑ Ⓒ Ⓓ
14. Ⓐ Ⓑ Ⓒ Ⓓ
15. Ⓐ Ⓑ Ⓒ
16. Ⓐ Ⓑ Ⓒ Ⓓ
17. Ⓐ Ⓑ Ⓒ Ⓓ
18. _____
19. Ⓐ Ⓑ Ⓒ
20. Ⓐ Ⓑ Ⓒ
21. Ⓐ Ⓑ Ⓒ Ⓓ
22. Ⓐ Ⓑ Ⓒ Ⓓ
23. Ⓐ Ⓑ Ⓒ Ⓓ
24. Ⓐ Ⓑ Ⓒ Ⓓ
25. Ⓐ Ⓑ Ⓒ Ⓓ
26. Ⓐ Ⓑ Ⓒ Ⓓ
27. Ⓐ Ⓑ Ⓒ Ⓓ
28. Ⓐ Ⓑ Ⓒ Ⓓ
29. Ⓐ Ⓑ Ⓒ Ⓓ
30. _____
31. Ⓐ Ⓑ Ⓒ
32. Ⓐ Ⓑ
33. Ⓐ Ⓑ
34. Ⓐ Ⓑ Ⓒ Ⓓ

35. Ⓐ Ⓑ
36. Ⓐ Ⓑ Ⓒ Ⓓ
37. Ⓐ Ⓑ Ⓒ Ⓓ
38. Ⓐ Ⓑ Ⓒ Ⓓ
39. Ⓐ Ⓑ Ⓒ Ⓓ
40. Ⓐ Ⓑ Ⓒ Ⓓ
41. Ⓐ Ⓑ Ⓒ Ⓓ
42. Ⓐ Ⓑ Ⓒ Ⓓ
43. Ⓐ Ⓑ Ⓒ Ⓓ
44. Ⓐ Ⓑ Ⓒ Ⓓ
45. Ⓐ Ⓑ Ⓒ
46. Ⓐ Ⓑ Ⓒ
47. Ⓐ Ⓑ Ⓒ
48. Ⓐ Ⓑ Ⓒ Ⓓ
49. Ⓐ Ⓑ Ⓒ Ⓓ
50. Ⓐ Ⓑ Ⓒ Ⓓ
51. Ⓐ Ⓑ Ⓒ Ⓓ
52. Ⓐ Ⓑ Ⓒ Ⓓ
53. Ⓐ Ⓑ Ⓒ
54. Ⓐ Ⓑ Ⓒ
55. Ⓐ Ⓑ Ⓒ Ⓓ
56. _____
57. _____
58. _____
59. Ⓐ Ⓑ Ⓒ Ⓓ
60. Ⓐ Ⓑ Ⓒ Ⓓ
61. Ⓐ Ⓑ
62. Ⓐ Ⓑ Ⓒ Ⓓ
63. Ⓐ Ⓑ Ⓒ Ⓓ
64. Ⓐ Ⓑ Ⓒ Ⓓ
65. Ⓐ Ⓑ Ⓒ Ⓓ
66. Ⓐ Ⓑ Ⓒ Ⓓ
67. Ⓐ Ⓑ Ⓒ Ⓓ
68. Ⓐ Ⓑ Ⓒ

69. _____
70. Ⓐ Ⓑ Ⓒ
71. Ⓐ Ⓑ Ⓒ
72. Ⓐ Ⓑ Ⓒ
73. Ⓐ Ⓑ Ⓒ
74. Ⓐ Ⓑ Ⓒ
75. Ⓐ Ⓑ Ⓒ
76. Ⓐ Ⓑ Ⓒ
77. _____
78. _____
79. _____
80. Ⓐ Ⓑ Ⓒ Ⓓ
81. Ⓐ Ⓑ Ⓒ Ⓓ
82. Ⓐ Ⓑ Ⓒ Ⓓ
83. Ⓐ Ⓑ Ⓒ Ⓓ
84. Ⓐ Ⓑ Ⓒ Ⓓ
85. Ⓐ Ⓑ Ⓒ Ⓓ
86. Ⓐ Ⓑ Ⓒ Ⓓ
87. Ⓐ Ⓑ Ⓒ Ⓓ
88. Ⓐ Ⓑ Ⓒ Ⓓ
89. Ⓐ Ⓑ Ⓒ Ⓓ
90. Ⓐ Ⓑ Ⓒ Ⓓ
91. Ⓐ Ⓑ Ⓒ Ⓓ
92. Ⓐ Ⓑ Ⓒ Ⓓ
93. Ⓐ Ⓑ Ⓒ Ⓓ
94. Ⓐ Ⓑ Ⓒ Ⓓ
95. Ⓐ Ⓑ Ⓒ Ⓓ
96. _____
97. _____
98. _____
99. Ⓐ Ⓑ Ⓒ Ⓓ Ⓔ Ⓕ
    Ⓖ Ⓗ Ⓘ Ⓙ Ⓚ
100. Ⓐ Ⓑ Ⓒ Ⓓ

answer sheet

Practice Test 5

1. First priority is given to

   (A) coordinating.
   (B) issuing traffic.
   (C) separating aircraft.
   (D) vectoring.

2. Non-radar separation is used in preference to radar separation when

   (A) an operational advantage will be gained.
   (B) the aircraft is not transponder-equipped.
   (C) secondary radar is out of service.
   (D) controller is not radar-qualified.

3. Automated Flight Service Stations (AFSS) receive and process IFR flight plans.

   (A) True
   (B) False

4. A/an _____ consists of white arrows that point in the direction of landing, replacing the runway centerline and beginning at the non-landing portion to the threshold bar.

   (A) stabilized area
   (B) abandoned runway
   (C) relocated threshold
   (D) displaced threshold

5. A _____ is identified by large chevrons pointing in the direction of the threshold bar.

   (A) blast pad
   (B) closed runway
   (C) relocated threshold
   (D) dislocated threshold

6. Two thousand feet vertical separation is required for IFR flight above _____ to FL600.

   (A) FL410
   (B) FL290
   (C) FL240
   (D) FL180

7. To apply the lateral departure divergence rule, you must assign headings that diverge by at least _____ degrees.

   (A) 15
   (B) 30
   (C) 45
   (D) 60

8. Responsibility for validating NOTAM data and operating the National NOTAM System belongs to

   (A) National Aeronautics and Space Administration (NASA).
   (B) National Flight Data Center (NFDC).
   (C) ARTCCs.
   (D) FSSs.

9. What causes temperature inversion clutter on primary radar systems?

   (A) Particles in the air slowing the radar signal
   (B) Moisture in the air bending the radar signal
   (C) Warm air over cold air deflecting the radar signal
   (D) Cold air over warm air reflecting the radar signal

10. The primary radar clutter caused by dropping large amounts of shredded foil is called _____ jamming.

    (A) active
    (B) inactive
    (C) passive
    (D) static

11. What is the name of the secondary radar interference caused by an improperly adjusted transponder operating near the antenna?

    (A) Ring around
    (B) Anomalous propagation
    (C) Range interference
    (D) Inversion

12. In what document would you find factors affecting flight safety?

    (A) Order 7110.10
    (B) Order 7210.3
    (C) *Aeronautical Information Manual*
    (D) *Terminal Phraseology Guide*

13. Which contraction is used to identify General Notices issued by Washington Headquarters?

    (A) GANOT
    (B) GENOT
    (C) GENNOT
    (D) GNOT

14. Which contraction is used to identify Regional Notices Issued by Washington Headquarters?

    (A) RENOT
    (B) RANOT
    (C) RNTE
    (D) RENIT

15. A Letter of Agreement is required to implement the delegation of responsibility for _____ control service.

    (A) approach
    (B) local
    (C) ground

16. What is generally the vertical limit of Class D airspace?

    (A) FL450
    (B) 18,000 MSL
    (C) 2,500 feet above airport
    (D) 3,500 AGL

17. The upper vertical limit of Class A airspace is

    (A) FL180.
    (B) FL240.
    (C) FL450.
    (D) FL600.

18. The upper limit of Class G airspace is _____.

19. What is the maximum speed of an aircraft operating within Class C or D airspace?

    (A) 156 knots
    (B) 200 knots
    (C) 250 knots

20. At what number should the altimeter be set in an aircraft maintaining FL310?

    (A) 29.92
    (B) 29.94
    (C) 29.98

21. A pilot operating below 18,000 feet MSL shall set the altimeter to

    (A) the current altimeter setting of a station along the route and within 100 NM of the aircraft.
    (B) the current altimeter setting of a station along the route and within 200 NM of the aircraft.
    (C) the elevation of the arrival airport.
    (D) 29.92 for entire route of flight.

22. A pilot-in-command operating in VFR conditions shall NOT cancel an IFR flight plan while operating in Class _____ airspace.

    (A) D
    (B) C
    (C) E
    (D) A

23. An appropriate magnetic course for an aircraft flying VFR at 6,500 feet MSL and more than 3,000 feet AGL would be _____ degrees.

    (A) 190
    (B) 100
    (C) 060
    (D) 010

24. If takeoff minimums are NOT prescribed for a particular airport, the minimum visibility required for an air taxi aircraft having two engines or less is _____ statute mile(s).

    (A) .5
    (B) 1
    (C) 1.5
    (D) 2

25. What are the two requirements necessary to operate an aircraft in IFR flight in controlled airspace?

    (A) File an IFR flight plan and have two-way radio communication.
    (B) Request ATC clearance and have Mode C.
    (C) File an IFR flight plan and request ATC clearance.
    (D) File an IFR flight plan and receive an appropriate ATC clearance.

26. What force in flight counteracts lift?

    (A) Pressure
    (B) Thrust
    (C) Weight
    (D) Relative wind

27. What is used to determine the angle of attack?

    (A) Wing chord and the ground
    (B) Flight path and wing chord
    (C) Flight path and relative wind
    (D) Flight path and upper camber

28. What three factors affect the density of the air?

    (A) Temperature, atmospheric pressure, and humidity
    (B) Temperature, atmospheric pressure, and altitude
    (C) Temperature, altitude, and airspeed
    (D) Atmospheric pressure, altitude, and humidity

29. The forces that are acting on a helicopter in flight are lift, thrust, _____, and _____.

    (A) torque; drag
    (B) weight; gravity
    (C) angle of attack; drag
    (D) weight; drag

30. Why is the controller NOT responsible for anticipating the existence or effects of wake turbulence?

31. Wake turbulence has the greatest impact on ATC in the areas of

    (A) damage and money.
    (B) resources and delays.
    (C) increased separation and traffic management delays.

32. Every aircraft generates a wake turbulence while in flight regardless of its size.

    (A) True
    (B) False

33. Vortices are generated at the moment an aircraft begins to taxi.

    (A) True
    (B) False

34. A small business jet aircraft will fall into which aircraft category?

(A) Twin
(B) Category S
(C) Category B
(D) Category III

35. Helicopters do NOT fall into a category because they are NOT fixed-wing aircraft.

(A) True
(B) False

36. What are the weight classes of aircraft?

(A) Ultra light, small, large, heavy
(B) Small, large, heavy
(C) Small, medium, large
(D) Small, large, heavy, jumbo

37. Who is responsible for ensuring the uniform designations of aircraft throughout the world?

(A) FAA
(B) ICAO
(C) Owner
(D) Manufacturer

38. "An airspace assignment of defined vertical and lateral dimensions established outside Class A airspace to separate/segregate certain military activities from IFR traffic and to identify for VFR traffic where these activities are conducted." This is the definition of a/an

(A) Military Operations Area (MOA).
(B) IFR military training route.
(C) VFR military training route.
(D) air refueling track.

39. What is the call sign for civilian air ambulance flights?

(A) AIR EVAC
(B) MED EVAC
(C) LIFEGUARD
(D) GARDEN PLOT

40. How do you convert local daylight savings time to UTC?

(A) Subtract the conversion factors.
(B) Add the conversion factor, then subtract 1 hour.
(C) Subtract the conversion factor, then add 1 hour.
(D) Add the conversion factor, then add 1 hour.

41. The angular difference between true and magnetic north at a given location is called

(A) correction.
(B) variation.
(C) compensation.
(D) deviation.

42. What type of lines connect points of equal difference between true and magnetic north?

(A) Agonic
(B) Isochronous
(C) Isogonic
(D) Isobaric

43. True heading is the

(A) true course corrected for magnetic variation.
(B) actual path of an aircraft over the ground.
(C) true course corrected for the effects of the wind.
(D) intended path of an aircraft over the ground.

44. An aircraft travels at 600 knots for 1 hour, 15 minutes. How many nautical miles has the aircraft traveled?

(A) 600
(B) 650
(C) 700
(D) 750

45. What DME equipment on the ground is required to respond to the aircraft interrogator?

(A) Transmitter
(B) Transponder
(C) VOR

46. How are all NDBs, except compass locators, identified?

    (A) Three-letter identifier in Morse code
    (B) Two-letter identifier in Morse code
    (C) Aural tone

47. An ILS approach becomes a non-precision approach when the _____ fail(s).

    (A) localizer
    (B) localizer and glideslope
    (C) glideslope

48. The component of the ILS that gives lateral course guidance to the runway is the

    (A) localizer.
    (B) marker beacon.
    (C) glideslope.
    (D) DME.

49. The vertical dimensions of the Jet Route System are from

    (A) 18,000 feet MSL up to and including FL450.
    (B) 18,000 feet MSL up to and including 60,000 feet MSL.
    (C) 17,000 feet AGL up to and including 45,000 feet AGL.
    (D) 18,000 feet AGL up to but not including FL600.

50. The primary use for sectional aeronautical charts is _____ navigation by _____ speed aircraft.

    (A) IFR; slow- and medium-
    (B) VFR; high-
    (C) IFR; high-
    (D) VFR; slow- and medium-

51. Terrain contour lines on a sectional aeronautical chart are depicted every _____ feet.

    (A) 100
    (B) 500
    (C) 1,000
    (D) 2,000

52. The airport/facility directory is published every _____ days.

    (A) 28
    (B) 56
    (C) 112
    (D) 180

53. IFR area charts are published

    (A) every 56 days.
    (B) every 6 months.
    (C) at the same time as the terminal area charts.

54. An IFR area chart displays communications information for airports with

    (A) approach and departure control services.
    (B) a hard-surfaced runway at least 5,000 feet long.
    (C) an approved low-altitude instrument approach procedure.

55. When no altitude is depicted, the MEA on a jet airway is

    (A) 14,500 feet.
    (B) 18,000 feet.
    (C) FL240.
    (D) the same as the minimum obstruction clearance altitude (MOCA).

56. Identify this map symbol:

57. Identify this map symbol:

58. Identify this map symbol:

59. Instrument approach procedures (IAPs) are designed to

    (A) be used only by aircraft in IFR conditions.
    (B) transition an aircraft from the en route segment of the flight to a point where the runway is in sight.
    (C) expedite air traffic in terminal areas.
    (D) provide an IFR descent from the en route environment to a point where a safe landing can be made.

60. A non-precision approach does NOT provide

 (A) electronic glideslope information.
 (B) azimuth guidance to Category D aircraft.
 (C) height and visibility minima.
 (D) missed approach instructions.

61. Minimum sector altitudes (MSAs) are for emergency use only and do NOT ensure NAVAID frequency reception.

 (A) True
 (B) False

62. What information may be obtained from the attitude indicator?

 (A) Rate of turn
 (B) Degrees of bank
 (C) Height above sea level
 (D) Rate of climb

63. Which of the following is a gyroscopic instrument?

 (A) Heading indicator
 (B) Altimeter
 (C) Airspeed indicator
 (D) Vertical speed indicator

64. What is the minimum required information for handling an emergency?

 (A) Aircraft identification and type, nature of the emergency, and pilot's desires
 (B) Aircraft identification, altitude, fuel remaining in time
 (C) Aircraft identification and type, altitude, color of aircraft
 (D) Aircraft identification, airspeed, number of people on board

65. Which facility is responsible for receiving and relaying all pertinent ELT signal information to the appropriate authorities?

 (A) AFSS/FSS
 (B) ARTCC
 (C) RCC
 (D) ATCT

66. The pilot of an aircraft that has been hijacked can be expected to squawk Code

 (A) 7300.
 (B) 7500.
 (C) 7600.
 (D) 7700.

67. Emergency locator transmitters (ELTs) are designed to operate continuously for at least _____ hours.

 (A) 6
 (B) 12
 (C) 24
 (D) 48

68. A provision for the effective use of all available facilities for search-and-rescue missions is called a

 (A) Search and Rescue Facility.
 (B) National Search and Rescue Plan.
 (C) Rescue Coordination Center.

69. Why might the same turbulence be considered "light" by one aircraft and "severe" by another?

70. What type of turbulence is caused by any obstruction placed in the path of wind?

 (A) Wake turbulence
 (B) Obstruction turbulence
 (C) Mechanical turbulence

71. What type of aviation hazard is considered cumulative in nature?

 (A) Low clouds and ceilings
 (B) Icing
 (C) Turbulence

72. A form of induction system icing would be

 (A) fuel freezing in the fuel lines between the tank and engine.
 (B) water freezing in the radiator system.
 (C) ice blocking air flow into an engine carburetor.

73. What can contain almost all the phenomena that create hazards to aviation?

    (A) Thunderstorms
    (B) Volcanic eruptions
    (C) Widespread IFR

74. Intensity levels for icing are

    (A) light, moderate, severe, and extreme.
    (B) trace, moderate, severe, and extreme.
    (C) trace, light, moderate, and severe.

75. Precipitation begins in which stage of a thunderstorm?

    (A) Initial
    (B) Mature
    (C) Dissipating

76. Most tornadoes are a product of which type of thunderstorm?

    (A) Single-cell
    (B) Multi-cell
    (C) Super-cell

77. What is the difference between a funnel cloud and a tornado?

78. What weather phenomenon encompasses almost every hazard to aviation?

79. A tropical storm is reclassified as a hurricane when the wind speeds exceed what?

80. What phenomenon is most likely to reduce visibility to near zero?

    (A) Blowing dust
    (B) Blowing snow
    (C) Blowing sand
    (D) Haze

81. What phenomenon rarely reduces visibility to less than 1 mile?

    (A) Fog
    (B) Low clouds
    (C) Rain
    (D) Snow

82. Which characteristic is typical of clear ice?

    (A) Smooth
    (B) Rough
    (C) Easy to remove
    (D) Granular

83. For structural icing to form on an aircraft in flight, which of the following must occur?

    (A) The aircraft must be above 2,000 feet.
    (B) The aircraft must have all de-icing equipment off.
    (C) Air temperatures must be below freezing.
    (D) The aircraft must be flying through visible moisture.

84. What type of turbulence is caused by very warm surface temperature and uneven heating of the earth's surface?

    (A) Mechanical
    (B) Wake
    (C) Convective
    (D) Clear air

85. Turbulence intensities are classified as

    (A) smooth, rough, moderate, and severe.
    (B) light, moderate, severe, and extreme.
    (C) choppy, light, severe, and hazardous.
    (D) smooth, rough, severe, and extreme.

86. A change in wind speed and/or direction in a short distance is

    (A) the jet stream.
    (B) a frontal passage.
    (C) convection.
    (D) wind shear.

87. A funnel-shaped cloud moving along the ground is a

    (A) funnel cloud.
    (B) hurricane.
    (C) tornado.
    (D) waterspout.

88. Name the words you would use to interrupt a lower-priority message when you have an emergency or control message to transmit.

    (A) "Clearance" and "breaking in"
    (B) "Interrupt" and "urgent"
    (C) "Emergency" and "control"
    (D) "MAYDAY" and "PAN"

89. An action to transfer radar identification of an aircraft from one controller to another when the aircraft will enter the receiving controller's airspace and radio communication is transferred is a

    (A) point out.
    (B) handover.
    (C) handoff.
    (D) transfer.

90. Who/What is responsible for initiating coordination and obtaining approval of an aircraft to cross an active runway?

    (A) The local controller
    (B) Flight data
    (C) The supervisor
    (D) The ground controller

91. "VV 61783" and "VV 16783" (similar call signs) are both on frequency. To transmit a message to VV 61783, you would state

    (A) NAVY SIX ONE SEVEN EIGHT THREE.
    (B) NAVY SEVEN EIGHT THREE.
    (C) NAVY JET SEVEN EIGHT THREE.
    (D) NAVY SIX ONE SEVEN.

92. The terminology for stating an altimeter of 28.72 is

    (A) ALTIMETER TWO EIGHT POINT SEVEN TWO.
    (B) ALTIMETER TWO EIGHT DECIMAL SEVEN TWO.
    (C) ALTIMETER TWO EIGHT SEVEN TWO.
    (D) ALTIMETER TWENTY-EIGHT POINT SEVENTY-TWO.

93. The surface wind is from 170 degrees at 20 knots. This would be stated as

    (A) WIND ONE SEVENTY AT TWENTY KNOTS.
    (B) WIND FROM SOUTH AT TWENTY KNOTS.
    (C) SOUTH WIND AT TWENTY.
    (D) WIND ONE SEVEN ZERO AT TWO ZERO.

94. What is the term for the physical or automated action to transfer identification of an aircraft from one controller to another if the aircraft will or may enter the airspace of another controller, but radio communications will NOT be transferred?

    (A) Point out
    (B) Transfer of control
    (C) Handover
    (D) Forwarding of arrival information

95. A controller monitors assigned radio frequencies

    (A) once every hour.
    (B) intermittently.
    (C) continuously.
    (D) from sunset to sunrise.

96. When stating flight levels, an aircraft at 28,000 feet would be said to be at an altitude of _____.

97. Runway 31C would be spoken as _____.

98. The phraseology for contacting Columbia Automated Flight Service Station would be _____.

99. Clearance authorizing pilots to make intermediate stops while en route to a final destination is called _____.

    (A) taxi clearance
    (B) approach clearance
    (C) composite flight plan clearance
    (D) landing clearance
    (E) takeoff clearance
    (F) amended clearance
    (G) departure clearance
    (H) cruise clearance
    (I) holding clearance
    (J) altitude reservation clearance
    (K) through clearance

100. Which item is always included in a clearance?

    (A) Aircraft identification
    (B) Departure procedure
    (C) Holding instructions
    (D) Altitude

ANSWER KEY

1. C	44. D
2. A	45. B
3. A	46. A
4. D	47. C
5. A	48. A
6. A	49. A
7. C	50. D
8. B	51. B
9. C	52. B
10. C	53. A
11. A	54. A
12. C	55. B
13. B	56. VORTAC
14. A	57. minimum en route altitude
15. A	58. transition route
16. C	59. D
17. D	60. A
18. the base of overlying airspace	61. A
19. B	62. B
20. A	63. A
21. A	64. A
22. A	65. B
23. A	66. B
24. B	67. D
25. D	68. B
26. C	69. The effect on the aircraft varies depending on the size and weight. Light/small aircraft are generally affected more severely than larger/heavier aircraft.
27. B	
28. A	
29. D	
30. because it is unpredictable	
31. C	70. C
32. A	71. B
33. B	72. C
34. D	73. A
35. B	74. C
36. B	75. B
37. B	76. C
38. A	77. Funnel clouds do not touch the ground; tornadoes do.
39. C	
40. B	78. thunderstorms
41. B	79. 64 knots, or 74 miles per hour
42. C	80. B
43. C	81. C

82. A
83. D
84. C
85. B
86. D
87. C
88. C
89. C
90. D
91. A

92. C
93. D
94. A
95. C
96. FLIGHT LEVEL TWO EIGHT ZERO
97. RUNWAY THREE ONE CENTER
98. COLUMBIA RADIO
99. K
100. A

ANSWER SHEET PRACTICE TEST 6

1. (A) (B) (C) (D)	35. (A) (B) (C) (D)	69. (A) (B) (C) (D)
2. (A) (B) (C) (D)	36. (A) (B)	70. (A) (B) (C) (D)
3. (A) (B) (C) (D)	37. (A) (B)	71. (A) (B) (C) (D)
4. (A) (B) (C) (D)	38. (A) (B) (C) (D)	72. (A) (B) (C) (D)
5. (A) (B) (C) (D)	39. (A) (B) (C) (D)	73. (A) (B) (C) (D)
6. (A) (B) (C) (D)	40. (A) (B) (C) (D)	74. (A) (B) (C) (D)
7. (A) (B) (C) (D)	41. (A) (B) (C) (D)	75. (A) (B) (C) (D)
8. (A) (B) (C) (D)	42. (A) (B) (C) (D)	76. (A) (B) (C) (D)
9. (A) (B) (C) (D)	43. (A) (B) (C) (D)	77. (A) (B) (C) (D)
10. (A) (B) (C) (D) (E)	44. (A) (B) (C) (D)	78. (A) (B) (C) (D)
11. (A) (B) (C) (D) (E)	45. (A) (B) (C) (D)	79. (A) (B) (C) (D)
12. (A) (B) (C) (D)	46. (A) (B) (C)	80. (A) (B) (C) (D)
13. (A) (B) (C) (D)	47. (A) (B) (C)	81. (A) (B) (C) (D)
14. (A) (B) (C) (D)	48. (A) (B) (C) (D)	82. (A) (B) (C) (D)
15. (A) (B) (C)	49. (A) (B) (C) (D)	83. (A) (B) (C) (D)
16. (A) (B) (C) (D)	50. (A) (B) (C) (D)	84. (A) (B) (C) (D)
17. (A) (B) (C) (D)	51. (A) (B) (C) (D)	85. (A) (B) (C) (D)
18. (A) (B) (C)	52. (A) (B) (C) (D)	86. (A) (B) (C) (D)
19. (A) (B) (C) (D) (E)	53. (A) (B) (C) (D)	87. (A) (B) (C)
20. (A) (B) (C) (D) (E)	54. (A) (B) (C) (D)	88. (A) (B) (C) (D)
21. (A) (B) (C) (D)	55. (A) (B) (C) (D)	89. (A) (B) (C) (D)
22. (A) (B) (C) (D)	56. _____	90. (A) (B) (C) (D)
23. (A) (B) (C) (D)	57. _____	91. (A) (B) (C) (D)
24. (A) (B) (C) (D)	58. _____	92. _____
25. (A) (B) (C) (D)	59. (A) (B) (C) (D)	93. (A) (B) (C)
26. (A) (B) (C) (D)	60. (A) (B) (C) (D)	94. (A) (B) (C)
27. (A) (B) (C) (D)	61. (A) (B)	95. (A) (B) (C) (D)
28. (A) (B) (C) (D)	62. (A) (B) (C) (D)	96. (A) (B) (C) (D)
29. (A) (B) (C) (D)	63. (A) (B) (C) (D)	97. (A) (B) (C) (D)
30. (A) (B) (C) (D)	64. (A) (B) (C)	98. (A) (B) (C) (D)
31. (A) (B) (C) (D)	65. (A) (B) (C) (D)	99. (A) (B) (C) (D) (E) (F)
32. (A) (B) (C) (D)	66. (A) (B) (C) (D)	(G) (H) (I) (J) (K)
33. (A) (B) (C) (D)	67. (A) (B) (C) (D)	100. (A) (B) (C) (D) (E) (F)
34. (A) (B)	68. (A) (B) (C) (D)	(G) (H) (I) (J) (K)

answer sheet

Practice Test 6

1. What position in the Automated Flight Service Station (AFSS) is responsible for recording and disseminating HIWAS summaries?

   (A) Weather Observer
   (B) Broadcast
   (C) Flight Data/NOTAM Coordinator
   (D) Preflight

2. Which of the following duties is NOT the function of the Clearance Delivery position in the Tower?

   (A) Operating communication equipment
   (B) Processing and forwarding flight plan information
   (C) Compiling statistical data
   (D) Issuing clearances and ensuring accuracy of readback

3. What position in the Tower initiates control instructions?

   (A) Local Control
   (B) Clearance Delivery
   (C) Flight Data
   (D) Tower Associate

4. A taxiway _____ is identified by a continuous yellow line.

   (A) holding line
   (B) parking area
   (C) centerline
   (D) closed for repair

5. An "H" inside a large cross is the recommended marking for _____ heliports.

   (A) civil
   (B) closed
   (C) hospital
   (D) some civil and military

6. Radar separation at or above FL600 requires _____ miles separation between aircraft.

   (A) 3
   (B) 5
   (C) 10
   (D) 20

7. An en route facility providing radar separation between two aircraft at FL270 must provide no less than _____ miles separation.

   (A) 3
   (B) 5
   (C) 10
   (D) 20

8. Who is responsible for observing and reporting the conditions of the landing area of an airport?

   (A) Airport Manager/Operator
   (B) Tower Controller
   (C) Airport Maintenance Officer
   (D) Flight Service Specialist

9. Which of the following is an advantage of a Secondary Radar System?

(A) Displays weather echoes
(B) Only displays aircraft with transponders
(C) Displays are not degraded by weather echoes or ground clutter
(D) Signal strength is affected by aircraft orientation

10. Which device broadcasts interrogator transmissions?

(A) Transponder
(B) Radar display
(C) Interrogator
(D) Antenna
(E) Decoder

11. Which device processes transponder replies and forwards data to the radar display?

(A) Transponder
(B) Radar display
(C) Interrogator
(D) Antenna
(E) Decoder

12. What document is used to consolidate instructions from different levels into a single directive to avoid having instructions scattered among several directives?

(A) Order 7110.65
(B) Notices
(C) Supplements
(D) Changes

13. Which document prescribes air traffic procedures and phraseology used by Flight Service Specialists?

(A) Order 7210.3
(B) Order 7110.10
(C) *Aeronautical Information Manual*
(D) *Terminal Phraseology Guide*

14. Which document contains approved words and phrase contractions used by the FAA?

(A) Order 7340.1
(B) Order 7110.65
(C) *Aeronautical Information Manual*
(D) Order 7350.7

15. One purpose of Standard Operating Procedures is to

(A) specify jurisdictional boundaries for each position/sector.
(B) establish coordination between facilities.
(C) coordinate between government and nongovernment facilities.

16. A prohibited area is identified by the letter _____ and a number.

(A) R
(B) M
(C) P
(D) W

17. A warning area is established beyond _____ miles from the coast of the United States.

(A) 1
(B) 3
(C) 5
(D) 10

18. When may a pilot deviate from an ATC clearance?

(A) At the pilot's discretion
(B) In an emergency
(C) Under no condition

19. A service operated by appropriate authority to promote the safe, orderly, expeditious flow of air traffic is known as

(A) aircraft.
(B) airport.
(C) air traffic control.
(D) air traffic clearance.
(E) flight plan.

20. Specified information relating to the intended flight of an aircraft that is filed orally or in writing with air traffic control is known as

(A) aircraft.
(B) airport.
(C) air traffic control.
(D) air traffic clearance.
(E) flight plan.

21. When operating an aircraft at an airport that has an operating control tower, the pilot must have

(A) a transponder with Mode C.
(B) a transponder only.
(C) radar contact and two-way communications.
(D) two-way radio communications with the tower.

22. The minimum age required to obtain an ATC tower certificate is

(A) 18.
(B) 21.
(C) 30.
(D) No age requirement

23. The minimum IFR altitude at which a pilot may fly over a designated mountainous area is _____ feet above the highest obstacle within a horizontal distance of _____ nautical miles.

(A) 1,000; 3
(B) 2,000; 4
(C) 3,000; 4
(D) 3,000; 5

24. An aircraft on an IFR flight plan is in VFR conditions when a two-way radio failure occurs. The pilot shall

(A) proceed VFR and land as soon as practicable.
(B) return IFR to point of departure.
(C) squawk code 7500.
(D) proceed to nearest airport and execute an IFR approach.

25. A pilot flying under IFR conditions experiences a radio failure. If a route has NOT been assigned and/or ATC has NOT advised a route to be expected, what action should the pilot take?

(A) Proceed by the route filed in the flight plan.
(B) Land at nearest available airport.
(C) Climb to VFR-on-top and continue flight.
(D) Proceed to alternate airport.

26. For an aircraft to maintain a constant airspeed and maintain straight and level flight, what must be in balance?

(A) Thrust and drag; weight and gravity
(B) Thrust and gravity; lift and drag
(C) Thrust and drag; lift and weight
(D) Lift and drag; thrust and weight

27. Which are the primary control surfaces on an airplane?

(A) Ailerons, elevator, and flaps
(B) Elevator, flaps, and trim tabs
(C) Rudder, ailerons, and elevator
(D) Flaps, ailerons, and propeller

28. Movement around the vertical axis is controlled by the

(A) ailerons.
(B) rudder.
(C) elevator.
(D) flaps.

29. What term defines a maneuver in which a helicopter is in motionless flight over a reference point and maintaining a constant heading and altitude?

(A) Autorotation
(B) Blade stall
(C) Hovering
(D) Ground effect

30. Which three aircraft characteristics represent the greatest generated wake turbulence?

   (A) Heavy, dirty, slow
   (B) Small, clean, fast
   (C) Large, dirty, slow
   (D) Heavy, clean, slow

31. Which factor has the greatest impact on wake turbulence?

   (A) Speed
   (B) Weight
   (C) Wing configuration
   (D) Pilot capabilities

32. With zero wind, vortices near the ground will travel laterally at a speed of _____ knots.

   (A) 10 to 20
   (B) 5 to 10
   (C) 2 to 3
   (D) 0

33. Another name for jet blast is

   (A) turbine wash.
   (B) burner blast.
   (C) jet fuel burn.
   (D) thrust stream turbulence.

34. Most Category I aircraft will generally operate within the 300 to 550 knots speed range.

   (A) True
   (B) False

35. What are the three basic types of engines found on aircraft today?

   (A) Reciprocating, piston, and internal combustion
   (B) Reciprocating, turboprop, and turbojet
   (C) Diesel, steam, and nuclear
   (D) Reciprocating, impulse, radial

36. High-wing, mid-wing, and low-wing are the three basic wing placements found on aircraft.

   (A) True
   (B) False

37. An aircraft's design function, type of power plant or engine used, and materials used are all factors that influence the shape of the fuselage.

   (A) True
   (B) False

38. The call sign used by the Civil Air Reserve Fleet is

   (A) NIGHT WATCH.
   (B) FLYNET.
   (C) GARDEN PLOT.
   (D) MARSA.

39. More than one aircraft departing at intervals of 1 minute or less is the definition of a

   (A) cell departure.
   (B) formation departure.
   (C) cell flight.
   (D) MARSA.

40. Who is responsible for separation of aircraft within a formation?

   (A) ATC
   (B) Only the flight leader
   (C) The flight leader and the pilots in the other aircraft
   (D) The en route controller

41. The navigational method based solely on computing air speed, course, wind, ground speed, and elapsed time is

   (A) dead reckoning.
   (B) VFR navigation.
   (C) pilotage.
   (D) radio navigation.

42. The method of navigation that requires the use of ground-based transmitters is called

   (A) ground computation.
   (B) pilotage.
   (C) dead reckoning.
   (D) radio navigation.

43. An aircraft travels at 450 knots for 2 hours, 30 minutes. How many nautical miles has the aircraft traveled?

(A) 1,050
(B) 1,075
(C) 1,100
(D) 1,125

44. An aircraft flies for 4 hours at 220 knots. How many nautical miles has the aircraft covered?

(A) 820
(B) 880
(C) 900
(D) 980

45. An aircraft flies for 5 hours at 200 knots. How many nautical miles has the aircraft covered?

(A) 800
(B) 900
(C) 1,000
(D) 1,100

46. Which of the following components of an ILS is designed to provide the pilot with directional azimuth guidance to the runway?

(A) Markers
(B) Glidepath
(C) Localizer

47. The purpose of the marker beacon is to

(A) provide directional information.
(B) identify a particular location.
(C) provide airborne radio direction finding.

48. Which component of an ILS makes the ILS approach NOT authorized if it fails?

(A) Localizer
(B) Glideslope
(C) Outer marker (OM)
(D) Middle marker (MM)

49. DME equipment measures the

(A) horizontal distance in statute miles.
(B) horizontal distance in nautical miles.
(C) slant range in statute miles.
(D) slant range in nautical miles.

50. The ability to offset and relocate a VOR in order to provide a more direct route is an advantage of _____ navigation equipment.

(A) ILS
(B) NDB
(C) RNAV
(D) VOR

51. Frequencies placed just above a communication box on a sectional aeronautical chart are used to contact which type of facility?

(A) En Route Center
(B) Approach Control
(C) Tower
(D) Flight Service Station

52. Ground control frequencies for airports with control towers are found

(A) in the sectional aeronautical chart legend.
(B) next to the depiction of the airport on the chart.
(C) on the reverse flap of the sectional aeronautical chart legend.
(D) only in the airport/facility directory.

53. Solid triangles indicate

(A) VOR changeover points.
(B) DME fixes.
(C) compulsory reporting points.
(D) substitute route structure.

54. Frequencies for approach and departure control functions can be found on what charts?

   (A) En route low-altitude chart
   (B) En route high-altitude chart
   (C) IFR area chart
   (D) (A) and (C)

55. An asterisk (*) before an altitude along a low-altitude airway indicates a

   (A) MOCA.
   (B) MCA.
   (C) MEA.
   (D) MRA.

56. Identify this map symbol:

◄——— R-275 ———

57. Identify this map symbol: ⟨

58. Identify this map symbol: ▭▭▭

59. The decision height (DH)

   (A) must be followed by a runway visual range (RVR) number.
   (B) is always AGL.
   (C) represents the lowest altitude to which an aircraft may descend when cleared for a non-precision approach.
   (D) is the height at which a decision must be made either to continue the approach or execute a missed approach.

60. Which of the following is an optional component of an ILS?

   (A) Inner marker beacon
   (B) Approach lights
   (C) Glideslope
   (D) Localizer

61. Nondirectional radio beacons are adversely affected by lightning and precipitation static.

   (A) True
   (B) False

62. Which instrument would be affected if the pitot tube became clogged?

   (A) Altimeter
   (B) Vertical speed indicator
   (C) Heading indicator
   (D) Airspeed indicator

63. Which instrument is NOT connected to the pitot-static system?

   (A) Airspeed indicator
   (B) Vertical speed indicator
   (C) Attitude indicator
   (D) Altimeter

64. The exclusive transponder code for hijacked aircraft is

   (A) 7700.
   (B) 7600.
   (C) 7500.

65. An aircraft threatened by serious and/or imminent danger that requires immediate assistance is considered as a/an _____ condition.

   (A) urgent
   (B) distress
   (C) concerned
   (D) lost

66. The universal emergency frequencies are _____ VHF and _____ UHF.

   (A) 121.0; 243.5
   (B) 119.5; 245.0
   (C) 121.5; 243.5
   (D) 121.5; 243.0

67. Who has the final responsibility for the course of action to be followed in an emergency?

   (A) ARTCC
   (B) FSS specialist
   (C) Pilot
   (D) Aircraft owner

68. An emergency situation exists if declared by the

    (A) pilot, facility personnel, or aircraft operator.
    (B) pilot, supervisor, or RCC.
    (C) pilot, ARTCC, or facility personnel.
    (D) ARTCC, aircraft operator, or Red Flag Warning (RFW).

69. The atmospheric layer containing most of the earth's weather is the

    (A) mesophere.
    (B) stratosphere.
    (C) troposphere.
    (D) tropopause.

70. The standard lapse rate within the troposphere is a 2-degree Celsius decrease in temperature with each increase of _____ feet in altitude.

    (A) 2,000
    (B) 1,500
    (C) 1,000
    (D) 500

71. The force that deflects air to the right in the Northern Hemisphere is called the _____ Force.

    (A) Northern
    (B) Southern
    (C) Gradient
    (D) Coriolis

72. The wind circulation around an area of low pressure in the Northern Hemisphere is

    (A) clockwise and toward the center.
    (B) clockwise and outward from the center.
    (C) counterclockwise and toward the center.
    (D) counterclockwise and outward from the center.

73. An elongated area of high pressure is called a/an

    (A) ridge.
    (B) trough.
    (C) front.
    (D) air mass.

74. The jet stream is a narrow, high-speed river of wind found near the

    (A) troposphere.
    (B) tropopause.
    (C) mesosphere.
    (D) exosphere.

75. An extensive body of air within which temperature and moisture in a horizontal plane are essentially the same is described as a/an

    (A) air mass.
    (B) cold front.
    (C) warm front.
    (D) jet stream.

76. An air mass may be modified by

    (A) heating from above only.
    (B) cooling from below only.
    (C) heating or cooling from above.
    (D) heating or cooling from below.

77. Which characteristic is typical of a stable air mass?

    (A) Turbulence
    (B) Smooth air
    (C) Cumulus clouds
    (D) Good visibility

78. When a cold front overtakes a warm front, a/an _____ front is formed.

    (A) mixed
    (B) moderate
    (C) stationary
    (D) occluded

79. A cloud type belonging to the low cloud family and occurring ONLY at the surface to 6,500 feet is

    (A) altostratus.
    (B) cirrostratus.
    (C) cirrus.
    (D) stratus.

80. What type of cloud has the prefix of nimbo or the suffix of nimbus?

(A) Fragmented
(B) Convective
(C) Precipitation
(D) Fair weather

81. What cloud type frequently produces an anvil shape and is most hazardous to aviation?

(A) Altocumulus
(B) Cumulonimbus
(C) Nimbostratus
(D) Cirrostratus

82. Which of the following is NOT a form of precipitation?

(A) Snow
(B) Fog
(C) Hail
(D) Drizzle

83. Convective currents are usually caused by

(A) thunderstorms.
(B) thick fog.
(C) uneven heating of the earth's surface.
(D) sea breezes being forced up the side of a mountain.

84. The "standard" surface temperature at sea level is considered _____ degrees Celsius (_____ degrees Fahrenheit).

(A) 13; 57
(B) 14; 58
(C) 15; 59
(D) 16; 60

85. The "standard" surface pressure at sea level is considered _____ inches of mercury (_____ millibars).

(A) 29.90; 1,013.2
(B) 29.92; 1,013.2
(C) 29.95; 1,015.3
(D) 30.02; 1,015.3

86. In the standard atmosphere, the troposphere extends from the surface of the earth to approximately _____ feet.

(A) 26,000
(B) 30,000
(C) 32,000
(D) 36,000

87. What is the most common and persistent weather hazard encountered in aviation?

(A) Low clouds
(B) Fog
(C) Haze and smoke

88. What would 651224 indicate in the FD?

(A) Wind from 120 degrees at 24 knots, temperature −24°C
(B) Temperature −65°C, temperature −24°C
(C) Wind 150 degrees at 112 knots, temperature −24°C
(D) Wind 151 degrees at 22 knots, temperature −24°C

89. FD forecast altitudes are in true altitude through _____ feet.

(A) 12,000
(B) 18,000
(C) 24,000
(D) 30,000

90. When an in-flight advisory has NOT yet been issued but conditions meet the criteria to issue an advisory, a/an _____ may be issued.

(A) AIRMET
(B) SIGMET
(C) CWA
(D) Meteorological Impact Statement (MIS)

91. A flow control and flight operations planning forecast of conditions expected to begin beyond 2 hours, but within 12 hours of issuance is a/an

(A) AIRMET.
(B) SIGMET.
(C) CWA.
(D) MIS.

92. If the specialist being relieved recognizes an inaccuracy immediately after relinquishing position responsibility, who should be notified?

93. Before receiving a verbal briefing from the specialist being relieved, the relieving specialist shall

(A) indicate that he/she has assumed position responsibility.
(B) sign onto the position.
(C) preview the position.

94. Briefing on applicable traffic is accomplished during which step of the briefing process?

(A) Previewing the position
(B) Verbal briefing
(C) Visual briefing

95. The terminology for stating the frequency 121.5 would be

(A) "ONE TWENTY-ONE FIVE."
(B) "ONE TWO ONE FIVE."
(C) "ONE TWO ONE POINT FIVE."
(D) "ONE TWO ONE DECIMAL FIVE."

96. A Mach speed of .8 is spoken as

(A) "POINT EIGHT MACH."
(B) "MACH POINT EIGHT."
(C) "MACH EIGHT."
(D) "MACH PERIOD EIGHT."

97. What is the call sign for a civil aircraft with the President of the United States aboard?

(A) "AIR FORCE ONE"
(B) "EXECUTIVE ONE PRESIDENT"
(C) "PRESIDENT ONE"
(D) "EXECUTIVE ONE"

98. Jet route 35 would be spoken as

(A) "J THIRTY-FIVE."
(B) "JET ROUTE THREE FIVE."
(C) "VICTOR THIRTY-FIVE."
(D) "J THREE FIVE."

99. What type of clearance keeps aircraft within a specified airspace, specified ground area, or at a specified point while waiting further clearance?

(A) Taxi clearance
(B) Approach clearance
(C) Composite flight plan clearance
(D) Landing clearance
(E) Takeoff clearance
(F) Amended clearance
(G) Departure clearance
(H) Cruise clearance
(I) Holding clearance
(J) Altitude reservation clearance
(K) Through clearance

100. What type of clearance authorizes an aircraft to proceed via a preapproved flight plan?

(A) Taxi clearance
(B) Approach clearance
(C) Composite flight plan clearance
(D) Landing clearance
(E) Takeoff clearance
(F) Amended clearance
(G) Departure clearance
(H) Cruise clearance
(I) Holding clearance
(J) Altitude reservation clearance
(K) Through clearance

practice test

ANSWER KEY

1. B		44. B	
2. C		45. C	
3. A		46. C	
4. C		47. B	
5. C		48. A	
6. C		49. D	
7. B		50. C	
8. A		51. D	
9. C		52. C	
10. D		53. C	
11. E		54. D	
12. C		55. A	
13. B		56. Departure-Arrival Route	
14. A		57. distance not to scale	
15. A		58. airport	
16. C		59. D	
17. B		60. A	
18. B		61. A	
19. C		62. D	
20. E		63. C	
21. D		64. C	
22. A		65. B	
23. B		66. D	
24. A		67. C	
25. A		68. A	
26. C		69. C	
27. C		70. C	
28. B		71. D	
29. C		72. C	
30. D		73. A	
31. B		74. B	
32. C		75. A	
33. D		76. D	
34. B		77. B	
35. B		78. D	
36. A		79. D	
37. A		80. C	
38. C		81. B	
39. B		82. B	
40. C		83. C	
41. A		84. C	
42. D		85. B	
43. D		86. D	

87. B
88. C
89. A
90. C
91. D
92. the relieving specialist and any other appropriate position
93. C

94. B
95. C
96. B
97. D
98. A
99. I
100. J

answers

practice test 6

ANSWER SHEET PRACTICE TEST 7

1. Ⓐ Ⓑ Ⓒ Ⓓ
2. Ⓐ Ⓑ Ⓒ Ⓓ
3. Ⓐ Ⓑ Ⓒ Ⓓ
4. Ⓐ Ⓑ Ⓒ Ⓓ
5. Ⓐ Ⓑ Ⓒ Ⓓ
6. Ⓐ Ⓑ Ⓒ Ⓓ
7. Ⓐ Ⓑ
8. Ⓐ Ⓑ Ⓒ Ⓓ
9. Ⓐ Ⓑ Ⓒ Ⓓ Ⓔ
10. Ⓐ Ⓑ Ⓒ Ⓓ Ⓔ
11. Ⓐ Ⓑ Ⓒ Ⓓ Ⓔ
12. Ⓐ Ⓑ Ⓒ Ⓓ
13. Ⓐ Ⓑ Ⓒ Ⓓ
14. Ⓐ Ⓑ Ⓒ Ⓓ
15. Ⓐ Ⓑ Ⓒ Ⓓ
16. Ⓐ Ⓑ Ⓒ Ⓓ
17. Ⓐ Ⓑ Ⓒ Ⓓ
18. Ⓐ Ⓑ Ⓒ Ⓓ Ⓔ
19. Ⓐ Ⓑ Ⓒ Ⓓ Ⓔ
20. Ⓐ Ⓑ Ⓒ Ⓓ Ⓔ
21. Ⓐ Ⓑ Ⓒ Ⓓ
22. Ⓐ Ⓑ Ⓒ Ⓓ
23. Ⓐ Ⓑ Ⓒ Ⓓ
24. Ⓐ Ⓑ Ⓒ Ⓓ
25. Ⓐ Ⓑ Ⓒ Ⓓ
26. Ⓐ Ⓑ Ⓒ Ⓓ
27. Ⓐ Ⓑ Ⓒ Ⓓ
28. Ⓐ Ⓑ Ⓒ Ⓓ
29. Ⓐ Ⓑ Ⓒ Ⓓ
30. _____
    _____
    _____
31. _____
32. _____
    _____
33. _____
    _____
34. _____

35. Ⓐ Ⓑ Ⓒ Ⓓ
36. Ⓐ Ⓑ
37. _____
38. _____
39. _____
40. _____
41. _____
42. _____
43. Ⓐ Ⓑ Ⓒ Ⓓ
44. Ⓐ Ⓑ Ⓒ Ⓓ
45. Ⓐ Ⓑ
46. Ⓐ Ⓑ Ⓒ
47. Ⓐ Ⓑ Ⓒ Ⓓ
48. Ⓐ Ⓑ Ⓒ Ⓓ
49. Ⓐ Ⓑ Ⓒ Ⓓ
50. Ⓐ Ⓑ Ⓒ Ⓓ
51. Ⓐ Ⓑ Ⓒ Ⓓ
52. Ⓐ Ⓑ Ⓒ Ⓓ
53. Ⓐ Ⓑ Ⓒ Ⓓ
54. Ⓐ Ⓑ Ⓒ Ⓓ
55. Ⓐ Ⓑ
56. Ⓐ Ⓑ Ⓒ
57. Ⓐ Ⓑ Ⓒ
58. Ⓐ Ⓑ Ⓒ Ⓓ
59. Ⓐ Ⓑ Ⓒ Ⓓ
60. Ⓐ Ⓑ Ⓒ Ⓓ
61. Ⓐ Ⓑ Ⓒ Ⓓ
62. Ⓐ Ⓑ Ⓒ Ⓓ
63. Ⓐ Ⓑ Ⓒ Ⓓ
64. Ⓐ Ⓑ Ⓒ Ⓓ
65. Ⓐ Ⓑ Ⓒ Ⓓ
66. Ⓐ Ⓑ Ⓒ Ⓓ
67. Ⓐ Ⓑ Ⓒ Ⓓ
68. _____
69. Ⓐ Ⓑ Ⓒ
70. Ⓐ Ⓑ Ⓒ
71. Ⓐ Ⓑ Ⓒ
72. Ⓐ Ⓑ Ⓒ

73. _____
74. Ⓐ Ⓑ Ⓒ
75. Ⓐ Ⓑ Ⓒ
76. _____
77. _____
78. Ⓐ Ⓑ Ⓒ Ⓓ
79. Ⓐ Ⓑ Ⓒ Ⓓ
80. Ⓐ Ⓑ Ⓒ Ⓓ
81. Ⓐ Ⓑ Ⓒ Ⓓ
82. Ⓐ Ⓑ Ⓒ Ⓓ
83. Ⓐ Ⓑ Ⓒ Ⓓ
84. Ⓐ Ⓑ Ⓒ Ⓓ
85. Ⓐ Ⓑ Ⓒ Ⓓ
86. Ⓐ Ⓑ Ⓒ Ⓓ
87. Ⓐ Ⓑ Ⓒ Ⓓ
88. Ⓐ Ⓑ Ⓒ Ⓓ
89. Ⓐ Ⓑ Ⓒ Ⓓ
90. _____
91. _____
    _____
92. _____
    _____
    _____
93. Ⓐ Ⓑ Ⓒ
94. Ⓐ Ⓑ Ⓒ
95. Ⓐ Ⓑ Ⓒ Ⓓ Ⓔ Ⓕ
    Ⓖ Ⓗ Ⓘ Ⓙ Ⓚ
96. Ⓐ Ⓑ Ⓒ Ⓓ Ⓔ Ⓕ
    Ⓖ Ⓗ Ⓘ Ⓙ Ⓚ
97. Ⓐ Ⓑ Ⓒ Ⓓ Ⓔ Ⓕ
    Ⓖ Ⓗ Ⓘ Ⓙ Ⓚ
98. Ⓐ Ⓑ Ⓒ Ⓓ Ⓔ Ⓕ
    Ⓖ Ⓗ Ⓘ Ⓙ Ⓚ
99. Ⓐ Ⓑ Ⓒ Ⓓ Ⓔ Ⓕ
    Ⓖ Ⓗ Ⓘ Ⓙ Ⓚ
100. Ⓐ Ⓑ Ⓒ Ⓓ Ⓔ Ⓕ
    Ⓖ Ⓗ Ⓘ Ⓙ Ⓚ

answer sheet

Practice Test 7

1. The ATC facility that provides air traffic control services to aircraft on IFR flight plans during the en route phase of flight is

   (A) ATCT.
   (B) AFSS.
   (C) TRACON.
   (D) ARTCC.

2. The En Route Sector team member who scans and manages the flight progress strips and also may accept handoffs via landline communications is the _____ position.

   (A) Radar Coordinator
   (B) Radar Associate
   (C) Radar
   (D) Radar Flight Data

3. In a terminal radar facility, who has the responsibility for the safe and efficient operation of a facility sector?

   (A) Facility Manager
   (B) Radar Position
   (C) Radar Associate Position
   (D) Radar Team

4. Direction signs have a yellow background with a _____ inscription.

   (A) red
   (B) white
   (C) black
   (D) pink

5. Taxiway edge lights are

   (A) white.
   (B) amber.
   (C) blue.
   (D) red.

6. For a terminal facility to provide visual separation between two arriving IFR aircraft, the following condition must exist:

   (A) One of the aircraft must be visually observed by the tower.
   (B) Both aircraft must be visually observed by the tower.
   (C) Communications must be maintained with both aircraft.
   (D) The pilots of both aircraft must see each other.

7. When separating a departing aircraft from a preceding departing aircraft using the same runway, ensure that the takeoff roll does NOT begin until the preceding departing aircraft has crossed the runway end.

   (A) True
   (B) False

223

8. A NOTAM that is locally disseminated is classified as a

   (A) NOTAM D.
   (B) NOTAM M.
   (C) NOTAM L.
   (D) NOTAM C.

9. Which device is the ground-based
   transmitter/receiver?

   (A) Transponder
   (B) Radar display
   (C) Interrogator
   (D) Antenna
   (E) Decoder

10. Which device is the airborne receiver/
    transmitter?

    (A) Transponder
    (B) Radar display
    (C) Interrogator
    (D) Antenna
    (E) Decoder

11. Which device provides the electronic
    presentation of radar-derived infor-
    mation?

    (A) Transponder
    (B) Radar display
    (C) Interrogator
    (D) Antenna
    (E) Decoder

12. Which document lists location
    identifiers authorized by the FAA?

    (A) Order 7340.1
    (B) Order 7110.65
    (C) *Aeronautical Information
        Manual*
    (D) Order 7350.7

13. Which document provides the
    aviation community with basic flight
    information and ATC procedures?

    (A) Order 7340.1
    (B) Order 7110.65
    (C) *Aeronautical Information
        Manual*
    (D) Order 7350.7

14. The addition, deletion, or modifica-
    tion of information or instructions
    within an order are made through a

    (A) change.
    (B) notice.
    (C) supplement.
    (D) amendment.

15. After approval by the Service Area
    Office, the Air Traffic Manager is
    responsible for

    (A) preparing the Letter of Agree-
        ment (LOA) in final form.
    (B) establishing effective date.
    (C) delivering signed LOA to each
        participating facility.
    (D) all of the above

16. Military Operations Areas (MOAs)
    consist of airspace of defined dimen-
    sions established for the purpose of

    (A) separating certain military
        training activities from
        IFR traffic.
    (B) restricting VFR flights.
    (C) providing airspace in the event
        of national emergencies.
    (D) protecting military airports.

17. What airspace contains federal VOR
    airways?

    (A) Class A
    (B) Class C
    (C) Class E
    (D) Class G

18. A device that is used or intended to
    be used for flight in the air is
    known as

    (A) aircraft.
    (B) airport.
    (C) air traffic control.
    (D) air traffic clearance.
    (E) flight plan.

19. An area of land or water that is used or intended to be used for the landing and takeoff of aircraft is known as

    (A) aircraft.
    (B) airport.
    (C) air traffic control.
    (D) air traffic clearance.
    (E) flight plan.

20. An authorization by air traffic control for the purpose of preventing collision between known aircraft for an aircraft to proceed under specified traffic conditions within controlled airspace is known as

    (A) aircraft.
    (B) airport.
    (C) air traffic control.
    (D) air traffic clearance.
    (E) flight plan.

21. Upon request of authorized officials, personnel holding an ATC tower operators certificate shall

    (A) be given 48 hours to provide the certificate for inspection.
    (B) present the certificate for inspection.
    (C) control traffic without regard to medical restrictions.
    (D) control traffic with inadequate equipment.

22. An ATC specialist who is 41 years old and works in the terminal option is required to have a medical examination every

    (A) year.
    (B) two years.
    (C) three years.
    (D) five years.

23. What is the requirement for supplemental oxygen above 15,000 MSL?

    (A) Only the pilot is provided with supplemental oxygen.
    (B) None.
    (C) Each occupant of aircraft is provided with supplemental oxygen.
    (D) Pilot and co-pilot are provided with supplemental oxygen.

24. Which one of the following items is NOT required on a VFR flight plan?

    (A) Pilot's name and address
    (B) Fuel on board
    (C) Name of each occupant
    (D) Type of aircraft

25. A pilot should file a defense VFR (DVFR) flight plan if the flight will

    (A) be in instrument flight conditions.
    (B) enter positive control airspace.
    (C) enter coastal Air Defense Identification Zone (ADIZ).
    (D) enter a restricted area.

26. Movement around the longitudinal axis is called

    (A) roll.
    (B) yaw.
    (C) crab.
    (D) pitch.

27. Which action would cause a change in pitch?

    (A) Pushing on a rudder pedal
    (B) Turning the control yoke
    (C) Pushing the control yoke
    (D) Adjusting the rudder trim

28. Which control allows the pilot to relieve manual pressure on the primary controls?

    (A) Trim tab
    (B) Flaps
    (C) Control yoke
    (D) Elevator

29. What is the basic purpose of the autorotation maneuver?

    (A) To make emergency landings
    (B) To conserve fuel
    (C) To maintain constant altitude
    (D) To maintain rearward flight

30. Three factors that affect the strength of wake turbulence are _____, _____, and _____.

31. The phenomenon created by an aircraft passing through the atmosphere is called _____.

32. Vortices from large aircraft will sink at a rate of approximately _____ to _____ feet per minute.

33. The ability of an aircraft to counteract the effects of induced roll is based on the _____ and _____ of the aircraft.

34. For a helicopter to generate trailing vortices, it must be in _____.

35. What are the three basic types of landing gear?

    (A) Uni-gear, bicycle gear, and tricycle gear
    (B) Tricycle gear, conventional gear, and tandem gear
    (C) Pontoon gear, skid rail gear, and mesh gear
    (D) Cycle gear, tandem gear, and random gear

36. The two configurations of landing gear are fixed and retractable.

    (A) True
    (B) False

37. An aircraft weighing 300,000 pounds will fall into the _____ weight class.

38. An aircraft with a certified takeoff weight of _____ pounds or less will fall into the small weight class.

39. Name one factor that affects aircraft performance.

40. Name two types of ALTRVs.

41. What does "TO" mean when referring to an altitude or flight level?

42. What condition exists whereby the military service involved assumes responsibility for separation between participating military aircraft in the ATC system?

43. To travel a distance of 650 nautical miles, an aircraft would have to maintain a ground speed of 130 knots for how long?

    (A) 4 hours, 30 minutes
    (B) 5 hours
    (C) 5 hours, 30 minutes
    (D) 6 hours

44. The purpose of parallels of latitude lines is to measure degrees of latitude

    (A) east and west of the equator.
    (B) north and south of the equator.
    (C) north and south of the Prime Meridian.
    (D) east and west of the Prime Meridian.

45. On a hot, humid day, an aircraft's landing ground speed is slower than on a cool, dry day.

    (A) True
    (B) False

46. MLS identification is a four-letter designation starting with the letter

    (A) I.
    (B) M.
    (C) N.

47. The GPS constellation of _____ satellites is designed so that a minimum of five are always observable by a user anywhere on Earth.

    (A) 18
    (B) 21
    (C) 24
    (D) 27

48. The GPS receiver needs at least _____ satellites to yield three-dimensional information, including position, velocity, time, and altitude.

(A) 3
(B) 4
(C) 5
(D) 6

49. Using Lines of Position (LOPs) to determine an aircraft's location is a characteristic of _____ navigation.

(A) VOR
(B) GPS
(C) INS
(D) LORAN

50. Where are Class B airspace operating rules found?

(A) On the reverse side of a terminal area chart
(B) On the inside flap of a sectional aeronautical chart
(C) In the world aeronautical chart legend
(D) Only in the airport/facility directory

51. The world aeronautical chart and the sectional aeronautical chart are alike in that they

(A) use similar symbols in the chart legends.
(B) depict minimum IFR altitudes.
(C) are used primarily by high-speed aircraft.
(D) provide the pilot with information about services available at various airports.

52. If no changeover point is depicted along an airway, it means that

(A) the airway segment crosses through uncontrolled airspace.
(B) either NAVAID can be used for the entire length of the route segment.
(C) there is a gap in NAVAID signal coverage along the airway.
(D) the changeover is to be made at the halfway point between the two NAVAIDs.

53. How is Class A airspace depicted on an en route low-altitude chart?

(A) As a solid white background
(B) In blue, with a solid blue border
(C) With a hatched blue line around the boundary
(D) None of the above

54. IFR area charts use the same symbols as those found in the

(A) terminal area charts.
(B) en route low- and high-altitude charts.
(C) sectional charts.
(D) airport/facility directory.

55. All airports have Standard Instrument Departures (SID) to allow transition from the terminal environment to the en route environment.

(A) True
(B) False

56. U.S. Terminal Procedure Charts are published every _____ days.

(A) 28
(B) 56
(C) 112

57. After locating the correct volume, the specialist should verify

(A) whether the airport has a SID.
(B) the currency of the volume.
(C) whether the desired SID is a Vector or Pilot Navigational SID.

58. When the glideslope component of an ILS is inoperative,

    (A) the entire approach is unusable.
    (B) it is classified as a localizer approach.
    (C) the altitude minima are lower but the visibility minima are higher.
    (D) the altitude minima are lower and the visibility minima remain the same.

59. DME arcs are depicted in the

    (A) profile view.
    (B) airport diagram.
    (C) plan view.
    (D) circling section.

60. Height of obstructions depicted on IAP charts are

    (A) always AGL.
    (B) found only in the plan view section.
    (C) sometimes AGL.
    (D) always MSL.

61. A transponder code consists of four numbers from zero to seven with _____ possible codes.

    (A) 4,006
    (B) 4,066
    (C) 4,086
    (D) 4,096

62. The FMS constantly updates its position information by

    (A) selecting the most appropriate combination of conventional navigational aids.
    (B) placing primary dependence on satellite-based information.
    (C) following established airways, but with a much greater degree of accuracy.
    (D) using onboard Mode S data link equipment.

63. The destination location tie-in FSS is responsible for SAR for aircraft on a VFR flight plan when the

    (A) destination location tie-in FSS acknowledges receipt of the flight notification message.
    (B) pilot files a VFR flight plan.
    (C) departure message is sent.
    (D) the aircraft departure time is received by the departure location tie-in FSS.

64. An aircraft on a VFR flight plan is considered overdue when it fails to arrive _____ minutes after its ETA and communications or location cannot be established.

    (A) 15
    (B) 30
    (C) 45
    (D) 60

65. An aircraft NOT on a flight plan fails to arrive at its destination, and a reliable source reports that the flight was due to arrive at 1500 UTC. This aircraft is considered overdue at

    (A) 1500.
    (B) 1530.
    (C) 1600.
    (D) 1700.

66. An aircraft is overdue on a VFR flight plan. An INREQ will be sent _____ after ETA if the aircraft has NOT been found.

    (A) 30 minutes
    (B) 1 hour
    (C) 1 1/2 hours
    (D) 2 hours

67. A pilot requesting Lake Island Reporting Service will report every 10 minutes. Search and rescue must be initiated if no report is received in _____ minutes.

    (A) 10
    (B) 15
    (C) 30
    (D) 60

68. In a METAR, winds are reported to a pilot as "calm" when the winds are less than how many knots?

69. Unrestricted visibility is coded as

(A) +6SM.
(B) P5SM.
(C) P6SM.

70. What contraction denotes wind shear?

(A) WND SHR
(B) WDSR
(C) WS

71. Widespread IFR conditions from ceiling and fog would be described by what type of aviation weather advisory?

(A) AIRMET
(B) SIGMET
(C) Convective SIGMET

72. AIRMET advisory bulletins are issued

(A) only as required.
(B) hourly.
(C) every 6 hours.

73. Which advisory would be used to describe moderate to occasionally severe turbulence?

74. Convective SIGMETs advisories are issued

(A) only as required.
(B) hourly.
(C) every 4 to 6 hours.

75. The maximum valid time for a CWA is _____ hours.

(A) 2
(B) 4
(C) 6

76. What is the difference between a Center Weather Advisory (CWA) and a Meteorological Impact Statement (MIS)?

77. Winds aloft forecasts are used by the pilot for what purpose?

78. Which of the following is a correctly formatted valid time for a TAF forecast from 0000Z on June12 to 0000Z on June13?

(A) 120024
(B) 120000
(C) 120024Z
(D) 0000Z

79. As part of the TAF sky conditions, which cloud type(s) is/are forecast?

(A) Towering cumulus clouds (TCU)
(B) Cumulonimbus clouds (CB)
(C) Altocumulus castellanus clouds (ACC)
(D) Rotor clouds

80. Obscurations to vision are always included in TAF reports when visibility is

(A) 5 statute miles or less.
(B) less than 5 statute miles.
(C) 6 statute miles or less.
(D) less than 6 statute miles.

81. In a TAF, wind shear is given in hundreds of feet AGL up to and including _____ feet.

(A) 1,000
(B) 1,500
(C) 2,000
(D) 3,000

82. In a TAF, PROB30 is used when the occurrence of an event is _____ percent.

(A) 20 to 30
(B) 30 to 39
(C) 30
(D) greater than 30

83. In a TAF, events forecast to last less than an hour are encoded with what contraction?

(A) OCNL
(B) CHC
(C) EXPD
(D) TEMPO

84. In a TAF, the FM contraction is used to indicate

    (A) rapid changes.
    (B) gradual changes.
    (C) temporary.
    (D) an outlook forecast.

85. In a TAF, what does the four-digit time appended to the FM contraction indicate?

    (A) The hour and minute the change is expected to begin
    (B) The duration of the FM event
    (C) The time period during which the change will occur
    (D) The ending hour and minute of the FM event

86. AIRMET TANGO advisories are issued for which condition?

    (A) IFR
    (B) Turbulence
    (C) Icing
    (D) Thunderstorms

87. SIGMET advisories are issued

    (A) when required.
    (B) hourly.
    (C) every 2 hours.
    (D) every 4 hours.

88. Which weather advisory would be used to describe embedded thunderstorms over Indiana and Ohio?

    (A) AIRMET
    (B) SIGMET
    (C) Convective SIGMET
    (D) International SIGMET

89. Severe icing NOT associated with thunderstorms is criteria for issuance of what type of aviation weather advisory?

    (A) AIRMET SIERRA
    (B) AIRMET ZULU
    (C) SIGMET
    (D) Convective SIGMET

90. The Flight Service Option has _____ designations for their strips.

91. Compared to terminal or en route strips, flight service strips are _____ yet have _____ blocks.

92. Use authorized symbols or abbreviations for recording _____, _____, and _____.

93. What prefix phrase should you use to relay a clearance to an aircraft through another aircraft?

    (A) "ATC CLEARS."
    (B) "ATC RELAYS."
    (C) "ATC ADVISES."

94. The pilot-in-command of an aircraft may NOT deviate from a clearance unless an amendment has been obtained or

    (A) an early departure is required.
    (B) Instrument Flight Rules (IFR) are in effect.
    (C) an emergency exists.

95. Which type of clearance provides aircraft/vehicles a route to follow while on movement area of airport?

    (A) Taxi clearance
    (B) Approach clearance
    (C) Composite flight plan clearance
    (D) Landing clearance
    (E) Takeoff clearance
    (F) Amended clearance
    (G) Departure clearance
    (H) Cruise clearance
    (I) Holding clearance
    (J) Altitude reservation clearance
    (K) Through clearance

96. Which type of clearance authorizes aircraft to execute a particular procedure for the purpose of landing at an airport?

(A) Taxi clearance
(B) Approach clearance
(C) Composite flight plan clearance
(D) Landing clearance
(E) Takeoff clearance
(F) Amended clearance
(G) Departure clearance
(H) Cruise clearance
(I) Holding clearance
(J) Altitude reservation clearance
(K) Through clearance

97. Which type of clearance is required by a combination of a VFR and IFR flight?

(A) Taxi clearance
(B) Approach clearance
(C) Composite flight plan clearance
(D) Landing clearance
(E) Takeoff clearance
(F) Amended clearance
(G) Departure clearance
(H) Cruise clearance
(I) Holding clearance
(J) Altitude reservation clearance
(K) Through clearance

98. Which type of clearance provides authorization for an aircraft to land at a specified airport?

(A) Taxi clearance
(B) Approach clearance
(C) Composite flight plan clearance
(D) Landing clearance
(E) Takeoff clearance
(F) Amended clearance
(G) Departure clearance
(H) Cruise clearance
(I) Holding clearance
(J) Altitude reservation clearance
(K) Through clearance

99. Which type of clearance authorizes the pilot to depart the airport?

(A) Taxi clearance
(B) Approach clearance
(C) Composite flight plan clearance
(D) Landing clearance
(E) Takeoff clearance
(F) Amended clearance
(G) Departure clearance
(H) Cruise clearance
(I) Holding clearance
(J) Altitude reservation clearance
(K) Through clearance

100. Which type of clearance changes a previously issued clearance?

(A) Taxi clearance
(B) Approach clearance
(C) Composite flight plan clearance
(D) Landing clearance
(E) Takeoff clearance
(F) Amended clearance
(G) Departure clearance
(H) Cruise clearance
(I) Holding clearance
(J) Altitude reservation clearance
(K) Through clearance

ANSWER KEY

1. D
2. B
3. D
4. C
5. C
6. B
7. A
8. C
9. C
10. A
11. B
12. D
13. C
14. A
15. D
16. A
17. C
18. A
19. B
20. D
21. B
22. A
23. C
24. C
25. C
26. A
27. C
28. A
29. A
30. weight; shape of the wing; speed
31. wake turbulence
32. 300; 500
33. wingspan; counter control capabilities
34. forward flight
35. B
36. A
37. heavy
38. 41,000
39. any of the following: weather conditions, load, pilot's ability, aircraft configuration, aircraft speed, aircraft altitude, aircraft climb rate, aircraft weight class

40. stationary and moving
41. to and including that altitude or flight level
42. MARSA
43. B
44. B
45. B
46. B
47. C
48. B
49. D
50. A
51. A
52. D
53. D
54. B
55. B
56. B
57. B
58. B
59. C
60. D
61. D
62. A
63. A
64. B
65. C
66. B
67. B
68. 3
69. C
70. C
71. A
72. C
73. SIGMET
74. B
75. A
76. A CWA is a short-term "nowcast" for up to 2 hours; an MIS is a forecast of conditions expected to begin beyond 2 hours but within 12 hours of issuance.

77. to select the best altitude for a flight, determine aircraft performance, and calculate ground speed
78. A
79. B
80. C
81. C
82. C
83. D
84. A
85. A
86. B
87. A

88. C
89. C
90. two
91. larger; fewer
92. clearances; reports; instructions
93. A
94. C
95. A
96. B
97. C
98. D
99. E
100. F

answers

practice test 7

APPENDIXES

A Glossary of Air Traffic Controller/Pilot Terms

AERODROME—A defined area on land or water (including any buildings, installations, and equipment) intended to be used either wholly or in part for the arrival, departure, and movement of aircraft.

AERONAUTICAL BEACON—A visual NAVAID displaying flashes of white and/or colored light to indicate the location of an airport, a heliport, a landmark, a certain point of a federal airway in mountainous terrain, or an obstruction.

AERONAUTICAL CHART—A map used in air navigation containing all or part of the following: topographic features, hazards and obstructions, navigation aids, navigation routes, designated airspace, and airports. Commonly used aeronautical charts are:

- Sectional Aeronautical Chart (scale 1:500,000)—Designed for visual navigation of slow- or medium-speed aircraft. Topographic information on this chart features the portrayal of relief and a judicious selection of visual checkpoints for VFR flight. Aeronautical information includes visual and radio aids to navigation, airports, controlled airspace, restricted areas, obstructions, and related data.

- VFR Terminal Area Chart (scale 1:250,000)—Depicts Class B airspace, which provides for the control or segregation of all the aircraft within this class of airspace. This chart depicts topographic information and aeronautical information, including visual and radio aids to navigation, airports, controlled airspace, restricted areas, obstructions, and related data.

- World Aeronautical Chart (WAC) (scale 1:1,000,000)—Provides a standard series of aeronautical charts covering land areas of the world at a size and scale convenient for navigation by moderate-speed aircraft. Topographic information includes cities and towns, principal roads, railroads, distinctive landmarks, drainage, and relief. Aeronautical information includes visual and radio aids to navigation, airports, airways, restricted areas, obstructions, and other pertinent data.

- En Route Low-Altitude Chart—Provides aeronautical information for en route instrument navigation (IFR) in the low-altitude stratum. Information includes the portrayal of airways, limits of controlled airspace, position identification and frequencies of radio aids, selected airports, minimum en route and minimum obstruction clearance altitudes, airway distances, reporting points, restricted areas, and related data. Area charts, which are a part of this series, furnish terminal data at a larger scale in congested areas.

- En Route High-Altitude Chart—Provides aeronautical information for en route instrument navigation (IFR) in the high-altitude stratum. Information includes the portrayal of jet routes, identification and frequencies of radio aids, selected airports, distances, time zones, special-use airspace, and related information.

- Instrument Approach Procedures (IAP) Chart—Portrays the aeronautical data required to execute an instrument approach to an airport. These charts depict the procedures (including all related data) and the airport diagram. Each procedure is designated for use with a specific type of electronic navigation system, including NDB, TACAN, VOR, ILS/MLS, and RNAV. IAP charts are identified by the type of navigational aid(s) that provide final approach guidance.

- Instrument Departure Procedure (DP) Chart—Designed to expedite clearance delivery and to facilitate transition between takeoff and en route operations. Each DP is presented as a separate chart and may serve a single airport or more than one airport in a given geographical location.

- Standard Terminal Arrival Route (STAR) Chart—Designed to expedite air traffic control arrival procedures and to facilitate transition between en route and instrument approach operations. Each STAR procedure is presented as a separate chart and may serve a single airport or more than one airport in a given geographical location.

- Airport Taxi Chart—Designed to expedite the efficient and safe flow of ground traffic at an airport. These charts are identified by the official airport name (e.g., Ronald Reagan Washington National Airport).

AERONAUTICAL INFORMATION MANUAL (AIM)—This primary FAA publication with the purpose of instructing aviation workers about operating in the National Airspace System of the United States provides basic flight information, air traffic control procedures, and general instructional information concerning health, medical facts, factors affecting flight safety, accident and hazard reporting, and types of aeronautical charts and their use.

AIR DEFENSE IDENTIFICATION ZONE (ADIZ)—The area of airspace over land or water extending upward from the surface within which the ready identification, location, and control of aircraft are required in the interest of national security. Types of ADIZs are:

- Domestic Air Defense Identification Zone—An ADIZ within the United States along an international boundary of the United States.

- Coastal Air Defense Identification Zone—An ADIZ over U.S. coastal waters.

- Distant Early Warning Identification Zone (DEWIZ)—An ADIZ over the coastal waters of the state of Alaska.

- Land-Based Air Defense Identification Zone—An ADIZ over U.S. metropolitan areas. It is activated and deactivated as needed, with dimensions, activation dates, and other relevant information disseminated via NOTAM.

AIR NAVIGATION FACILITY—Any facility used, available for use, or designed for use in aid of air navigation, including landing areas; lights; any apparatus or equipment for disseminating weather information, signaling, radio-directional finding, or radio or other electrical communication; and any other structure or mechanism having a similar purpose for guiding or controlling flight in the air or during aircraft landing and takeoff.

AIR ROUTE SURVEILLANCE RADAR (ARSR)—Air Route Traffic Control Center (ARTCC) radar, used primarily to detect and display an aircraft's position while en route between terminal areas. The ARSR enables controllers to provide radar air traffic control service when aircraft are within the ARSR coverage. In some instances, ARSR may enable an ARTCC to provide terminal radar services that are similar to but usually more limited than those provided by a radar approach control.

AIR ROUTE TRAFFIC CONTROL CENTER (ARTCC)—A facility established to provide air traffic control service to aircraft operating on IFR flight plans within controlled airspace and principally during the en route phase of flight. When equipment capabilities and controller workload permit, certain advisory/assistance services may be provided to VFR aircraft.

AIR TRAFFIC CLEARANCE—An authorization by air traffic control for the purpose of preventing collision between known aircraft, for an aircraft to proceed under specified traffic conditions within controlled airspace. The pilot-in-command of an aircraft may not deviate from the provisions of a Visual Flight Rules (VFR) or Instrument Flight Rules (IFR) air traffic clearance except in an emergency or unless an amended clearance has been obtained. Additionally, the pilot may request a different clearance from what has been issued by air traffic control if information available to the pilot makes another course of action more practicable, or if aircraft equipment limitations or company procedures forbid compliance with the clearance issued. Pilots may also request clarification or amendment, as appropriate, any time a clearance is not fully understood or is considered unacceptable because of safety of flight.

Controllers should, in such instances and to the extent of operational practicality and safety, honor the pilot's request. As 14 CFR Part 91.3(a) states: "The pilot-in-command of an aircraft is directly responsible for, and is the final authority as to, the operation of that aircraft." **The pilot is responsible to request an amended clearance** if air traffic control issues a clearance that would cause a pilot to deviate from a rule or regulation or, in the pilot's opinion, would place the aircraft in jeopardy.

AIR TRAFFIC CONTROL (ATC)—A service operated by appropriate authority to promote the safe, orderly, and expeditious flow of air traffic.

AIR TRAFFIC CONTROL SYSTEM COMMAND CENTER (ATCSCC)—An Air Traffic Tactical Operations facility responsible for monitoring and managing the flow of air traffic throughout the NAS, producing a safe, orderly, and expeditious flow of traffic while minimizing delays. The following functions are located at the ATCSCC:

- Central Altitude Reservation Function (CARF)—Responsible for coordinating, planning, and approving special user requirements under the altitude reservation (ALTRV) concept.

- Airport Reservation Office (ARO)—Responsible for approving IFR flights at designated high-density traffic airports (John F. Kennedy, LaGuardia, and Ronald Reagan Washington National) during specified hours.

- U.S. Notice to Airmen (NOTAM) Office—Responsible for collecting, maintaining, and distributing NOTAMs for the U.S. civilian and military, as well as for international aviation communities.

- Weather Unit—Monitors all aspects of weather for the United States that might affect aviation, including cloud cover, visibility, winds, precipitation, thunderstorms, icing, turbulence, and more. Provides forecasts based on observations and discussions with meteorologists from various National Weather Service offices, FAA facilities, airlines, and private weather services.

AIRCRAFT APPROACH CATEGORY—A grouping of aircraft based on a speed of 1.3 times the stall speed in the landing configuration at maximum gross landing weight. An aircraft must fit in only one category. If it is necessary to maneuver at speeds in excess of the upper limit of a speed range for a category, the minimums for the category for that speed must be used. For example, an aircraft that falls under Category A but is circling to land at a speed in excess of 91 knots must use the approach Category B minimums when circling to land. The categories are as follows:

- Category A—speed less than 91 knots

- Category B—speed 91 knots or more but less than 121 knots

- Category C—speed 121 knots or more but less than 141 knots

- Category D—speed 141 knots or more but less than 166 knots

- Category E—speed 166 knots or more

AIRCRAFT CLASSES—For the purposes of Wake Turbulence Separation Minima, air traffic control classifies aircraft as heavy, large, and small, as follows:

- Heavy—Aircraft capable of takeoff weights of more than 255,000 pounds, whether or not they are operating at this weight during a particular phase of flight.

- Large—Aircraft of more than 41,000 pounds, maximum certificated takeoff weight up to 255,000 pounds.

- Small—Aircraft of 41,000 pounds or less maximum certificated takeoff weight.

AIRPORT—An area on land or water used or intended to be used for the landing and takeoff of aircraft; it includes its buildings and facilities, if any.

AIRPORT ELEVATION—The highest point of an airport's usable runways measured in feet from mean sea level.

AIRPORT/FACILITY DIRECTORY—A publication designed primarily as a pilot's operational manual, containing listings of all airports, seaplane bases, and heliports open to the public, including communications data, navigational facilities, and certain special notices and procedures. This publication is issued in seven volumes according to geographical area.

AIRPORT LIGHTING—Various lighting aids that may be installed on an airport. Types of airport lighting include:

- Approach Light System (ALS)—An airport lighting facility that provides visual guidance to landing aircraft by radiating light beams in a directional pattern. The pilot can use the pattern to align the aircraft with the extended centerline of the runway on his/her final approach for landing. Condenser-Discharge Sequential Flashing Lights/Sequenced Flashing Lights may be installed in conjunction with the ALS at some airports. There are nine types of Approach Light Systems:

  1 ALSF-1—Approach Light System with Sequenced Flashing Lights in ILS Cat-I configuration.

  2 ALSF-2—Approach Light System with Sequenced Flashing Lights in ILS Cat-II configuration. The ALSF-2 may operate as an SSALR (see below) when weather conditions permit.

  3 SSALF—Simplified Short Approach Light System with Sequenced Flashing Lights.

  4 SSALR—Simplified Short Approach Light System with Runway Alignment Indicator Lights.

  5 MALSF—Medium-Intensity Approach Light System with Sequenced Flashing Lights.

  6 MALSR—Medium-Intensity Approach Light System with Runway Alignment Indicator Lights.

  7 LDIN—Lead-in-light System: Consists of one or more series of flashing lights installed at or near ground level, providing positive visual guidance along a curving or straight approach path where special problems exist with hazardous terrain, obstructions, or noise abatement procedures.

  8 RAIL—Runway Alignment Indicator Lights: Sequenced Flashing Lights installed only in combination with other light systems.

  9 ODALS—Omni-directional Approach Lighting System: Consists of seven omni-directional flashing lights in the approach area of a non-precision runway. Five lights are located on the runway centerline, extended with the first light located 300 feet from the threshold and running at equal intervals up to 1,500 feet from the threshold. The other two lights are located one on each side of the runway threshold, at a lateral distance of 40 feet from the runway edge or 75 feet from the runway edge when installed on a runway equipped with a VASI.

- Runway Lights/Runway Edge Lights—Lights having a prescribed angle of emission, used to define the lateral limits of a runway. Runway lights are uniformly spaced at intervals of approximately 200 feet, and their intensity may be controlled or preset.

- Touchdown Zone Lighting—Two rows of transverse light bars located symmetrically about the runway centerline normally at 100-foot intervals. The basic system extends 3,000 feet along the runway.

- Runway Centerline Lighting—Flush centerline lights spaced at 50-foot intervals beginning 75 feet from the landing threshold and extending to within 75 feet of the opposite end of the runway.

- Threshold Lights—Fixed green lights arranged symmetrically left and right of the runway centerline, identifying the runway threshold.

- Runway End Identifier Lights (REIL)—Two synchronized flashing lights, one on each side of the runway threshold, which provide rapid and positive identification of the approach end of a particular runway.

- Visual Approach Slope Indicator (VASI)—An airport lighting facility providing vertical visual approach slope guidance to aircraft during approach to landing by radiating a directional pattern of high-intensity red and white focused light beams. The beams indicate to the pilot that he/she is "on path" if the pilot sees red/white, "above path" if white/white, and "below path" if red/red. Some airports serving large aircraft have three-bar VASIs, which provide two visual glidepaths to the same runway.

- Precision Approach Path Indicator (PAPI)—An airport lighting facility, similar to VASI, providing vertical approach slope guidance to aircraft during approach to landing. PAPIs consist of a single row of either two or four lights, normally installed on the left side of the runway, and have an effective visual range of about 5 miles during the day and up to 20 miles at night. PAPIs radiate a directional pattern of high-intensity red and white focused light beams. The beams indicate that the pilot is "on path" if he/she sees an equal number of white lights and red lights (with white to the left of red); "above path" if the pilot sees more white than red lights; and "below path" if the pilot sees more red than white lights.

- Boundary Lights—Lights defining the perimeter of an airport or landing area.

AIRPORT ROTATING BEACON—A visual NAVAID operated at many airports. At civil airports, alternating white and green flashes indicate the location of the airport. At military airports, the beacons flash alternately white and green, but are differentiated from civil beacons by dual peaked (two quick) white flashes between the green flashes.

AIRPORT SURFACE DETECTION EQUIPMENT—Radar equipment specifically designed to detect all principal features on the surface of an airport, including aircraft and vehicular traffic, and to present the entire image on a radar indicator console in the control tower. Used to augment visual observation by tower personnel of aircraft and/or vehicular movements on runways and taxiways.

AIRPORT SURVEILLANCE RADAR (ASR)—Approach control radar used to detect and display an aircraft's position in the terminal area. ASR provides range and azimuth information but does not provide elevation data. Coverage of the ASR can extend up to 60 miles.

AIRSPEED—The speed of an aircraft relative to its surrounding air mass. The unqualified term "airspeed" means one of the following:

- Indicated Airspeed—The speed shown on the aircraft airspeed indicator. This is the speed used in pilot/controller communications under the general term "airspeed."

- True Airspeed—The airspeed of an aircraft relative to undisturbed air, used primarily in flight planning and the en route portion of flight. When used in pilot/controller communications, it is referred to as "true airspeed" and not shortened to "airspeed."

AIRWAY—A Class E airspace area established in the form of a corridor, the centerline of which is defined by radio navigational aids.

ALTITUDE—The height of a level, point, or object measured in feet above ground level (AGL) or from mean sea level (MSL).

- MSL Altitude—Altitude expressed in feet from mean sea level.

- AGL Altitude—Altitude expressed in feet above ground level.

- Indicated Altitude—The altitude as shown by an altimeter. On a pressure or barometric altimeter, indicated altitude is shown uncorrected for instrument error and uncompensated for variation from standard atmospheric conditions.

APPROACH CLEARANCE—Authorization by air traffic control for a pilot to conduct an instrument approach. The type of instrument approach for which a clearance is given and other pertinent information is provided in the approach clearance when required.

APPROACH CONTROL SERVICE—Air traffic control service provided by an approach control facility for arriving and departing VFR/IFR aircraft and, on occasion, en route aircraft. At some airports that are not served by an approach control facility, the ARTCC provides limited approach control service.

APPROACH GATE—An imaginary point used within air traffic control as a basis for vectoring aircraft to the final approach course. The gate is established along the final approach course 1 mile from the final approach fix on the side away from the airport and will be no closer than 5 miles from the landing threshold.

APPROACH SPEED—The recommended speed, according to aircraft manuals, used by pilots when making an approach to landing. This speed will vary for different segments of an approach, as well as for aircraft weight and configuration.

AREA NAVIGATION (ICAO)—A method of navigation that permits aircraft operation on any desired flight path within the coverage of station-referenced navigation aids or within the limits of the capability of self-contained aids, or a combination of these.

AREA NAVIGATION (RNAV)—Provides enhanced navigational capability to the pilot. RNAV equipment can compute the airplane position and actual track and ground speed, and then provide meaningful information relative to a flight route selected by the pilot. Typical equipment will provide the pilot with distance, time, bearing, and crosstrack error relative to the selected "TO" or "active" waypoint and the selected route. Several distinctly different navigational systems with different navigational performance characteristics are capable of providing area navigational functions. Present-day RNAV includes INS, LORAN-C, VOR/DME, and GPS. Modern multi-sensor systems can integrate one or more of these systems to provide a more accurate and reliable navigational system. Because of differing levels of performance, area navigational capabilities can satisfy various levels of Required Navigational Performance (RNP). The major types of equipment are the following:

- VORTAC referenced or Course Line Computer (CLC) systems account for the greatest number of RNAV units in use. To function, the CLC must be within the service range of a VORTAC.

- OMEGA/VLF, although it is comprised of two separate systems, can be considered as one operationally. This is a long-range navigation system based upon very-low-frequency (VLF) radio signals transmitted from a total of 17 stations worldwide.

- Inertial Navigation Systems (INSs) are totally self-contained and require no information from external references. They provide aircraft position and navigation information in response to signals resulting from inertial effects on components within the system.

- MLS Area Navigation (MLS/RNAV) provides area navigation with reference to an MLS ground facility.

- Long-range radio navigation system (LORAN-C) uses ground waves transmitted at low frequency to provide user position information at ranges of 600 to 1,200 nautical miles at both en route and approach altitudes. The usable signal coverage areas are determined by the signal-to-noise ratio, the envelope-to-cycle difference, and the geometric relationship between the positions of the user and the transmitting stations.

- Global Positioning System (GPS) is a space-based radio positioning, navigation, and time-transfer system that provides highly accurate position and velocity information and precise time, on a continuous global basis, to an unlimited number of properly equipped users. The system is unaffected by weather and provides a worldwide common grid reference system. (See ICAO term AREA NAVIGATION.)

AREA NAVIGATION (RNAV) APPROACH CONFIGURATION:

- STANDARD T—An RNAV approach in which the design allows direct flight to any one of three initial approach fixes (IAFs) and eliminates the need for procedure turns. The standard design is to align the procedure on the extended centerline with the missed approach point (MAP) at the runway threshold, the final approach fix (FAF), and the initial approach/intermediate fix (IAF/IF). The other two IAFs will be established perpendicular to the IF.

- MODIFIED T—An RNAV approach design for single or multiple runways where terrain or operational constraints do not allow for the standard T. The T may be modified by increasing or decreasing the angle from the corner IAF(s) to the IF or by eliminating one or both corner IAFs.

- STANDARD I—An RNAV approach design for a single runway with both corner IAFs eliminated. Course reversal or radar vectoring may be required at busy terminals with multiple runways.

- TERMINAL ARRIVAL AREA (TAA)—The TAA is controlled airspace established in conjunction with the Standard or Modified T and I RNAV approach configurations. The standard TAA has three areas: straight-in, left base, and right base. The arc boundaries of these three areas are published portions of the approach; they allow aircraft to transition from the en route structure direct to the nearest IAF. TAAs will also eliminate or reduce feeder routes, departure extensions, and procedure turns or course reversal.

    1. STRAIGHT-IN AREA—A 30-NM arc centered on the IF, bounded by a straight line extending through the IF perpendicular to the intermediate course.

    2. LEFT BASE AREA—A 30-NM arc centered on the right corner IAF. The area shares a boundary with the straight-in area except that it extends out for 30 NM from the IAF and is bounded on the other side by a line extending from the IF through the FAF to the arc.

    3. RIGHT BASE AREA—A 30-NM arc centered on the left corner IAF. The area shares a boundary with the straight-in area except that it extends out for 30 NM from the IAF and is bounded on the other side by a line extending from the IF through the FAF to the arc.

AUTOMATED RADAR TERMINAL SYSTEMS (ARTS)—The generic term for the ultimate in functional capability afforded by several automation systems. Each system differs in functional capabilities and equipment. An ARTS plus a suffixed Roman numeral denotes a specific system. A suffixed letter indicates a major modification to that system. In general, an ARTS displays for the terminal controller the aircraft identification, flight plan data, and other flight-associated information (e.g., altitude, speed, and aircraft position symbols in conjunction with his/her radar presentation). Normal radar coexists with the alphanumeric display. In addition to enhancing visualization of the air traffic situation, ARTSs facilitate intra-facility and inter-facility transfer and coordination of flight information. These capabilities are enabled by specially designed computers and subsystems tailored to the radar and communications equipment and operational requirements of each automated facility. Modular design permits adoption of improvements in computer software and electronic technologies as they become available, while retaining the unique characteristics of each system.

- ARTS II—A programmable nontracking, computer-aided display subsystem capable of modular expansion. An ARTS II provides a level of automated air traffic control capability at terminals with low-to-medium activity. Flight identification and altitude may be associated with the display of secondary radar targets. The system has the capability of communicating with ARTCCs and other ARTS II, IIA, III, and IIIA facilities.

- ARTS IIA—A programmable radar-tracking computer subsystem capable of modular expansion. The ARTS IIA detects, tracks, and predicts secondary radar targets. The targets are displayed by means of computer-generated symbols, ground speed, and flight plan data. Although primary radar targets are not tracked, they are displayed coincident with the secondary radar, along with the symbols and alphanumerics. The system has the capability of communicating with ARTCCs and other ARTS II, IIA, III, and IIIA facilities.

- ARTS III—The Beacon Tracking Level (BTL) of the modular, programmable automated radar terminal system used at medium-to-high activity terminals. An ARTS III detects, tracks, and predicts secondary radar-derived aircraft targets. These are displayed with computer-generated symbols and alphanumeric characters depicting flight identification, aircraft altitude, ground speed, and flight plan data. Although primary radar targets are not tracked, they are displayed coincident with the secondary radar, along with the symbols and alphanumerics. The system has the capability of communicating with ARTCCs and other ARTS III facilities.

- ARTS IIIA—The Radar Tracking and Beacon Tracking Level (RT&BTL) of the modular, programmable automated radar terminal system. An ARTS IIIA detects, tracks, and predicts primary and secondary radar-derived aircraft targets. This more sophisticated computer-driven system upgrades the existing ARTS III by providing improved tracking, continuous data recording, and fail-soft capabilities (meaning that in the event of a failure, it is designed to shut down any nonessential components but to keep the system and programs running on the computer).

AUTOMATIC DEPENDENT SURVEILLANCE (ADS)—A surveillance technique in which aircraft automatically provide, via a data link, information from on-board navigation and position fixing systems. This includes aircraft identification, four-dimensional position, and additional data as appropriate.

AUTOMATIC DEPENDENT SURVEILLANCE-BROADCAST (ADS-B)—A surveillance system in which an aircraft or vehicle to be detected is fitted with cooperative equipment in the form of a data link transmitter. The aircraft or vehicle periodically broadcasts its GPS-derived position and other information (such as velocity) over the data link. The information is received by a ground-based transmitter/receiver ("transceiver") for processing and display at an air traffic control facility.

AUTOMATIC DIRECTION FINDER (ADF)—An aircraft radio navigation system that senses and indicates direction to an L/MF nondirectional radio beacon (NDB) ground transmitter. Direction is indicated to the pilot as a magnetic bearing or as a relative bearing to the longitudinal axis of the aircraft, depending on the type of indicator installed in the aircraft. In certain applications (e.g., military), ADF operations may be based on airborne and ground transmitters in the VHF/UHF frequency spectrum.

BEARING—The horizontal direction to or from any point, usually measured clockwise from true north, magnetic north, or some other reference point, through 360 degrees.

CEILING—The height above the earth's surface of the lowest layer of clouds or obscuring phenomena. It is reported as "broken," "overcast," or "obscuration," and not classified as "thin" or "partial."

CENTER RADAR ARTS PRESENTATION/PROCESSING—A computer program developed to provide a backup system for airport surveillance radar in the event of a failure or malfunction. The program uses air route traffic control center radar for the processing and presentation of data on the ARTS IIA or IIIA displays.

CENTER RADAR ARTS PRESENTATION/PROCESSING-PLUS—A computer program developed to provide a backup system for airport surveillance radar in the event of a terminal secondary radar system failure. The program uses a combination of ARTCC radar and terminal airport surveillance radar primary targets, displayed simultaneously for processing and presenting data on the ARTS IIA or IIIA displays.

CENTER TRACON AUTOMATION SYSTEM (CTAS)—A computerized set of programs designed to aid ARTCCs and TRACONs in managing and controlling air traffic.

CENTER WEATHER ADVISORY (CWA)—An unscheduled weather advisory issued by Center Weather Service Unit (CWSU) meteorologists for air traffic control use to alert pilots of existing or anticipated adverse weather conditions within the upcoming 2 hours. A CWA may modify or redefine a SIGMET.

CIRCLE-TO-LAND MANEUVER—A maneuver initiated by the pilot to align an aircraft with a runway for landing when a straight-in landing from an instrument approach is not possible or desirable. At tower-controlled airports, this maneuver is made only after air traffic control authorization has been obtained and the pilot has established required visual reference to the airport.

CIRCLE TO RUNWAY (RUNWAY NUMBER)—Terminology used by air traffic control to inform a pilot that he/she must circle to land, because the runway in use is other than the runway aligned with the instrument approach procedure. When the direction of the circling maneuver in relation to the airport/runway is required, the controller will state the direction (in the 8 cardinal compass points) and specify a left or right downwind or base leg as appropriate. For example, "Cleared VOR Runway Three Six Approach Circle to Runway Two Two," or "Circle northwest of the airport for a right downwind to Runway Two Two."

CLEARED (Type of) APPROACH—Air traffic control authorization for an aircraft to execute a specific instrument approach procedure to an airport. For example, "Cleared ILS Runway Three Six Approach."

CLEARED AS FILED—The aircraft is cleared to proceed in accordance with the route of flight filed in the flight plan. This clearance does not include the altitude, DP, or DP Transition.

CLEARED FOR TAKEOFF—Air traffic control authorization for an aircraft to depart. It is predicated on known traffic and known physical airport conditions.

CLEARED FOR THE OPTION—Air traffic control authorization for an aircraft to make a touch-and-go, low approach, missed approach, stop-and-go, or full stop landing at the discretion of the pilot. It is normally used in training so that an instructor can evaluate a student's performance under changing situations.

CLEARED TO LAND—Air traffic control authorization for an aircraft to land. It is predicated on known traffic and known physical airport conditions.

CLUTTER—In radar operations, the reception and visual display of radar returns caused by precipitation, chaff, terrain, numerous aircraft targets, or other phenomena. Such returns may limit or preclude air traffic control from providing services based on radar.

COMBINED CENTER-RAPCON—An air traffic facility that combines the functions of an ARTCC and a radar approach control facility.

COMMON TRAFFIC ADVISORY FREQUENCY (CTAF)—A frequency designed for carrying out airport advisory practices while operating to or from an airport without an operating control tower. The CTAF may be a UNICOM, MULTICOM, FSS, or tower frequency and is identified in appropriate aeronautical publications.

COMPASS LOCATOR—A low-power, low- or medium-frequency (L/MF) radio beacon installed at the site of the outer or middle marker of an Instrument Landing System (ILS). It can be used for navigation at distances of approximately 15 miles, or as authorized in the approach procedure.

- Outer Compass Locator (LOM)—Compass locator installed at the site of the outer marker of an ILS.

- Middle Compass Locator (LMM)—Compass locator installed at the site of the middle marker of an ILS.

CONFLICT ALERT—A function of certain air traffic control automated systems that is designed to alert radar controllers to existing or pending situations between tracked targets (known IFR or VFR aircraft) that require his/her immediate attention or action.

CONFLICT RESOLUTION—The resolution of potential conflicts between aircraft that are radar identified and in communication with air traffic control by ensuring that radar targets do not touch. Pertinent traffic advisories shall be issued when this procedure is applied.

CONTACT APPROACH—An approach wherein an aircraft on an IFR flight plan, having an air traffic control authorization, operating clear of clouds with at least 1 mile flight visibility and a reasonable expectation of continuing to the destination airport in those conditions, may deviate from the instrument approach procedure and proceed to the destination airport by visual reference to the surface. This approach will only be authorized when requested by the pilot and when the reported ground visibility at the destination airport is at least 1 statute mile.

CONTROL SECTOR—An airspace area of defined horizontal and vertical dimensions for which a controller or group of controllers has air traffic control responsibility, normally within an air route traffic control center or an approach control facility. Sectors are established based on predominant traffic flows, altitude strata, and controller workload. Pilot communications during operations within a sector are normally maintained on discrete frequencies assigned to each sector.

CONTROLLED AIRSPACE—An airspace of defined dimensions within which air traffic control service is provided to IFR flights and to VFR flights in accordance with the airspace classification.

- Controlled airspace is a generic term that covers Class A through Class E airspace.

- Controlled airspace is also the airspace within which all aircraft operators are subject to certain pilot qualifications, operating rules, and equipment requirements, according to Title 14 CFR Part 91 (for specific operating requirements, refer to this document). For IFR operations in any class of controlled airspace, a pilot must file an IFR flight plan and receive an appropriate air traffic control clearance. Each Class B, Class C, and Class D airspace area designated for an airport contains at least one primary airport around which the airspace is designated (for specific designations and descriptions of the airspace classes, please refer to 14 CFR Part 71).

- Controlled airspace in the United States is designated as five classes:

  1 CLASS A—Generally, the airspace from 18,000 feet MSL up to and including FL 600, including the airspace overlying waters within 12 nautical miles of the coast of the 48 contiguous United States and Alaska. Unless otherwise authorized, all pilots must operate their aircraft under IFR.

  2 CLASS B—Generally, the airspace from the surface to 10,000 feet MSL surrounding the nation's busiest airports in terms of airport operations or passenger enplanements. The configuration of each Class B airspace area is individually tailored and consists of a surface area and two or more layers (some Class B airspace areas resemble upside-down wedding cakes), and is designed to contain all published instrument procedures once an aircraft enters the airspace. An air traffic control clearance is required for all aircraft to operate in the area, and all aircraft that are so cleared receive separation services within the airspace. The cloud clearance requirement for VFR operations is "clear of clouds."

  3 CLASS C—Generally, the airspace from the surface to 4,000 feet above the airport elevation (charted in MSL) surrounding airports that have an operational control tower, are serviced by a radar approach control, and have a certain number of IFR operations or passenger enplanements. Although the configuration of each Class C area is individually tailored, the airspace usually consists of a surface area with a 5-NM radius, a circle with a 10-NM radius that extends no lower than 1,200 feet up to 4,000 feet above the airport elevation, and an outer area that is not charted. Each person must establish two-way radio communications with the air traffic control facility that is providing air traffic services before entering the airspace, and must thereafter maintain those communications while within the airspace. VFR aircraft are only separated from IFR aircraft within the airspace.

  4 CLASS D—Generally, the airspace from the surface to 2,500 feet above the airport elevation (charted in MSL) surrounding airports that have an operational control tower. The configuration of each Class D airspace area is individually tailored, and when instrument procedures are published the airspace will normally be designed to contain the procedures. Arrival extensions for instrument approach procedures may be Class D or Class E airspace. Unless otherwise authorized, each person must establish two-way radio communications with the air traffic control facility providing air traffic services before entering Class D airspace and must thereafter maintain communications while in the airspace. No separation services are provided to VFR aircraft.

⑤ CLASS E—Generally, if the airspace is not Class A, B, C, or D, and it is controlled airspace, it is Class E airspace. This class extends upward, either from the surface or a designated altitude, to the overlying or adjacent controlled airspace. When designated as a surface area, the airspace is configured to contain all instrument procedures. Also in this class are federal airways, airspace beginning at either 700 or 1,200 feet AGL used to transition to/from the terminal or en route environment, en route domestic, and offshore airspace areas designated below 18,000 feet MSL. Unless designated at a lower altitude, Class E airspace begins at 14,500 MSL over the United States, including that airspace overlying the waters within 12 nautical miles of the coast of the 48 contiguous states and Alaska, up to but not including 18,000 feet MSL, and the airspace above FL 600.

CROSS (FIX) AT (ALTITUDE)—Used by air traffic control when a specific altitude restriction at a specified fix is required.

CROSS (FIX) AT OR ABOVE (ALTITUDE)—Used by air traffic control when an altitude restriction at a specified fix is required. It does not prohibit the aircraft from crossing the fix at a higher altitude than specified; however, the higher altitude may not be one that will violate a succeeding altitude restriction or altitude assignment.

CROSS (FIX) AT OR BELOW (ALTITUDE)—Used by air traffic control when a maximum crossing altitude at a specific fix is required. It does not prohibit the aircraft from crossing the fix at a lower altitude; however, it must be at or above the minimum IFR altitude.

CRUISE—Used in an air traffic control clearance to authorize a pilot to conduct flight at any altitude from the minimum IFR altitude up to and including the altitude specified in the clearance. The pilot may level off at any intermediate altitude within this block of airspace. Climb/descent within the block is to be made at the discretion of the pilot.

However, once the pilot starts descent and verbally reports leaving an altitude in the block, he/she may not return to that altitude without additional air traffic control clearance. Further, it is approval for the pilot to proceed to and make an approach at the destination airport and can be used in conjunction with:

- An airport clearance limit at locations with a standard/special instrument approach procedure. The Code of Federal Regulations (CFR) require that if an instrument letdown to an airport is necessary, the pilot shall make the letdown in accordance with a standard/special instrument approach procedure for that airport.

- An airport clearance limit at locations that are within/below/outside controlled airspace and without a standard/special instrument approach procedure. Such a clearance is NOT AUTHORIZATION for the pilot to descend under IFR conditions below the applicable minimum IFR altitude, nor does it imply that air traffic control is exercising control over aircraft in Class G airspace. However, it provides a means for the aircraft to proceed to destination airport, descend, and land in accordance with applicable CFRs governing VFR flight operations. Also, this provides search-and-rescue protection until such time as the IFR flight plan is closed.

DEAD RECKONING—As applied to flying, the navigation of an airplane solely by means of computations based on airspeed, course, heading, and wind direction, as well as speed, ground speed, and elapsed time.

DECISION HEIGHT (DH)—As applied to operating aircraft, the height at which a decision must be made during an ILS, MLS, or PAR instrument approach either to continue the approach or to execute a missed approach.

DIRECTION FINDER (DF)—A radio receiver equipped with a directional sensing antenna to take bearings on a radio transmitter. Specialized radio direction finders are used in aircraft as air navigation aids. Others are ground-based, primarily to obtain a "fix" on a pilot requesting orientation assistance or to locate downed aircraft. A location "fix" is established by the intersection of two or more bearing lines plotted on a navigational chart, using either two separately located Direction Finders (DFs) to obtain a fix on an aircraft or a pilot plotting the bearing indications of his/her DF on two separately located ground-based transmitters, both of which can be identified on the pilot's chart. UDFs receive signals in the ultra-high–frequency radio broadcast band; VDFs in the very high-frequency band; and UVDFs in both bands. Air traffic control provides DF service at the towers and Flight Service Stations (FSSs) listed in the airport/facility directory and the DOD FLIP IFR en route supplement.

DISTANCE MEASURING EQUIPMENT—Equipment (airborne and ground-based) for measuring, in nautical miles, the slant range distance of an aircraft from the DME navigational aid.

DIVERSE VECTOR AREA—In a radar environment, the area in which a prescribed departure route is not required as the only suitable route to avoid obstacles. It is the area in which random radar vectors below the minimum vector altitude/minimum IFR altitude (MVA/MIA)—established in accordance with the TERPS criteria for diverse departures, obstacles, and terrain avoidance—may be issued to departing aircraft.

DME FIX—A geographical position determined by reference to a navigational aid that provides distance and azimuth information. A DME fix is defined by a specific distance in nautical miles and a radial, azimuth, or course (i.e., localizer) in degrees magnetic from that aid.

DME SEPARATION—Spacing of aircraft in terms of distances (nautical miles) determined by reference to distance-measuring equipment (DME).

EMERGENCY LOCATOR TRANSMITTER—A radio transmitter attached to the aircraft structure and operating on its own power source on 121.5 MHz and 243.0 MHz. The emergency locator transmitter aids in locating downed aircraft by radiating a downward-sweeping audio tone 2 to 4 times per second. It is designed to function without human action after an accident.

FINAL APPROACH COURSE—A bearing/radial/track of an instrument approach leading to a runway or an extended runway centerline, all without regard to distance.

FINAL APPROACH FIX (FAE)—The fix from which the final approach (IFR) to an airport is executed. It identifies the beginning of the final approach segment and is designated on government charts by a Maltese cross for non-precision approaches and a lightning bolt for precision approaches. When air traffic control directs a lower-than-published glideslope/glidepath intercept altitude, the final approach fix is the resultant actual point of the glideslope/glidepath intercept.

FINAL APPROACH-IFR—The flight path of an aircraft that is inbound to an airport on a final instrument approach course, beginning at the final approach fix or point and extending to the airport or the point where a circle-to-land maneuver or a missed approach is executed.

FINAL APPROACH POINT—The point, applicable only to a non-precision approach with no depicted FAF (such as an on airport VOR), where the aircraft is established inbound on the final approach course from the procedure turn and where the final approach descent may be commenced. The FAP serves as the FAF and identifies the beginning of the final approach segment.

FINAL MONITOR CONTROLLER—An air traffic control specialist assigned to radar monitor the flight path of aircraft during simultaneous parallel and simultaneous close parallel ILS approach operations. Each runway is assigned a final monitor controller during simultaneous parallel and simultaneous close parallel ILS approaches. Final monitor controllers shall utilize the Precision Runway Monitor (PRM) system during simultaneous close parallel ILS approaches.

FLIGHT LEVEL (FL)—A level of constant atmospheric pressure related to a reference datum of 29.92 inches of mercury. Each flight level is stated in three digits representing hundreds of feet. For example, FL250 represents a barometric altimeter indication of 25,000 feet; FL255 represents a barometric altimeter indication of 25,500 feet.

FLY HEADING (in degrees)—Informs the pilot of the heading he/she should fly. The pilot may have to turn to or continue on a specific compass direction to comply with the instructions. The pilot is expected to turn in the shorter direction to the heading, unless otherwise instructed by air traffic control.

FLY-BY WAYPOINT—Requires the use of turn anticipation to avoid overshooting the next flight segment.

FLY-OVER WAYPOINT—Precludes any turn until the waypoint is overflown and is followed by an intercept maneuver of the next flight segment.

GATE HOLD PROCEDURES—Procedures at selected airports to hold aircraft at the gate or other ground location whenever departure delays exceed or are anticipated to exceed 15 minutes. The sequence for departure is maintained in accordance with initial call-up unless modified by flow control restrictions. Pilots should monitor the ground control/clearance delivery frequency for engine start/taxi advisories or new proposed start/taxi time if the delay changes.

GENERAL AVIATION—The portion of civil aviation encompassing all facets of aviation, except air carriers who hold a certificate of public convenience and necessity from the Civil Aeronautics Board and large aircraft commercial operators.

GLIDESLOPE—Provides vertical guidance for aircraft during approach and landing. The glideslope/glidepath is based on one of the following:

- Electronic components emitting signals that provide vertical guidance by reference to airborne instruments during instrument approaches such as ILS/MLS.

- Visual ground aids, such as Visual Approach Slope Indicator (VASI), which provide vertical guidance for a VFR approach or for the visual portion of an instrument approach and landing.

- PAR, which is used by air traffic control to inform an aircraft of its vertical position (elevation) relative to the descent profile.

GLOBAL POSITIONING SYSTEM (GPS)—A space-based radio positioning, navigation, and time-transfer system. It provides highly accurate position and velocity information and precise time, on a continuous global basis, to an unlimited number of properly equipped users. The system is unaffected by weather and provides a worldwide common grid reference system. The GPS concept is predicated on accurate and continuous knowledge of the spatial position of each satellite in the system with respect to time and distance from a transmitting satellite to the user. The GPS receiver automatically selects appropriate signals from the satellites in view and translates these into three-dimensional position, velocity, and time. System accuracy for civil users is normally 100 meters horizontally.

GROUND CLUTTER—A pattern produced on the radar scope by ground returns that may degrade other radar returns in the affected area. The effect of ground clutter is minimized by the use of moving target indicator (MTI) circuits in the radar equipment resulting in a radar presentation that displays only targets in motion.

GROUND CONTROLLED APPROACH (GCA)—A radar approach system operated from the ground by air traffic control personnel transmitting instructions to the pilot by radio. The approach may be conducted with surveillance radar (ASR) only or with surveillance and precision approach radar (PAR). Usage of the term "GCA" by pilots is discouraged, except when referring to a GCA facility. Pilots should specifically request a "PAR" approach when a precision radar approach is desired, or request an "ASR" or "surveillance" approach when a non-precision radar approach is desired.

GROUND DELAY PROGRAM (GDP)—A traffic management (TM) process administered by the ATCSCC when aircraft are held on the ground. The purpose is to support the TM mission and limit airborne holding. It is a flexible program and may be implemented in various forms, depending upon the needs of the air traffic system. Ground delay programs provide for equitable assignment of delays to all system users.

GROUND SPEED—The speed of an aircraft relative to the surface of the earth.

GROUND STOP (GS)—A process requiring aircraft that meet a specific criteria to remain on the ground. The criteria may be airport specific, airspace specific, or equipment specific. For example: all departures to San Francisco; all departures entering Yorktown sector; all Category I and II aircraft going to Charlotte, etc. GSs normally occur with little or no warning.

HANDOFF—The transfer of radar identification of an aircraft from one controller to another if the aircraft will enter the receiving controller's airspace and radio communications.

HOLD PROCEDURE—A predetermined maneuver that keeps aircraft within a specified airspace while awaiting further clearance from air traffic control. Also used during ground operations to keep aircraft within a specified area or at a specified point while awaiting further clearance from air traffic control.

HOLDING FIX—A specified fix identifiable to a pilot by NAVAIDs or visual reference to the ground; used as a reference point in establishing and maintaining the position of an aircraft while holding.

IFR AIRCRAFT—An aircraft conducting flight in accordance with Instrument Flight Rules (IFR).

IFR CONDITIONS—Weather conditions below the minimum for flight under Visual Flight Rules (VFR).

ILS CATEGORIES—ILS Category I is an approach procedure that provides for approach to a height above touchdown of not less than 200 feet and with runway visual range of not less than 1,800 feet. ILS Category II is an approach procedure that provides for approach to a height above touchdown of not less than 100 feet and with runway visual range of not less than 1,200 feet. ILS Category III is divided into three subcategories:

- IIIA—An ILS approach procedure that provides for approach without a decision height minimum and with runway visual range of not less than 700 feet.

- IIIB—An ILS approach procedure that provides for approach without a decision height minimum and with runway visual range of not less than 150 feet.

- IIIC—An ILS approach procedure that provides for approach without a decision height minimum and without runway visual range minimum.

INERTIAL NAVIGATION SYSTEM—An RNAV system that is a form of self-contained navigation.

INITIAL APPROACH FIX (IAF)—The fix depicted on instrument approach procedure (IAP) charts that identifies the beginning of the initial approach segment(s).

INNER MARKER—A marker beacon used with an ILS (CAT II) precision approach, located between the middle marker and the end of the ILS runway. The beacon transmits a radiation pattern keyed at six dots per second and indicates to the pilot, aurally and visually, that he/she is at the designated decision height (DH)—normally 100 feet above the touchdown zone elevation on the ILS CAT II approach. It also marks progress during a CAT III approach.

INSTRUMENT APPROACH PROCEDURE (IAP)—A series of predetermined maneuvers for the orderly transfer of an aircraft under instrument flight conditions from the beginning of the initial approach to a landing or to a point from which a landing may be made visually. It is prescribed and approved for a specific airport by competent authority.

INSTRUMENT DEPARTURE PROCEDURE (DP)—A preplanned Instrument Flight Rules (IFR) departure procedure published for pilot use, in graphic or textual format, that provides information on obstruction clearance from the terminal area to the appropriate en route structure. The two types of DP are Obstacle Departure Procedures (ODP), printed textually or graphically, and Standard Instrument Departures (SID), which is always printed graphically.

INSTRUMENT FLIGHT RULES (IFR)—Rules governing the procedures for conducting instrument flight. Also a term used by pilots and controllers to indicate a type of flight plan.

INSTRUMENT LANDING SYSTEM (ILS)—A precision instrument approach system that normally consists of the following electronic components and visual aids:

- Localizer

- Glideslope

- Outer marker

- Middle marker

- Approach lights

INSTRUMENT METEOROLOGICAL CONDITIONS—Meteorological conditions expressed in terms of visibility, distance from cloud, and ceiling less than the minima specified for visual meteorological conditions.

INSTRUMENT RUNWAY—A runway equipped with electronic and visual navigation aids for which a precision or non-precision approach procedure having straight-in landing minimums has been approved.

INTERMEDIATE FIX (IF)—The fix that identifies the beginning of the intermediate approach segment of an instrument approach procedure. The fix is not normally identified on the instrument approach chart as an intermediate fix (IF).

INTERROGATOR—The ground-based surveillance radar beacon transmitter-receiver that normally scans in synchronism with a primary radar, transmitting discrete radio signals that repetitiously request all transponders on the mode in use to reply. The replies are mixed with the primary radar returns and displayed on the same plan position indicator (radarscope). The term is also applied to the airborne element of the TACAN/DME system.

INTERSECTING RUNWAYS—Two or more runways that cross or meet within their lengths:

- A point defined by any combination of courses, radials, or bearings of two or more navigational aids.

- A description of the point at which two runways, a runway and a taxiway, or two taxiways cross or meet.

INTERSECTION DEPARTURE—A departure from any runway intersection except the end of the runway.

JAMMING—Electronic or mechanical interference that may disrupt the display of aircraft on radar or the transmission/reception of radio communications/navigation.

JET BLAST—Jet engine exhaust (thrust stream turbulence).

JET ROUTE—A route designed to serve aircraft operations from 18,000 feet MSL up to and including FL450. The routes are referred to as "J" routes with subsequent numbering to identify the designated route (e.g., "J105" for jet route 105).

LAND AND HOLD SHORT OPERATIONS—Include simultaneous takeoffs and landings and/or simultaneous landings when a landing aircraft is able and is instructed by the controller to hold short of the intersecting runway/taxiway or designated hold-short point. Pilots are expected to inform the controller promptly if the hold-short clearance cannot be accepted.

LANDING AREA—Any locality on land, water, or structures, including airports/heliports and intermediate landing fields, used or intended to be used for landing and takeoff of aircraft, whether or not facilities are provided for shelter, servicing, or receiving or discharging passengers or cargo.

LANDING MINIMUMS—The minimum visibility prescribed for landing a civilian aircraft while using an instrument approach procedure. The minimum applies with other limitations set forth in Title 14 CFR Part 91 with respect to the minimum descent altitude (MDA) or decision height (DH), prescribed in the IAPs as follows:

- Straight-in landing minimums—A statement of MDA and visibility or DH and visibility, required for a straight-in landing on a specified runway.

- Circling minimums—A statement of MDA and visibility required for the circle-to-land maneuver.

LATERAL NAVIGATION (LNAV)—A function of area navigation (RNAV) equipment that calculates, displays, and provides lateral guidance to a profile or path.

LATERAL SEPARATION—Lateral spacing of aircraft at the same altitude by requiring operation on different routes or in different geographical locations.

LOCALIZER—The component of an ILS that provides course guidance to the runway.

LONGITUDINAL SEPARATION—Longitudinal spacing of aircraft at the same altitude by a minimum distance, expressed in units of time or miles.

LOW-ALTITUDE AIRWAY STRUCTURE—The network of airways serving aircraft operations up to but not including 18,000 feet MSL.

LOW APPROACH—An approach over an airport or runway following an instrument approach or a VFR approach, including the go-around maneuver where the pilot intentionally does not make contact with the runway.

LPV—A type of approach with vertical guidance (APV) based on WAAS, published on RNAV (GPS) approach charts. This procedure takes advantage of the precise lateral guidance available from WAAS. The minima is published as a decision altitude (DA).

MACH NUMBER—The ratio of true airspeed to the speed of sound; e.g., MACH .82, MACH 1.6. (See AIRSPEED.)

MARKER BEACON—An electronic navigation facility transmitting a 75-MHz vertical fan- or bone-shaped radiation pattern. Marker beacons are identified by their modulation frequency and keying code; when received by compatible airborne equipment, they indicate to the pilot both aurally and visually that he/she is passing over the facility.

METERING—A method of time-regulating arrival traffic flow into a terminal area so as not to exceed a predetermined terminal acceptance rate.

MIDDLE MARKER—A marker beacon that defines a point along the glideslope of an ILS, normally located at or near the point of decision height (ILS Category I). The beacon is keyed to transmit alternate dots and dashes keyed at the rate of 95 dot/dash combinations per minute on a 1,300-Hz tone that is received aurally and visually by compatible airborne equipment.

MINIMUM CROSSING ALTITUDE (MCA)—The lowest altitude at certain fixes at which an aircraft must cross when proceeding in the direction of a higher minimum en route IFR altitude (MEA).

MINIMUM DESCENT ALTITUDE (MDA)—The lowest altitude, expressed in feet above mean sea level, to which descent is authorized on final approach or during circle-to-land maneuvering in execution of a standard instrument approach procedure where no electronic glideslope is provided.

MINIMUM EN ROUTE ALTITUDE (MEA)—The lowest published altitude between radio fixes that assures acceptable navigational signal coverage and meets obstacle clearance requirements between those fixes. The MEA prescribed for a federal airway or segment thereof, an area navigation low or high route, or another direct route applies to the entire width of the airway, segment, or route between the radio fixes defining the airway, segment, or route.

MINIMUM IFR ALTITUDE (MIA)—Minimum altitude for IFR operations as prescribed in Title 14 CFR Part 91. MIAs are published on aeronautical charts; they are prescribed in Title 14 CFR Part 95 for airways and routes and in Title 14 CFR Part 97 for standard instrument approach procedures. If no applicable minimum altitude is prescribed in 14 CFR Part 95 or 14 CFR Part 97, the following MIAs apply:

- In designated mountainous areas—2,000 feet above the highest obstacle within a horizontal distance of 4 nautical miles from the course to be flown.

- Other than mountainous areas—1,000 feet above the highest obstacle within a horizontal distance of 4 nautical miles from the course to be flown.

- As otherwise authorized by the administrator or assigned by air traffic control.

MINIMUM OBSTRUCTION CLEARANCE ALTITUDE (MOCA)—The lowest published altitude in effect between radio fixes on VOR airways, off-airway routes, or route segments that meets obstacle clearance requirements for the entire route segment and assures acceptable navigational signal coverage within 25 SM (22 NM) miles of a VOR.

MINIMUM RECEPTION ALTITUDE (MRA)—The lowest altitude at which an intersection can be determined.

MINIMUM SAFE ALTITUDE (MSA)—The minimum altitude specified in Title 14 CFR Part 91 for various aircraft operations. MSAs are altitudes depicted on approach charts that provide at least 1,000 feet of obstacle clearance for emergency use within a specified distance from the navigation facility upon which a procedure is predicated. These altitudes will be identified as minimum sector altitudes or emergency safe altitudes and are established as follows:

- Minimum Sector Altitude—Depicted on approach charts; provides at least 1,000 feet of obstacle clearance within a 25-mile radius of the navigation facility upon which the procedure is predicated. Sectors depicted on approach charts must be at least 90° in scope. These altitudes are for emergency use only and do not necessarily assure acceptable navigational signal coverage.

- Emergency Safe Altitude—Depicted on approach charts; provides at least 1,000 feet of obstacle clearance in non-mountainous areas and 2,000 feet of obstacle clearance in designated mountainous areas within a 100-mile radius of the navigation facility upon which the procedure is predicated. These altitudes are normally used only in military procedures. They are identified on published procedures as "Emergency Safe Altitudes."

MINIMUM VECTOR ALTITUDE (MVA)—The lowest MSL altitude at which an IFR aircraft will be vectored by a radar controller, except as otherwise authorized for radar approaches, departures, and missed approaches. The altitude meets IFR obstacle clearance criteria. It may be lower than the published MEA along an airway or J-route segment. It may be used for radar vectoring only after the controller determines that an adequate radar return is being received from the aircraft being controlled. Charts depicting minimum vector altitudes are normally available only to controllers, not to pilots.

MISSED APPROACH POINT (MAP)—A point prescribed in each instrument approach procedure at which a missed approach procedure shall be executed if the required visual reference does not exist.

MODE—The letter or number assigned to a specific pulse spacing of radio signals transmitted or received by ground interrogator or airborne transponder components of the Air Traffic Control Radar Beacon System (ATCRBS). Mode A (military Mode 3) and Mode C (altitude reporting) are used in air traffic control.

MOVEMENT AREA—The runways, taxiways, and other areas of an airport/heliport used for taxiing/hover taxiing, air taxiing, takeoff, and landing aircraft, exclusive of loading ramps and parking areas. At airports/heliports with a tower, pilots must obtain specific approval for entry into the movement area from air traffic control.

NATIONAL AIRSPACE SYSTEM (NAS)—The common network of U.S. airspace; air navigation facilities, equipment and services; airports or landing areas; aeronautical charts, information, and services; rules, regulations, and procedures; technical information; and manpower and material. Some system components are shared jointly with the military.

NAVAID CLASSES—VOR, VORTAC, and TACAN aids are classified according to operational use. The three classes of NAVAIDs are:

- T—terminal
- L—low altitude
- H—high altitude

NAVIGATIONAL AID (NAVAID)—Any visual or electronic device airborne or on the surface that provides point-to-point guidance information or position data to aircraft in flight.

NONDIRECTIONAL BEACON—An L/MF or UHF radio beacon transmitting nondirectional signals, whereby the pilot of an aircraft equipped with direction-finding equipment can determine his/her bearing to or from the radio beacon, and then home in on or track to or from the station. A radio beacon installed in conjunction with an ILS marker is normally called a Compass Locator.

NON-MOVEMENT AREAS—Taxiways and apron (ramp) areas not under the control of air traffic.

NON-PRECISION APPROACH PROCEDURE—A standard instrument approach procedure in which no electronic glideslope is provided. Examples: VOR, TACAN, NDB, LOC, ASR, LDA, and Simplified Directional Facility (SDF) approaches.

NOTICE TO AIRMEN (NOTAM)—A notice containing information (not known sufficiently in advance to publicize by other means) concerning the establishment, condition, or change in any component of—facility of, service of, procedure of, or hazard in—the National Airspace System. The timely knowledge of which is essential to personnel concerned with flight operations.

- Distant Notice to Airmen (NOTAM D)—NOTAM given distant dissemination (in addition to local dissemination) beyond the area of responsibility of the FSS. These NOTAMs are stored and available until canceled.

- Local Notice to Airmen (NOTAM L)—NOTAM given local dissemination by voice and other means, such as teleautograph and telephone, to satisfy local user requirements.

- FDC NOTAM—Regulatory in nature, transmitted by the U.S. NOTAM Office (USNOF), and given systemwide dissemination.

OBSTACLE DEPARTURE PROCEDURE (ODP)—A preplanned IFR departure procedure printed for pilot use in text or graphic form to provide obstruction clearance via the least onerous route from the terminal area to the appropriate en route structure. ODPs are recommended for obstruction clearance, and they may be flown without air traffic control clearance unless an alternate departure procedure (SID or radar vector) has been specifically assigned by air traffic control.

OUTER MARKER (OM)—A marker beacon at or near the glideslope intercept altitude of an ILS approach. It is keyed to transmit two dashes per second on a 400-Hz tone, which is received aurally and visually by compatible airborne equipment. The OM is normally located 4 to 7 miles from the runway threshold on the extended centerline of the runway.

PARALLEL ILS APPROACHES—Approaches to parallel runways by IFR aircraft which, when established inbound toward the airport on the adjacent final approach courses, are radar-separated by at least 2 miles.

PARALLEL RUNWAYS—Two or more runways at the same airport whose centerlines are parallel. In addition to runway number, parallel runways are designated as L (left) and R (right) or, if three parallel runways exist, L (left), C (center), and R (right).

PRECISION APPROACH RADAR (PAR)—Radar equipment in some air traffic control facilities that is operated by the FAA and/or the military services at joint-use civil/military locations and separate military installations to detect and display azimuth, elevation, and range of aircraft on the final approach course to a runway. The equipment may be used to monitor certain non-radar approaches, but it is primarily used to conduct a precision instrument approach wherein the controller issues guidance instructions to the pilot based on the aircraft's position in relation to the final approach course (azimuth), the glidepath (elevation), and the distance (range) from the touchdown point on the runway, as displayed on the radar scope.

PREFERENTIAL ROUTES—Preferential routes (PDRs, PARs, and PDARs) are adapted in ARTCC computers to accomplish inter-facility/intra-facility controller coordination and to assure that flight data is posted at the proper control positions. Locations having a need for these specific inbound and outbound routes normally publish such routes in local facility bulletins, and their use by pilots minimizes FP route amendments. When the workload or traffic situation permits, controllers normally provide radar vectors or assign requested routes to minimize circuitous routing. Preferential routes are usually confined to one ARTCC's area and are referred to by the following names or acronyms:

- Preferential Departure Route (PDR)—A specific departure route from an airport or terminal area to an en route point where flow control is no longer necessary. It may be included in an instrument departure procedure (DP) or a Preferred IFR Route.

- Preferential Arrival Route (PAR)—A specific arrival route from an appropriate en route point to an airport or terminal area. It may be included in a STAR or a Preferred IFR Route. (The abbreviation "PAR" is used primarily within the ARTCC; it should not be confused with the abbreviation for Precision Approach Radar.)

- Preferential Departure and Arrival Route (PDAR)—A route between two terminals within or immediately adjacent to one ARTCC's area. PDARs are not synonymous with Preferred IFR Routes, but they may be listed as such since they accomplish essentially the same purpose.

PREFERRED IFR ROUTES—Routes established between busier airports to increase system efficiency and capacity. The routes typically extend through one or more ARTCC areas and are designed to achieve balanced traffic flows among high-density terminals. IFR clearances are issued on the basis of these routes, except when severe weather avoidance procedures or other factors dictate otherwise. Preferred IFR routes are listed in the airport/facility directory. If a flight is planned to or from an area having such routes, but the departure or arrival point is not listed in the airport/facility directory, pilots may use the part of a Preferred IFR route that is appropriate for the departure or arrival point listed. Preferred IFR routes are correlated with DPs and STARs and may be defined by airways, jet routes, direct routes between NAVAIDs, Waypoints, NAVAID radials/DME, or any combinations thereof.

PROCEDURE TURN—The maneuver prescribed when a pilot needs to reverse direction to establish an aircraft on the intermediate approach segment or final approach course. The outbound course, direction of turn, distance within which the turn must be completed, and minimum altitude are specified in the procedure. However, unless otherwise restricted, the point at which the turn may be commenced and the type and rate of turn are at the discretion of the pilot.

RADAR—A device that, by measuring the time interval between transmission and reception of radio pulses and correlating the angular orientation of the radiated antenna beam or beams in azimuth and/or elevation, provides information on range, azimuth, and/or elevation of objects in the path of the transmitted pulses.

- Primary Radar—A system in which a minute portion of a radio pulse transmitted from a site is reflected by an object and received at that site for processing and display at an air traffic control facility.

- Secondary Radar/Radar Beacon (ATCRBS)—A system in which the object to be detected is fitted with cooperative equipment in the form of a radio receiver/transmitter (transponder). Radar pulses transmitted from the searching transmitter/receiver (interrogator) site are received in the cooperative equipment and used to trigger a distinctive transmission from the transponder. This reply transmission, rather than a reflected signal, is then received at the transmitter/receiver site for processing and display at an air traffic control facility.

RADAR APPROACH CONTROL FACILITY—A terminal air traffic control facility that uses radar and non-radar capabilities to provide approach control services to aircraft arriving, departing, or transiting airspace controlled by the facility. Provides radar air traffic control services to aircraft operating in the vicinity of one or more civil and/or military airports in a terminal area. The facility may provide services of a ground-controlled approach (GCA); i.e., ASR and PAR approaches. A radar approach control facility may be operated by the FAA, the Air Force, the Army, the Navy, the Marines, or jointly by the FAA and any of these U.S. military services. Specific facility nomenclatures are used for administrative purposes only; they are related to the physical location of the facility and the operating service, as follows:

- Army Radar Approach Control (ARAC) (Army)

- Radar Air Traffic Control Facility (RATCF) (Navy/FAA)

- Radar Approach Control (RAPCON) (Air Force/FAA)

- Terminal Radar Approach Control (TRACON) (FAA)

- Air Traffic Control Tower (ATCT) (FAA)—Only the towers that have been delegated approach control authority.

RADAR ARRIVAL—An aircraft arriving at an airport served by a radar facility and in radar contact with the facility.

RNAV APPROACH—An instrument approach procedure that relies on aircraft area navigation equipment for guidance.

ROUTE—A defined path, consisting of one or more courses in a horizontal plane, that aircraft traverse over the surface of the earth.

RUNWAY—A defined rectangular area on a land airport prepared for the landing and takeoff run of aircraft along its length. Runways are normally numbered in relation to their magnetic direction rounded off to the nearest 10 degrees.

SEE AND AVOID—When weather conditions permit, pilots operating IFR or VFR are required to observe and maneuver to avoid other aircraft. Right-of-way rules are contained in Title 14 CFR Part 91.

SEGMENTS OF AN INSTRUMENT APPROACH PROCEDURE—An instrument approach procedure may have as many as four separate segments, depending on how the approach procedure is structured:

1. Initial Approach—The segment between the initial approach fix and the intermediate fix, or the point where the aircraft is established on the intermediate course or final approach course.

2. Intermediate Approach—The segment between the intermediate fix or point and the final approach fix.

3. Final Approach—The segment between the final approach fix or point and the runway, airport, or missed approach point.

4. Missed Approach—The segment between the missed approach point or the point of arrival at decision height and the missed approach fix at the prescribed altitude.

SEPARATION—In air traffic control, the spacing of aircraft to ensure their safe and orderly movement in flight and during landing and takeoff.

SEPARATION MINIMA—The minimum longitudinal, lateral, or vertical distances by which aircraft are spaced via air traffic control procedures.

SPECIAL-USE AIRSPACE—Airspace of defined dimensions identified by an area on the surface of the earth wherein activities must be confined because of their nature and/or wherein limitations may be imposed upon aircraft operations that are not a part of those activities. Types of special-use airspace are:

- Alert Area—Airspace that may contain a high volume of pilot training activities or an unusual type of aerial activity, neither of which is necessarily hazardous to other aircraft. Alert areas are depicted on aeronautical charts for the information of non-participating pilots. All activities within an alert area are conducted in accordance with FAA regulations. Pilots of participating aircraft and those transiting the area are equally responsible for collision avoidance.

- Controlled Firing Area—Airspace wherein activities are conducted under conditions so controlled as to eliminate hazards to nonparticipating aircraft and to ensure the safety of people and property on the ground.

- Military Operations Area (MOA)—Airspace established outside of Class A airspace to separate or segregate certain nonhazardous military activities from IFR traffic and to identify for VFR traffic where these activities are conducted.

- Prohibited Area—Airspace designated under Title 14 CFR Part 73 within which no person may operate an aircraft without the permission of the using agency.

- Restricted Area—Airspace designated under Title 14 CFR Part 73, within which the flight of aircraft, while not wholly prohibited, is subject to restriction. Most restricted areas are designated as joint use airspace, and IFR/VFR operations in the area may be authorized by the controlling air traffic control facility when it is not being used by the using agency. Restricted areas are depicted on en route charts. Where joint use is authorized, the name of the air traffic control facility is also shown.

- Warning Area—Airspace of defined dimensions, extending from 3 nautical miles outward from the coast of the United States, that contains activity that may be hazardous to nonparticipating aircraft. The purpose of warning areas is to notify non-participating pilots of potential danger. A warning area may be located over domestic or international waters or both.

SPECIAL VFR CONDITIONS—Meteorological conditions that are less problematic than those required for basic VFR flight in Classes B, C, D, or E surface areas, and in which some aircraft are permitted to navigate under VFR.

SPECIAL VFR OPERATIONS—Aircraft operating in accordance with clearances within Class B, C, D, and E surface areas in weather conditions less optimum than the basic VFR weather minima. Such operations must be requested by the pilot and approved by air traffic control.

STANDARD INSTRUMENT DEPARTURE (SID)—A preplanned Instrument Flight Rules (IFR) air traffic control departure procedure. SIDs are printed in graphic form for pilot/controller use to provide obstacle clearance and a transition from the terminal area to the appropriate en route structure. They are primarily designed for system enhancement to expedite traffic flow and to reduce pilot/controller workload. A pilot must always receive air traffic control clearance before flying a SID.

STANDARD TERMINAL ARRIVAL—A preplanned IFR air traffic control arrival procedure published for pilot use in graphic and/or textual form. STARs provide transition from the en route structure to an outer fix or an instrument approach fix/arrival waypoint in the terminal area.

SURVEILLANCE APPROACH—An instrument approach wherein the air traffic controller issues instructions for pilot compliance based on aircraft position in relation to the final approach course (azimuth) and the distance (range) from the end of the runway as displayed on the controller's radar scope. The controller will provide recommended altitudes on final approach, if requested by the pilot.

TACTICAL AIR NAVIGATION (TACAN)—An ultra-high–frequency electronic rho-theta air navigation aid that provides suitably equipped aircraft with a continuous indication of bearing and distance to the TACAN station.

TERMINAL AREA FACILITY (TAF)—A facility providing air traffic control service for arriving and departing IFR, VFR, Special VFR, and occasionally en route aircraft.

TITLE 14 CFR PART 91—The Code of Federal Regulations (CFR) is a codification of the general and permanent rules published in the Federal Register by the executive departments and agencies of the U.S. federal government. It is divided into 50 titles that represent broad areas subject to federal regulation. Each volume of the CFR is updated once each calendar year and is issued on a quarterly basis. Title 14 of the code, Aeronautics and Space, consists of 199 parts covering definitions, procedural rules, aircraft, airmen, airspace, air traffic and general operating rules, air carriers and operators for compensation or hire, schools and other certificated agencies, airports, navigational facilities, administrative regulations, and war risk insurance, all under the Federal Aviation Administration of the Department of Transportation. Part 91 (91.1 to 91.1443) covers general operating and flight rules. Each title in the CFR is updated annually; Title 14 is updated by January 1 of each year. The CFR is available in electronic form at http://www.gpoaccess.gov/cfr.

TOWER—A terminal facility that uses air/ground communications, visual signaling, and other equipment to provide air traffic control services to aircraft operating in the vicinity of an airport or movement area. Tower controllers authorize aircraft to land or takeoff at the airport controlled by the tower, or to transit the Class D airspace area regardless of flight plan or weather conditions (IFR or VFR). A tower may also provide approach control services (radar or non-radar).

TRAFFIC MANAGEMENT UNIT (TMU)—The entity in ARTCCs and designated terminals directly involved in actively managing facility traffic. The unit is usually under the direct supervision of an assistant manager for traffic management.

TRAFFIC PATTERN—The traffic flow prescribed for aircraft landing at, taxiing on, or taking off from an airport. The components of a typical traffic pattern are:

- Upwind Leg—A flight path parallel to the landing runway in the direction of landing.

- Crosswind Leg—A flight path at right angles to the landing runway off its upwind end.

- Downwind Leg—A flight path parallel to the landing runway in the direction opposite landing. The downwind leg normally extends between the crosswind leg and the base leg.

- Base Leg—A flight path at right angles to the landing runway off its approach end. The base leg normally extends from the downwind leg to the intersection of the extended runway centerline.

- Final Approach—A flight path in the direction of landing along the extended runway centerline. The final approach normally extends from the base leg to the runway. An aircraft making a straight-in approach VFR is also considered on final approach.

TRANSPONDER—The airborne radar beacon receiver/transmitter portion of the Air Traffic Control Radar Beacon System (ATCRBS) that automatically receives radio signals from interrogators on the ground and selectively replies with a specific pulse or pulse group only to interrogations received on the mode to which it is set to respond.

VFR AIRCRAFT—An aircraft conducting flight in accordance with Visual Flight Rules (VFR).

VFR CONDITIONS—Weather conditions equal to or better than the minimum for flight under Visual Flight Rules (VFR). The term may be used as an air traffic control clearance/instruction only when

- an IFR aircraft requests a climb/descent in VFR conditions.

- the clearance will result in noise abatement benefits where part of the IFR departure route does not conform to an FAA-approved noise abatement route or altitude.

- a pilot has requested a practice instrument approach and is not on an IFR flight plan.

VISUAL APPROACH—An approach conducted on an Instrument Flight Rules (IFR) flight plan that authorizes the pilot to proceed visually and clear of clouds to the airport. The pilot must, at all times, have either the airport or the preceding aircraft in sight. This approach must be authorized and under the control of the appropriate air traffic control facility. Reported weather at the airport must be ceiling at or above 1,000 feet and visibility of 3 miles or greater.

VISUAL FLIGHT RULES (VFR)—Govern the procedures for conducting flight under visual conditions. The abbreviation "VFR" is also used in the United States to indicate weather conditions equal to or greater than minimum VFR requirements. It may also be used by pilots and controllers to indicate type of flight plan.

VISUAL METEOROLOGICAL CONDITIONS—Meteorological conditions expressed in terms of visibility, distance from cloud, and ceiling equal to or better than specified minima.

VISUAL SEPARATION—A means employed by air traffic control to separate aircraft in terminal areas and en route airspace in the NAS. There are two ways to effect this separation:

- The tower controller sees the aircraft involved and issues instructions as necessary to ensure that the aircraft avoid each other.

- A pilot sees the other aircraft involved and, upon instructions from the controller, provides his/her own separation by maneuvering the aircraft as necessary. This may involve following another aircraft or keeping it in sight until avoidance is no longer a factor.

VOR—A ground-based electronic navigation aid transmitting very-high-frequency navigation signals, 360° azimuth, oriented from magnetic north. Used as the basis for navigation in the National Airspace System. The VOR periodically identifies itself by Morse code and may have an additional voice identification feature. Voice features may be used by air traffic control or FSSs for transmitting instructions/information to pilots.

VORTAC—A navigation aid providing VOR azimuth, TACAN azimuth, and TACAN distance measuring equipment (DME) at one site.

WIDE-AREA AUGMENTATION SYSTEM (WAAS)—A satellite navigation system consisting of the equipment and software that augments the GPS Standard Positioning Service (SPS). The WAAS provides enhanced integrity, accuracy, availability, and continuity over and above GPS SPS. The differential correction function provides improved accuracy required for precision approach.

Resources for Studying Air Traffic Control

PUBLICATIONS

For air traffic control–related publications other than those on this list, check with the FAA for advisory circulars. All circulars are cataloged in AC 00–2, Advisory Circular Checklist, which is issued annually. The circulars contain current information about availability, cost (if any), and ordering instructions. For a free copy of AC 00–2, contact:

U.S. Department of Transportation
General Services Section, M-443.2
Washington, DC 20590

1. FAA. AC 00–45E Aviation Weather Services. Available as downloadable PDF at http://www.airweb.faa.gov.

2. FAA. AC 61–12M Student Pilot Guide. Available as downloadable PDF at http://www.faa.gov/library/manuals/aviation or in HTML version at http://www.aviationwise.org/student_pilot/student_pilot_guide.htm

3. FAA. AC 61–27C Instrument Flying Handbook. Available as downloadable PDF at http://www.faa.gov/library/manuals/aviation.

4. FAA. *Aeronautical Information Manual*. Available as a downloadable PDF or online in an HTML version at http://www.faa.gov/airports_air-traffic/air_traffic/publications.

5. FAA. Pilot/Controller Glossary, addendum to Order 7110.65, Air Traffic Control, *Aeronautical Information Manual*. Available online at http://www.faa.gov/airports_airtraffic/air_traffic/publications.

6. Nolan, Michael S. *Fundamentals of Air Traffic Control*, Brooks Cole, 2004.

ON THE WEB

Air Traffic Control Association
http://www.atca.org

Code of Federal Regulations (CFR)
http://www.gpoaccess.gov/cfr/

Federal Aviation Administration
http://www.faa.gov/airports_airtraffic

Federal Aviation Administration
Air Traffic Division
http://www.ama500.jccbi.gov/

National Air Traffic Controllers
Association
http://www.natca.org

Contractions and Acronyms Used in Air Traffic Control

The *FAA Handbook 7340* contains the approved word and phrase contractions and acronyms typically used by both FAA controllers and other agencies that provide communication, weather, charting, and associated aviation-communication services. This includes the International Civil Aviation Organization (ICAO) and the National Weather Service (NWS).

These contractions and acronyms make it easier for controllers to communicate accurately and efficiently while performing their job duties. They also make written and printed communications more succinct while ensuring that each message's intent remains unambiguous. Contractions also save space on computer equipment, charts, drawings, and reports.

The list below is a greatly abridged version of the list used by the FAA, ICAO, NWS, and similar aviation-related organizations. In some cases, you will find that a particular contraction or acronym may have more than one meaning, or that two abbreviations have the same meaning. This usually occurs because different agencies may have originally developed their own abbreviations separately. However, you'll find that the meanings are still apparent based on the context of the rest of the communication in which they're used—whether the abbreviation is employed in air traffic, air traffic control, weather reporting, airline coding, or international circles.

appendix c

Contraction/Acronym	Meaning
A	
A/C	aircraft
A/C	approach control
A/D	arrival/departure
A/G	air to ground
AAF	airway facilities service
AAF	Army air field
AAITVL	arrival aircraft interval
AAP	advanced automation program
AAR	airport acceptance rate
AAR	airport arrival rate
AB	airborne
ABM	abeam
ABND	abandon
ABT	about
ABV	above
AC	advisory circular
AC	altocumulus (cloud formation)
AC, A/C, or ACFT	aircraft
ACC	Area Control Center
ACC	altocumulus castellanus (cloud formation)
ACDNT	accident
ACDO	Air Carrier District Office
ACE	Central Region, FAA
ACFT	aircraft
ACID	aircraft identification
ACK	acknowledge
ACLD	above clouds
ACLT	actual calculated landing time
ACPT	accept
ACTV	active

Contraction/Acronym	Meaning
ACTVT	activate
ADC	Air Defense Command
ADCUS	advise customs
ADF	automatic direction finder
ADIZ	Air Defense Identification Zone
ADO	Airline Dispatch Office
ADO	Airport District Office
ADR	advisory route
ADR	airport departure rate
ADS	automatic dependent surveillance
ADV	advise
ADVN	advance
ADVY, ADVZY, or ADZY	advisory
AEA	Eastern Region, FAA
AERO	aeronautical
AES	aircraft earth station
AEW	airborne early warning
AF	Air Force facilities
AF	airways facilities
AFB	Air Force Base
AFC	area forecast center
AFCT	affect
AFD	airport/facility directory
AFDK	after dark
AFIRM or AFM	affirmative
AFS	airways facilities sector
AFSS	Automated Flight Service Station
AFT	after
AG	air-ground
AGL	above ground level
AGL	Great Lakes Region, FAA

Contraction/Acronym	Meaning
AGN	again
AIM	*Aeronautical Information Manual*
AIP	*Aeronautical Information Publication*
AIRMET	airman's meteorological information
ALG	along
ALNOT	alert notice
ALPA	Airline Pilots Association
ALQDS	all quadrants
ALS	Approach Light System
ALSF	Approach Light System with sequenced flashing lights
ALSF-1	standard 2,400' high-intensity Approach Light System with sequenced flashers (Category I configuration)
ALSF-2	standard 2,400' high-intensity Approach Light System with sequenced flashers (Category II configuration)
ALT	altitude
ALTM	altimeter
ALTN	alternate
ALTRV	altitude reservation
AMASS	Airport Movement Area Safety System
AMCL	amended clearance
AMDT	amendment
AMS	air mass
ANE	New England Region, FAA
ANF	air navigation facility
ANG	Air National Guard
ANM	Northwest Mountain Region, FAA
ANMS	Automatic Network Management System
ANT	antenna
AO1	ASOS automated observation without precipitation discriminator (rain/snow)
AO2	ASOS automated observation with precipitation discriminator (rain/snow)

Contraction/Acronym	Meaning
AOA	at or above
AOA	at or after
AOAS	Advanced Oceanic Automation System
AOB	at or below
AOBF	at or before
AOC	Airline Operational Control Center
AOE	airport of entry
AOPA	Aircraft Owners and Pilots Association
AP	anomalous propagation
APCH	approach
APREQ	approval request
APV	approve
APVL	approval
ARAC	Army Radar Approach Control Facility
ARB	Air Reserve Base
ARCP	air refueling control point
AREA	automated en route air traffic control
AREP	air refueling egress point
AREX	air refueling exit
ARFF	aircraft rescue and fire fighting
ARINC	Aeronautical Radio, Inc.
ARIP	air refueling initiation point
ARO	Airport Reservations Office
ARPT	airport
ARSA	Airport Radar Service Area
ARSR	air route surveillance radar
ARTC	Air Route Traffic Control
ARTCC	Air Route Traffic Control Center
ARTS	Automated Radar Terminal Systems
AS	altostratus (cloud formation)
ASD	aircraft situational display

Contraction/Acronym	Meaning
ASDE	Airport Surface Detection Equipment
ASL	above sea level
ASO	Southern Region, FAA
ASOS	Automated Surface Observing System
ASP	arrival sequencing program
ASR	airport surveillance radar
ASW	Southwest Region, FAA
AT	air traffic
ATA	actual time of arrival
ATA	Air Transport Association of America
ATC	air traffic control
ATCA	Air Traffic Control Association
ATCA	ATC advises
ATCAA	ATC assigned airspace
ATCBI	ATC beacon interrogator
ATCC	ATC clears
ATCF	ATC facility
ATCRBS	ATC Radar Beacon System
ATCSCC	Air Traffic Control System Command Center
ATCT	airport traffic control tower
ATD	actual time of departure
ATIS	Automatic Terminal Information Service
ATM	air traffic management
ATM	air traffic manager
ATN	Aeronautical Telecommunications Network
ATO	air traffic operations
ATR	air transport rating
ATS	air traffic services
ATTM	at this time
ATTN	attention
AUTH	authority

Contraction/Acronym	Meaning
AUTH	authorized
AUTO	automatic
AVGAS	aviation gasoline
AVN	aviation
AWL	all weather landing
AWOS	Automatic Weather Observing/Reporting System
AWP	aviation weather processors
AWP	Western-Pacific Region, FAA
AWY	airway
AZM	azimuth
B	
B	base leg
B	beginning of precipitation
BASOPS	Base Operations Office
BC	back course
BCM	back course marker
BCN	beacon
BDR	border
BDRY	boundary
BECMG	becoming (expected between two-digit beginning hour and two-digit ending hour)
BFDK	before dark
BGN	began (or begin)
BGND	begin
BGND	beginning descent
BHND	behind
BIFR	before encountering IFR conditions
BINOVC	breaks in overcast
BKN	broken
BL	blowing
BLDG	building

Contraction/Acronym	Meaning
BLDU	blowing dust
BLN	balloon
BLO	below
BLSA	blowing sand
BLSN	blowing snow
BLZD	blizzard
BNDRY	boundary
BOVC	base of overcast
BR	mist
BRAF	braking action fair
BRAG	braking action good
BRAN	braking action nil
BRAP	braking action poor
BRG	bearing
BRGT	bright
BRITE	Bright Radar Indicator Tower Equipment
BT	back taxiing
BTL	between layers
BTN or BTWN	between
BY	blowing spray (weather reports only)
BYD	beyond
C	
C	Celsius
C	circling (approach and landing charts)
CA	conflict alert
CAA	Civil Aviation Authorities
CAAS	Class A airspace
CAASD	Center for Advanced Aviation System Development (Mitre Corporation)
CAD	computer-aided drawing
CAMI	Civil Aeronautical Medical Institute

Contraction/Acronym	Meaning
CANFORCE	Canadian Armed Forces
CAP	Civil Air Patrol
CAPT	captain
CARF	Central Altitude Reservation Function
CARIB	Caribbean
CAS	Collision Avoidance System
CASA	Controller Automated Spacing Aid
CAT	category
CAT	clear air turbulence
CAVOK	cloud and visibility OK
CAVU	clear or scattered clouds and visibility greater than 10 miles
CB	cumulonimbus (cloud formation)
CBAS	Class B airspace
CBI	computer-based instruction
CBMAM	cumulonimbus mamma (cloud formation)
CBSA	Class B surface area
CC	cirrocumulus (cloud formation)
CCAS	Class C airspace
CCC	Central Computer Complex
CCFP	Collaborative Convective Forecast Product
CCSL	standing lenticular cirrocumulus (cloud formation)
CCUS	cleared customs
CD	clearance delivery
CD	common digitizer
CDAS	Class D airspace
CDC	computer display channel
CDFNT	cold front
CDM	collaborative decision-making
CDR	coded departure routes
CDSA	Class D surface area

Contraction/Acronym	Meaning
CDT	controlled departure time
CEAS	Class E airspace
CENPAC	Central North Pacific
CENRAP	Center Radar Arts Presentation
CERAP	Center Radar Approach Control
CESA	Class E surface area
CFA	controlled firing area
CFAP	cleared for approach
CFM	confirm (or I confirm)
CFP	cold front passage
CFR	Code of Federal Regulations
CFWSU	Central Flow Weather Service Unit
CG	U.S. Coast Guard
CGAS	Class G airspace
CGAS	Coast Guard Air Station
CHC	chance
CI	cirrus (cloud formation)
CIC	controller in charge
CIFP	cancel IFR flight plan
CIFR	cancel IFR clearance previously given
CIG	ceiling
CIGS	ceilings
CIP	Capital Investment Plan
CLD	cloud
CLKWS	clockwise
CLNC	clearance
CLR	clear
CLSD	closed
CNCL or CNL	cancel
CNDN	Canadian
CNS	Communications, Navigation, And Surveillance

Contraction/Acronym	Meaning
CNTRLN	centerline
COB	close of business
CONTRAILS	condensation trails
COORD	coordinate
COP	changeover point
COTS	commercial off-the-shelf
CP	circular polarization
CP	conflict probe
CPDLC	Controller-Pilot Data Link Communications
CPTY	capacity
CRA	Conflict Resolution Advisory
CRAF	Civil Reserve Air Fleet
CRDA	converging runway display aid
CRS	course
CS	cirrostratus (cloud formation)
CTA	Control Area
CTAF	common traffic advisory frequency
CTAS	Center TRACON Automation System
CTGY	category
CTL	control
CU	cumulus (cloud formation)
CUST	customs
CVFP	cancel VFR flight plan
CVR	cockpit voice recorder
CW	continuous wave
CWP	Central Weather Processor
CWSU	Center Weather Service Unit
D	
DA	decision altitude
DA	Descent Advisor
DALGT	daylight

Contraction/Acronym	Meaning
DARC	Direct Access Radar Channel
DASI	digital altimeter setting indicator
D-ATIS	Data Link Automatic Terminal Information Service
DB	decibel
DBRITE	digital bright radar indicator tower equipment
DEFCON	defense readiness conditions
DEP	depart
DESTN	destination
DEV	deviation
DEWIZ	distant early warning identification zone
DF	direction finder
DFNT	definite
DGNSS	Differential Global Navigation Satellite System
DGPS	Differential Global Positioning System
DH	decision height
DISC	discontinue
DIST	distance
DLA	delay
DLT	delete
DME	distance measuring equipment
DMSH	diminish
DNWND	downwind
DOC	U.S. Department of Commerce
DoD or DOD	U.S. Department of Defense
DOE	U.S. Department of Energy
DOT	U.S. Department of Transportation
DP	deep
DPTH	depth
DR	direct route
DRFT	drift
DRG	during

Contraction/Acronym	Meaning
DRSA	low drifting sand
DRSN	low drifting snow
DRZL	drizzle
DS	dust storm
DSCNT	descent
DSIPT	dissipate
DSP	Departure Sequencing Program
DSP	display system replacement
DSRGD	disregard
DSS	Decision Support System
DSTC	distance
DTAM	descend to and maintain
DTAX	descend to and cross
DUATS	Direct User Access Terminal System
DURC	during climb
DURD	during descent
DURG	during
DURN	duration
DVFR	defense VFR
DVLP	develop
DVOR	Doppler Very-high-frequency Omni-directional Range
DVRS	Digital Voice Recorder System
DWNDFTS	downdrafts
DWPNT	dew point
E	
EARTS	En Route Automated Radar Tracking System
EB	eastbound
ECM	electronic counter measures
EDCT	estimated departure clearance (time)
EFAS	En Route Flight Advisory Service
EFC	expect further clearance

Contraction/Acronym	Meaning
EFF	effective
EHF	extremely high frequency (30,000 to 300,000 MHz)
ELT	emergency locator transmitter
EMBDD	embedded
EMERG	emergency
ENDCE	endurance
ENHNCD	enhanced
ENRT	en route
EPA	Environmental Protection Agency
EQPT or EQUIP	equipment
ERM, ERSP, or ESP	En Route Spacing Program
EST	estimate
EST	estimation
ETA	estimated time of arrival
ETD	estimated time of departure
ETE	estimated time en route
ETG	Enhanced Target Generator
ETMS	Enhanced Traffic Management System
EXPC	expect
EXPED	expedite
F	
F	cleared to fix
FA	Aviation Area Forecast
FA	final approach
FA	fuel advisory
FAA	Federal Aviation Administration
FAF	final approach fix
FANS	Future Air Navigation System
FAP	final approach point
FAR	Federal Aviation Regulations
FAST	final approach spacing tool

Contraction/Acronym	Meaning
FBO	fixed-base operator
FC	funnel cloud (cloud formation)
FCC	Federal Communications Commission
FCST	forecast
FCT	federal contract tower
FDC	Flight Data Center
FDIO	flight data input/output
FDP/RDP	flight data processing/radar data processing
FE	flight engineer
FEW	1 or 2 octas (eighths) cloud coverage
FG	fog
FIDO	Flight Inspection District Office
FIFO	Flight Inspection Field Office
FIR	Flight Information Region
FIS	Flight Information Services
FL	flight level
FLD	field
FLIP	*Flight Information Publication*
FLTCK	flight check
FLW	follow
FM	from
FMA	final monitor aid
FMS	Flight Management System
FOB	fuel on board
FP	flight plan
FPL	full performance level
FPM	feet per minute
FPR	flight plan route
FPS	flight progress strip
FRC	full route clearance
FRH	fly runway heading

Contraction/Acronym	Meaning
FROPA	frontal passage
FRZLVL	freezing level
FRZN	frozen
FSDO	Flight Standards District Office
FSL	full stop landing
FSS	Flight Service Station
FTS	Federal Telecommunications System
FU	smoke
FWD	forward
FZ	supercooled/freezing
FZDZ	freezing drizzle
FZFG	freezing fog
FZRA	freezing rain
FZRANO	freezing rain sensor not available
G	
G	gusts reaching (knots) (for weather reports only)
G/A	ground to air
G/A/G	ground to air and air to ground
GA	general aviation
GAO	Government Accountability Office
GC	ground control
GCA	ground control approach
GCI	ground control intercept
GDP	Ground Delay Program
GEN	general
GENOT	General Notices Issued by Washington Headquarters
GHz	gigahertz
GICG	glaze icing
GLD or GLDR	glider
GLFMEX	Gulf of Mexico
GLONASS	Global Orbiting Navigational Satellite System

Contraction/Acronym	Meaning
GMT	Greenwich mean time
GND	ground
GNDFG	ground fog
GNSS	Global Navigation Satellite System
GOVT	government
GP	glide path
GPS	Global Positioning System
GR	hail (greater than 3/4")
GRAD	gradient
GRDL	gradual
GS	ground stop
GS	glide slope
GS	ground speed
GS	snow pellets/small hail (weather reports)
GSA	General Services Administration
GSDO	General Safety District Office
GSTS	gusts
GSTY	gusty
GWT	gross weight
H	
HAA	height above airport
HAT	height above touchdown
HAZ	hazard
HCS	host computer system
HDG	heading
HDTA	high-density traffic airport
HDWND	headwind
HEL	helicopter
HELI	heliport
HF	high frequency
HFR	hold for release

Contraction/Acronym	Meaning
HI	high
HIALS	High-intensity Approach Light System
HIRL	high-intensity runway lights
HIWAS	Hazardous In-flight Weather Advisory Service
HLDG	holding
HLSTO	hailstones
HNGR	hangar
HP	holding pattern
HQ	headquarters
HUD	heads-up display
HVY	heavy
HZ	haze
Hz	hertz
I	
IAF	initial approach fix
IAP	instrument approach procedure
IAS	indicated air speed
IATA	International Air Transport Association
IBND	inbound
IC	ice crystals (weather reports only)
ICAO	International Civil Aviation Organization
ICG	icing
ICGIC	icing in clouds
ICGICIP	icing in clouds and precipitation
ICGIP	icing in precipitation
IF	intermediate fix
IFF	identification friend/foe
IFIM	International Flight Information Manual
IFR	Instrument Flight Rules
IFSS	International Flight Service Station
ILS	Instrument Landing System

Contraction/Acronym	Meaning
IM	inner marker
IMC	instrument meteorological conditions
IMDT	immediate
IN	inch
INBD	inbound
INC	in clouds
INCR	increase
INOP	inoperative
INREQ	information request
INS	Inertial Navigation System
INSTBY	instability
INT	intersection
INTCP	intercept
INTS	intense
INTSFY	intensify
INTST	intensity
INTXN	intersection
INVOF	in the vicinity of
IP	initial point
IPT	Integrated Product Team
IR	IFR Military Training Route
ITC	in-trail climb
ITD	in-trail descent
ITNRNT	itinerant
ITRY	itinerary
ITWS	Integrated Target Weather System
J	
JATO	jet-assisted take-off
J-BAR	jet runway barrier
JPDO	Joint Programs and Development Office
JSS	Joint Surveillance System

Contraction/Acronym	Meaning
JTST or JTSTR	jet stream
K	
KHz	kilohertz
KM	kilometers
KMH	kilometers per hour
KT	knots
L	
L	left
L	locator
L/MF	low or medium frequency
LA	low approach
LAAS	Local-Area Augmentation System
LAB	laboratory
LAHSO	land and hold short operations
LAN	local area network
LAT	latitude
LAWRS	Limited Aviation Weather Reporting Station
LC	local control
LDA	localizer-type directional aid
LDG	landing
LDIN	Lead-In Lighting System
LF	low frequency
LFT	lift
LGT	light
LGTD	lighted
LIFR	low IFR (weather reports only)
LIRL	low-intensity runway edge lights
LKLY	likely
LLWAS	Low-level Wind Shear Alert System
LLWS	low-level wind shear

Contraction/Acronym	Meaning
LMM	compass locator at ILS middle marker
LNAV	lateral navigation (from Terps-A1)
LNDG	landing
LO CIGS	low ceilings
LOA	Letter of Agreement
LOC	localizer
LOM	compass locator at ILS outer marker
LONG	longitude
LOP	line-of-position
LORAN	long-range navigation
LP	linear polarization
LRG	large
LRR	long-range radar
LSQ	line squall
LT	turn left after take-off
LTGCA	lightning cloud-to-air
LTGCC	lightning cloud-to-cloud
LTGCCCG	lightning cloud-to-cloud, cloud-to-ground
LTGCG	lightning cloud-to-ground
LTGCW	lightning cloud-to-water
LTGIC	lightning in clouds
LTL	little
LTLCG	little change
LTNG	lightning
LTR	later
LV	leaving
LVL	level
LWR	lower
LYR	layer
LYR	layered

Contraction/Acronym	Meaning
M	
M	Mach number (speed ratio to speed of sound)
MAA	maximum authorized (IFR) altitude
MAC	Military Airlift Command
MACH	Mach number (speed ratio to speed of sound)
MALS	Medium-intensity Approach Lighting System
MALSF	Medium-intensity Approach Lighting System with sequenced flashers
MALSR	Medium-intensity Approach Lighting System with runway alignment indicator lights
MALSR	Medium-intensity Approach Lighting System with runway alignment indicator
MANOP	manual of operations
MAP	missed approach procedure
MAPT	missed approach point
MARSA	Military Assumes Responsibility for Separation of Aircraft
MB	marker beacon
MB	millibars
MCA	minimum crossing altitude
MCAS	Marine Corps Air Station
MCI	Mode C intruder
MDA	minimum descent altitude
MDT	moderate
MEA	minimum en route altitude
MET	meteorological
METAR	aviation routine weather report
MF	medium frequency
MF	meter fix
MFOB	minimum fuel on board
MHA	minimum holding altitude
MHDF	medium- and high-frequency direction-finding station (same location)

Contraction/Acronym	Meaning
mHz or MHz	megahertz
MI	mile
MIDN	midnight
MIDPT	midpoint
MIFG	patches of shallow fog not deeper than 2 meters
MIFG	shallow fog
MIL	military
MIN	minute
MINIT	minutes in trail
MIRL	medium-intensity runway edge lights
MISC	miscellaneous
MISG	missing
MIT	miles in trail
MLS	Microwave Landing System
MM	middle marker
MNPS	Minimum Navigation Performance Specification
MNPSA	Minimum Navigation Performance Specification Airspace
MOA	Memorandum of Agreement
MOA	Military Operations Area
MOC	minimum obstacle clearance (required)
MOCA	minimum obstruction clearance altitude
MODE C	altitude-reporting mode of secondary radar
MODE S	Mode Select; Discrete Addressable Secondary Radar System with data link
MOGR	moderate or greater
MOT	Ministry of Transport (Canada)
MOU	Memorandum of Understanding
MPH	miles per hour
MRA	minimum reception altitude
MSA	minimum safe altitude

Contraction/Acronym	Meaning
MSAW	minimum safe altitude warning
MSL	mean sea level
MSTLY	mostly
MSTR	moisture
MT	mountain
MTCA	minimum terrain clearance altitude
MTD	moving target detection
MTI	moving target indicator
MTN	mountain
MTR	Military Training Route
MULTI-TAXI	many aircraft trying to taxi at once, creating congestion
MVA	minimum vector altitude
MVFR	maintain VFR
MXD	mixed
N	
NAATS	National Association of Air Traffic Control Specialists
NAES	Naval Air Engineering Station
NAFEC	National Aviation Facilities Experimental Center
NAR	North American Route
NAS	(United States) National Airspace System
NAS	Naval Air Station
NASA	National Aeronautics and Space Administration
NASP	National Airport System Plan
NAT	North Atlantic track
NATCA	National Air Traffic Controllers Association
NATS	National Air Traffic Service
NAV	navigation
NAVAID	navigational aid
NBAA	National Business Aviation Association
NBCAP	National Beacon Code Allocation Plan
NCDC	National Climatic Data Center

Contraction/Acronym	Meaning
NDB	nondirectional radio beacon
NEG	negative
NEXRAD	Next-Generation Weather Radar
NFDC	National Flight Data Center
NIL	none
NM	nautical miles
NMBR	number
NMC	National Meteorological Center
NMI	nautical miles
NOAA	National Oceanic and Atmospheric Administration
NOPAC	North Pacific
NOPT	no procedure turn required
NORAD	North American Aerospace Defense Command
NORDO	no radio
NOTAM	Notice to Airmen
NRP	North American Route Program
NS	nimbostratus (cloud formation)
NSSFC	National Severe Storm Forecast Center
NTAP	Notices To Airmen publication
NTSB	National Transportation Safety Board
NTZ	no transgression zone
NWS	National Weather Service
O	
OA	overhead approach
OARTS	Oceanic Air Route Tracking System
OAT	outside air temperature
OBND	outbound
OBS	observation
OBSC	obscure
OBST	obstacle
OBSTN	obstruction

Contraction/Acronym	Meaning
OC	on course
OCA	obstacle clearance altitude
OCFNT	occluded front
OCLD	occlude
OCNL	occasional
OCR	occur
ODALS	Omni-directional Approach Lighting System
ODAPS	Oceanic Display And Planning System
OFSHR	offshore
OG	on ground
OGN	originate
OHD	overhead
OJT	on-the-job training
OM	outer marker
OMB	U.S. Office of Management and Budget
OPN	open
ORD	Operational Readiness Demonstration
OSHA	Occupational Safety and Health Administration
OT	on time
OTLK	outlook
OTP	VFR conditions-on-top
OTR	other
OTS	Organized Track System
OTS	out of service
OV	over (location)
OVC	overcast
OVD	overdue
OVHD	overhead
P	
P	prohibited area
P/CG	*Pilot Controller Glossary*

Contraction/Acronym	Meaning
P6SM	visibility greater than 6 statute miles (TAF only)
PAPI	precision approach path indicator
PAR	precision approach radar
PAR	preferred arrival route
PARL	parallel
PASS	Professional Airway Systems Specialists
PATWAS	Pilots Automatic Telephone Weather Answering Service
PCD	proceed
PCL	pilot-controlled lighting
PCPN	precipitation
PCS	permanent change of station
PDAR	preferential arrival/departure route (Stage A)
PDC	pre-departure clearance
PDR	preferential departure route (Stage A)
PERM	permanent
PIC	pilot-in-command
PIREP	pilot weather report
PK WND	peak wind (weather reports only)
PL	ice pellets
PLASI	pulsating visual approach slope indicators
PLS	please
PN	prior notice required
PO	dust devils
POB	persons on board
POC	proceed
POC	proceeding on course
POS	positive
PPI	plan position indicator
PPINA	radar weather report not available (or omitted for a reason different than those otherwise stated)
PPINE	radar weather report no echoes observed

Contraction/Acronym	Meaning
PPINO	radar weather report equipment inoperative due to breakdown
PPIOK	radar weather report equipment operation resumed
PPIOM	radar weather report equipment inoperative due to maintenance
PPR	prior permission required
PRBL	probable
PRBLTY	probability
PRCHT	parachute
PRCTN	precaution
PREF	preferred
PRES	pressure
PRESFR	pressure falling rapidly
PRESRR	pressure rising rapidly
PREV	previous
PRFG	partial fog
PRIM	primary
PRM	precision runway monitor
PROB	probability
PROB30	probability 30 percent
PROB40	probability 40 percent
PROC	procedure
PROCD	proceed
PROG	prognosis or prognostic
PROP	propeller
PRSNT	present
PRST	persist
PRVD	provide
PSBL	possible
PSG	passage
PSN	position

Contraction/Acronym	Meaning
PSR	primary surveillance radar
PT	procedure turn
PTCHY	patchy
PTLY	partly
PTS	polar track structure
PUB	public
PUBL	publish
PVD	plan view display
PWI	proximity warning indicator
PWINO	precipitation identifier information not available (weather reports only)
PY	spray
Q	
QA	quality assurance
QFE	atmospheric pressure at airport elevation
QFLOW	quota flow control procedures
QNH	altimeter subscale setting to obtain elevation when on the ground
QSTNRY	quasi-stationary
QUAD	quadrant
R	
R	acknowledgement of receipt
R	restricted area
R	right
R	runway
R&D	research & development
RA	rain
RAF	Royal Air Force
RAGF	remote air-ground facility
RAIM	receiver autonomous integrity monitoring
RAPCON	radar approach control

Contraction/Acronym	Meaning
RAR	runway acceptance rate
RASH	rain showers
RASN	rain and snow
RASN	rain and snow showers
RATCF	Radar ATC Facility (USN)
RB	right base
RBDE	radar bright display equipment
RBN	radio beacon
RC	reverse course
RCAG	Remote Communications Air/Ground Facility
RCC	rescue coordination center
RCK	radio check
RCL	runway centerline
RCLL	runway centerline lights
RCO	remote communication outlet
RCPT	receipt
RCR	runway condition reading
RCV	receive
RCVNO	receiving capability out
RDC	reduce
RDG	ridge
RDL	radial
RDO	radio
RDS	radius
RE	regard
REC	receive
RECON	reconnaissance
REF	reference
REIL	runway end identifier lights
RENOT	Regional Notices Issued by Washington Headquarters
REQ	request

Contraction/Acronym	Meaning
RF	radio frequency
RFI	radio frequency interference
RGD	ragged
RH	relative humidity
RHI	range height indicator
RHINO	radar echo height information not available
RIF	reduction in force
RITC	request in trail climb
RITD	request in trail descent
RL	report immediately upon leaving
RLS	release
RLSD	released
RLTV	relative
RM	remarks (PIREP only)
RMLR	radar microwave link repeater
RMM	remote maintenance monitoring
RMMS	Remote Maintenance Monitoring Systems
RNAV	Area Navigation
RNP	Required Navigation Performance
RO	regional office
ROC	rate of climb
ROD	rate of descent
RON	remaining overnight
ROTG	rotating
RPD	rapid
RPM	rotation per minute
RPT	repeat
RPV	remotely piloted vehicle
RR	report immediately upon reaching
RSG	rising
RT	right turn after take-off

Contraction/Acronym	Meaning
RTE	route
RTR	remote transmitter/receiver
RTRN	return
RV	radar vector
RVR	runway visual range
RVRNO	RVR not available
RVSM	Reduced Vertical Separation Minimum
RVV	runway visibility value
RVVNO	RVV not available
RWY or RY	runway
RX	receiver
S	
SA	dust storm, sandstorm, rising dust or sand
SAFI	Semi-Automatic Flight Inspection
SALS	Short Approach Lighting System
SALSF	Short Approach Lighting System with sequenced flashing lights
SAR	search and rescue
SATCOM	satellite communication
SC	stratocumulus (cloud formation)
SCATANA	Security Control of Air Traffic and Air Navigation Aids
SCSL	standing lenticular stratocumulus (cloud formation)
SCT	scattered
SCTR	sector
SCTY	security
SDBY	standby
SDF	Simplified Directional Facility
SECT	sector
SELCAL	selective calling
SEPN	separation
SEQ	sequence

Contraction/Acronym	Meaning
SFL	sequence flashing lights
SH	showers
SHF	super-high frequency
SHGR	hail showers
SHGS	hail showers (small)
SHPL	ice pellet showers
SHRA	rain showers
SHRT	short
SHSN	snow showers
SHWR	shower
SI	straight-in approach
SIAP	Standard Instrument Approach Procedure
SID	Standard Instrument Departures
SIGMET	significant meteorological information
SIGWX	significant weather
SIMUL	simultaneous
SKC	sky clear
SKED	schedule
SL	sea level
SLO	slow
SLP	sea level pressure
SLS	side lobe suppression
SLT	sleet
SM	statute mile
SMA	Surface Movement Advisor
SML	small
SMTH	smooth
SN	snow
SNBNK	snowbank
SND	sand
SND	sanded

Contraction/Acronym	Meaning
SND	sanding
SNOINCR	snow depth increase in past hour
SNSH	snow showers
SNWFL	snowfall
SOB	souls on board
SOP	standard operating practice
SOP	standard operating procedure
SPD	speed
SPEC	specification
SPECI	nonroutine aviation selected special weather report
SPO	strategic plan of operation
SPRD	spread
SQ	squall
SQDN	squadron
SQK	squawk
SQLN	squall line
SR	sunrise
SRND	surround
SRY	secondary
SS	sandstorm
SS	sunset
SSALF	Simplified Short Approach Lighting System with sequenced flashers
SSALS	Simplified Short Approach Lighting System
SSB	single sideband
SSNO	request no SIDS or STARS
SSR	secondary surveillance radar
SST	Super Sonic Transport
ST	stratus (cloud formation)
STA	straight in approach
STAR	Standard Terminal Arrival Route

Contraction/Acronym	Meaning
STARS	Standard Terminal Automation Replacement System
STG	strong
STMP	Special Traffic Management Program
STNRY	stationary
STOL	short take-off and landing
STWY	stopway
SUA	special-use airspace
SUB	substitute
SUBJ	subject to
SUPSD	supersede
SUSP	suspend
SVC	service
SVFR	special VFR
SVR	severe
SVRL	several
SVRWX	severe weather
SWAP	Severe Weather Avoidance Plan
SWAP	Severe Weather Avoidance Procedures
SYNS	synopsis
SYS	system
T	
T	true (bearing)
TAC	Tactical Air Command (USAF)
TACAN	Tactical Air Navigation
TAF	terminal aerodrome forecast
TAIL	tail wind
TAS	true air speed
TBD	to be determined
TCAS	Traffic Alert and Collision Avoidance System
TCCC	tower control computer complex
TCH	threshold crossing height

Contraction/Acronym	Meaning
TCP	transfer of control point
TCU	towering cumulus (cloud formation)
TCVR	transceiver
TDWR	terminal Doppler weather radar
TDY	temporary duty
TDZ	touchdown zone
TDZE	touchdown zone elevation
TDZL	touchdown zone lights
TEC	tower en route control
TEL	telephone
TELCO	telephone company
TELCON	telephone conference
TEMP	temperature
TEMPO	temporary
TEND	trend
TERPS	Terminal Instrument Approach Procedure
TFC	traffic
TFM	traffic flow management
TFR	temporary flight restriction
THLD	threshold
TIL	until
TMA	Traffic Management Advisor
TMC	traffic management coordinator
TMI	traffic management initiatives
TMPRY	temporary
TMS	Traffic Management System
TMU	Traffic Management Unit
TOG	take-off gross weight
TOP	cloud top
TR	VFR low-altitude training routes
TRACON	Terminal Radar Approach Control

Contraction/Acronym	Meaning
TROF	trough
TROP	tropopause
TS	thunderstorm
TSA	Transportation Security Administration
TSD	traffic situation display
TSFR	transfer
TSGR	thunderstorm with hail
TSGS	thunderstorm with small hail
TSNT	transient
TSO	technical standard order
TSPL	thunderstorm with ice pellets
TSRA	thunderstorm with rain
TSSA	thunderstorm with dust storm or sandstorm
TSSN	thunderstorm with snow
TSTM	thunderstorm
TSTMS	thunderstorms
TURBC	turbulence
TVOR	terminal VOR
TWD	toward
TWEB	Transcribed Weather En Route Broadcast
TWR	control tower
TWY	taxiway
TX	transmitter
U	
UA	routine PIREP
UFA	until further advised
UFN	until further notice
UHF	ultra-high frequency
UN	unable
UNAVBL	unavailable
UNKN	unknown

Contraction/Acronym	Meaning
UNL	unlimited
UNMON	unmonitored
UNOFFL	unofficial
UNRDBL	unreadable
UNRELBL	unreliable
UNSKED	unscheduled
UNSTBL	unstable
UNSTDY	unsteady
UNUSBL	unusable
UP	unknown precipitation
UPDFTS	updrafts
UPDT	update
UPR	upper
URET	user request evaluation tool
URG	urgent
USA	U.S. Army
USAF	U.S. Air Force
USBL	usable
USCG	U.S. Coast Guard
USMC	U.S. Marine Corps
USN	U.S. Navy
USNO	U.S. Naval Observatory
UTC	Coordinated Universal Time
UUA	urgent PIREP
V	
V	variable (weather reports only)
V	Victor airway
VAPS	visual approaches
VAR	magnetic variation
VASI	visual approach slope indicator
VC	vicinity

Contraction/Acronym	Meaning
VCFG	fog in vicinity
VFR	Visual Flight Rules
VHF	very-high frequency
VIS	visibility
VLF	very-low frequency
VMC	visual meteorological conditions
VNAV	vertical navigation (from TERPS-A1)
VOL	volume
VOLMET	meteorological information for aircraft in flight
VOR	Very-high-frequency Omni-directional Range
VOR/DME	VHF Omni-directional Range collocated with distance measuring equipment
VORTAC	VOR and TACAN (collocated)
VOT	VOR test signal
VR	VFR military training routes
VRBL	variable
VSBY	visibility
VSTOL	vertical/short take-off and landing
VTOL	vertical take-off and landing
VV	vertical visibility (indefinite ceiling)
W	
WAAS	Wide-Area Augmentation System
WAC	World Aeronautical Chart
WADGPS	Wide-Area Differential Global Positioning System
WARP	weather and radar processor
WDLY	widely
WDSPRD	widespread
WGS	World Geodetic System
WILCO	will comply
WKN	weaken
WMO	World Meteorological Organization

Contraction/Acronym	Meaning
WMSC	Weather Message Switching Center
WND	wind
WO	without
WP	waypoint
WRMFNT	warm front
WRNG	warning
WS	SIGMET
WS	wind shear
WSFO	Weather Service Forecast Office
WSHFT	wind shift
WSR	weather surveillance radar
WW	Severe Weather Watch Bulletin
WX	weather
X	
X	cross
Z	
Z	Zulu time (essentially the same as Coordinated Universal Time or Greenwich mean time)
ZRNO	freezing rain information not available (weather reports only)

Aircraft Performance Characteristics and Abbreviations

It is vitally important that air traffic controllers understand the performance characteristics of all aircraft under their control. This includes each aircraft's speed capabilities, climb and descent rates, and landing and takeoff performance. It is also important that the controller have knowledge of each aircraft's configuration, including its engine type and number and its weight class. This appendix lists some of the more common aircraft operating in the U.S. air traffic control system. The information here is a subset of the FAA list included in Appendix A of the *FAA Air Traffic Control Handbook Order Number 7110.65*. Controllers are required to memorize this information, since they must use it daily in the performance of job duties.

MILITARY AIRCRAFT-TYPE DESIGNATORS

For air traffic control purposes, military aircraft are identified only by the mission type abbreviation, followed by the aircraft's model number. This designator is limited to four characters. The mission/type symbol is an alphabetical letter denoting the primary function or capability of an aircraft. The symbols currently used by the U.S. military services are listed below.

Abbreviation	Function
A	attack
B	bomber
C	cargo/transport
E	special electronic installation
F	fighter
H[1]	helicopter
K	tanker
O	observation
P	patrol
R	reconnaissance
S	antisubmarine
T	trainer

appendix d

Abbreviation	Function
U	utility
V[1]	VTOL and STOL
W	weather reconnaissance
X	research
Z	airship

The aircraft's military model number follows the mission/type symbol. The designator A-4, for example, would indicate an attack aircraft designated as "4" by the military. A P-3 aircraft is a patrol aircraft, and an F-16 is a fighter.

Sometimes, the designators are bundled together when describing multi-role or combination aircraft with a common airframe. For example, a very common military transport used by the Air Force is a C-135. If one of these aircraft is converted to reconnaissance work, it becomes an RC-135; if it is converted to use for electronic countermeasures, its designation becomes EC-135.

CIVIL AIRCRAFT DESIGNATORS

The tables below include information about aircraft manufacturers, place of origin, and specific model numbers for many civilian aircraft and some military aircraft. Each model of aircraft has a designated four-character letter/number code reserved for it.

The aircraft description column identifies the number of engines on the aircraft, the type of engines, and the aircraft weight class. Engine types include:

- P = piston
- T = turboprop
- J = jet

The weight designator classes are small, large, and heavy. These are based on the aircraft's certificated takeoff weight. They are used to determine the approach, landing, and departure wake turbulence separation of an aircraft. The weight ranges for these categories are as follows:

- Small = 41,000 lbs or less
- Large = from 41,000 to 255,000 lbs
- Heavy = more than 255,000 lbs

Aircraft performance information includes climb and descent rates and a landing and departure categorization known as Same Runway Separation (SRS). When an air traffic controller is departing or landing one aircraft after another on the same runway, he or she must apply specific separation rules based on each aircraft's SRS classification. As a rule of thumb, the lower the SRS classification, the less longitudinal distance the aircraft requires on the specified runway. For example, SRS Class I aircraft can land and stop within a much shorter distance than SRS Class II or Class III aircraft.

AEROSPATIALE (France)

Model	Type Designator	Description Number & Type Engines/Weight Class	Performance Information Climb Rate (fpm)	Descent Rate (fpm)	SRS Cat.
ATR-42–200/300/320	AT43	2T/L	2,000	2,000	III
ATR-42–400	AT44	2T/L	2,000	2,000	III
ATR-42–500	AT45	2T/L	2,000	2,000	III
ATR-72	AT72	2T/L	2,000	2,000	III

AIRBUS INDUSTRIES (International)

Model	Type Designator	Description Number & Type Engines/Weight Class	Performance Information Climb Rate (fpm)	Descent Rate (fpm)	SRS Cat.
A-300B2/4–1/2/100/200, A-300C4–200	A30B	2J/H	3,500	3,500	III
A-300B4–600	A306	2J/H	3,500	3,500	III
A-310 (CC-150 Polaris)	A310	2J/H	3,500	3,500	III
A-318	A318	2J/L	3,500	3,500	III
A-319, ACJ	A319	2J/L	3,500	3,500	III
A-320	A320	2J/L	3,500	3,500	III
A-321	A321	2J/L	3,500	3,500	III
A-330–200	A332	2J/H	3,500	3,500	III
A-330–300	A333	2J/H			III
A-340–200	A342	4J/H	3,500	3,500	III
A-340–300	A343	4J/H			III
A-340–500	A345	4J/H			III
A-340–600	A346	4J/H			III
A-380–800	A388	4J/H			III

BEECH AIRCRAFT COMPANY (USA)
(Also CCF, COLEMILL, DINFIA, EXCALIBUR, FUJI, HAMILTON, JETCRAFTERS, RAYTHEON, SWEARINGEN, VOLPAR)

Model	Type Designator	Description — Number & Type Engines/Weight Class	Performance Information — Climb Rate (fpm)	Descent Rate (fpm)	SRS Cat.
1900	B190	2T/S+	2,400	2,400	III
B300 Super King Air 350	B350	2T/S+	3,000	3,000	III
100 King Air	BE10	2T/S	2,250	2,250	II
19 Musketeer Sport, Sport	BE19	1P/S	680	680	IV
200	BE20	2T/S+	2,450	2,500	III
23 Musketeer, Sundowner	BE23	1P/S	740	800	I
24 Musketeer Super, Sierra	BE24	1P/S	1,000	1,000	I
300 Super King Air	BE30	2T/S+	3,000	3,000	III
33 Debonair, Bonanza	BE33	1P/S	1,000	1,000	I
35 Bonanza	BE35	1P/S	1,200	1,200	I
36 Bonanza	BE36	1P/S	1,100	1,100	I
400 Beechjet, Hawker 400 (T-1 Jayhawk, T-400)	BE40	2J/S+	3,300	2,200	III
58 Baron	BE58	2P/S	1,730	1,730	II
76 Duchess	BE76	2P/S	1,500	1,500	II
77 Skipper	BE77	1P/S	750	750	I
90, A90 to E90 King Air (T-44 V-C6)	BE9L	2T/S	2,000	2,000	II

BELLANCA AIRCRAFT (USA)

Model	Type Designator	Description	Performance Information		
		Number & Type Engines/Weight Class	Climb Rate (fpm)	Descent Rate (fpm)	SRS Cat.
Aeronca Chief/Super Chief, Pushpak	AR11	1P/S	500	500	I
17 Viking, Super Viking, Turbo Viking	BL17	1P/S	1,100	1,100	I
8 Decathlon, Scout	BL8	1P/S	1,000	1,000	I
7 ACA/ECA Champ, Citabria	CH7A	1P/S	750	750	I

BOEING COMPANY (USA)

Model	Type Designator	Description	Performance Information		
		Number & Type Engines/Weight Class	Climb Rate (fpm)	Descent Rate (fpm)	SRS Cat.
B-52 Stratofortress	B52	8J/H	3,000	3,000	III
717–200	B712	2J/L			III
737–300	B733	2J/L	5,500	3,500	III
737–900	B739	2J/L	4,000	4,000	III
747–400 (International, Winglets)	B744	4J/H	3,000	3,000	III
757–200 (C-32)	B752	2J/L	3,500	2,500	III
757–300	B753	2J/H	3,500	2,500	III
767–200	B762	2J/H	3,500	3,500	III
767–400	B764	2J/H	3,500	3,500	III
777–200	B772	2J/H	2,500	2,500	III
777–300	B773	2J/H	2,500	2,500	III
C-135B/C/E/K Stratolifter (EC-135, NKC-135, OC-135, TC-135, WC-135)	C135	4J/H	2,000	2,000	III
KC 135R/T, C-135FR, Stratotanker (CFM56 engines)	K35R	4J/H	5,000	3,000	III

BOEING COMPANY (USA) *(continued)*

Model	Type Designator	Number & Type Engines/Weight Class	Climb Rate (fpm)	Descent Rate (fpm)	SRS Cat.
		Description	**Performance Information**		
E-767	E767	2J/H	2,500	2,500	III

CESSNA AIRCRAFT COMPANY (USA)

Model	Type Designator	Number & Type Engines/Weight Class	Climb Rate (fpm)	Descent Rate (fpm)	SRS Cat.
		Description	**Performance Information**		
152, A152, Aerobat	C152	1P/S	750	1,000	I
172, P172, R172, Skyhawk, Hawk XP, Cutlass (T-41, Mescalero)	C172	1P/S	650	1,000	I
182, Skylane	C182	1P/S	890	1,000	I
207 (Turbo) Skywagon 207, (Turbo) Stationair 7/8	C207	1P/S	810	1,000	I
208 Caravan 1, (Super) Cargomaster, Grand Caravan (C-98, U27)	C208	1T/S	1,400	1,400	I
210, T210, (Turbo) Centurion	C210	1P/S	900	1,000	I
P210 Pressurized Centurion	P210	1P/S	1,000	1,000	I
310, T310 (U-3, L-27)	C310	2P/S	2,800	2,000	II
401, 402, Utililiner, Businessliner	C402	2P/S	2,500	2,000	II
421, Golden Eagle, Executive Commuter	C421	2P/S			II
421 (turbine)	C21T	2T/S			II
5000 Citation, Citation 1	C500	2J/S	3,100	3,500	III
501 Citation 1SP	C501	2J/S	4,300	3,000	III
525 Citationjet Citation CJ1	C525	2J/S	3,000		III

CESSNA AIRCRAFT COMPANY (USA) *(continued)*

Model	Type Designator	Description	Performance Information		
		Number & Type Engines/Weight Class	Climb Rate (fpm)	Descent Rate (fpm)	SRS Cat.
551 Citation 2SP	C551	2J/S	5,300	3,000	III
650 Citation 3/6/7	C650	2J/S+	3,900	4,000	III
680 Citation Sovereign	C680	2J/S+			III
750 Citation 10	C750	2J/S+	3,500	3,500	III
T37 (318A/B/C)	T37*	2J/S	3,000	3,000	III

CIRRUS (USA)

Model	Type Designator	Description	Performance Information		
		Number & Type Engines/Weight Class	Climb Rate (fpm)	Descent Rate (fpm)	SRS Cat.
SR-20	SR20	1P/S			I
SR-22	SR22	1P/S			I
VK-30 Cirrus	VK3P	1P/S			I

DEHAVILLAND (Canada/UK)

Model	Type Designator	Description	Performance Information		
		Number & Type Engines/Weight Class	Climb Rate (fpm)	Descent Rate (fpm)	SRS Cat.
DHC-7 Dash 7 (O-5, EO-5)	DHC7	4T/L	4,000	4,000	III
DHC8–100 Dash 8 (E-9, CT-142, CC-142)	DH8A	2T/L	1,500	1,500	III
DHC8–200 Dash 8	DH8B	2T/L	1,500	1,500	III
DHC8–300 Dash 8	DH8C	2T/L	1,500	1,500	III
DHC8–400 Dash 8	DH8D	2T/L	2,500	2,500	III

DIAMOND (Canada)

Model	Type Designator	Description Number & Type Engines/Weight Class	Performance Information Climb Rate (fpm)	Performance Information Descent Rate (fpm)	SRS Cat.
DA-20/22, DV-20 Katana, Speed Katana	DV20	1P/S	730		I
DA-42 TwinStar	DA42	2P/S	1,500	1,500	II

ECLIPSE AVIATION (USA)

Model	Type Designator	Description Number & Type Engines/Weight Class	Performance Information Climb Rate (fpm)	Performance Information Descent Rate (fpm)	SRS Cat.
Eclipse 500	EA50	2J/S			III

EMBRAER (Brazil)

Model	Type Designator	Description Number & Type Engines/Weight Class	Performance Information Climb Rate (fpm)	Performance Information Descent Rate (fpm)	SRS Cat.
CBA-123 Vector	VECT	2T/S+			III
EMB-110/111 Bandeirante (C-95, EC-95, P-95, R-95, SC-95)	E110	2T/S+	1,500	1,500	III
EMB-120 Brasilia (VC-97)	E120	2T/S+	2,300	2,300	III
EMB-135, ERJ-135/140	E135	2J/L	2,410	2,030	III
EMB-145, ERJ-145 (R-99)	E145	2J/L	2,350	2,190	III
EMB-170/175	E170	2J/L			III
EMB-190/195	E190	2J/L			III

GATES LEARJET CORP. (USA)

Model	Type Designator	Description Number & Type Engines/Weight Class	Performance Information Climb Rate (fpm)	Descent Rate (fpm)	SRS Cat.
35	LJ35	2J/S+	4,500	4,000	III
40	LJ40	2J/S+			III
45	LJ45	2J/S+			III
55	LJ55	2J/S+	5,000	4,000	III
60	LJ60	2J/S+	5,000	4,000	III

GRUMMAN AEROSPACE CORP. (USA)

Model	Type Designator	Description Number & Type Engines/Weight Class	Performance Information Climb Rate (fpm)	Descent Rate (fpm)	SRS Cat.
AA1 Trainer,Tr2, T-Cat, Lynx	AA1	1P/S	850	1,250	I
AA-5, Traveller, Cheetah Tiger	AA5	1P/S	660	1,000	I
GA-7 Cougar	GA7	2P/S	1,600	1,500	II

GULFSTREAM AEROSPACE CORP. (USA)

Model	Type Designator	Description Number & Type Engines/Weight Class	Performance Information Climb Rate (fpm)	Descent Rate (fpm)	SRS Cat.
AA-1 T-Cat, Lynx	AA1	1P/S	850	1,250	I
AA-5 Traveler, Cheetah, Tiger	AA5	1P/S	660	1,000	I
GA-7 Cougar	GA7	2P/S	1,600	1,500	II
GAC 159-C, Gulfstream 1	G159	2T/S+	2,000	2,000	III
G-1159, G-1159B/TT Gulfstream 2/2B/2SP/2TT	GLF2	2J/L	5,000	4,000	III

GULFSTREAM AEROSPACE CORP. (USA) *(continued)*

Model	Type Designator	Description — Number & Type Engines/Weight Class	Performance Information — Climb Rate (fpm)	Descent Rate (fpm)	SRS Cat.
G-1159A Gulfstream 3/SRA-1, SMA-3 (C20A/B/C/D/E)	GLF3	2J/L	5,000	4,000	III
G-1159C Gulfstream 300/4/4SP/ 400/SRA-4 (C-20F/G/H, S102, Tp102, U-4)	GLF4	2J/L	5,000	4,000	III
G-1159D Gulfstream 5/500/550 (C-37)	GLF5	2J/L	5,000	4,000	III

MITSUBISHI AIRCRAFT INTERNATIONAL, INC. (USA/Japan)

Model	Type Designator	Description — Number & Type Engines/Weight Class	Performance Information — Climb Rate (fpm)	Descent Rate (fpm)	SRS Cat.
MU-2, Marquise, Solitaire (LR-1)	MU2	2T/S	3,500	3,000	II
MU-300 Diamond	MU30	2J/S+	3,500	4,000	III

MOONEY AIRCRAFT CORP. (USA)

Model	Type Designator	Description — Number & Type Engines/Weight Class	Performance Information — Climb Rate (fpm)	Descent Rate (fpm)	SRS Cat.
M-20, M-20/A/B/C/D/E/ F/G/J/L/R/S, Mark 21, Allegro, Eagle, Ranger, Master, Super 21, Chaparral, Executive, Statesman, Ovation, 201, 202, 205, 220, ATS, MSE, PFM (non-turbocharged engine)	M20P	1P/S	1,000	1,000	I
M-22, Mustang	M22	1P/S	1,300	1,300	I

PIPER AIRCRAFT CORP. (USA)

Model	Type Designator	Description Number & Type Engines/Weight Class	Performance Information Climb Rate (fpm)	Descent Rate (fpm)	SRS Cat.
J-3 Cub (L-4, NE)	J3	1P/S	500	500	I
PA-18 Super Cub (L-18C, L-21, U-7)	PA18	1P/S	1,000	1,000	I
PA-24 Comanche	PA24	1P/S	900	1,000	I
PA-25 Pawnee	PA25	1P/S	650	650	I
PA-23–235/250 Aztec, Turbo Aztec (U-11, E-19, UC-26)	PA27	2P/S	1,500	1,500	II
PA-28–140/150/151/ 160/161/180/181Archer, Cadet, Cherokee, Cherokee Archer/ Challenger/ Chief/ Cruiser/ Flite Liner/ Warrior	P28A	1P/S	750	1,000	I
PA-28–201T/235/236 Cherokee, Cherokee Charger/Pathfinder, Dakota, Turbo Dakota	P28B	1P/S	900	1,000	I
PA-28R-1802/3, Turbo Arrow 3/200/201 Cherokee Arrow, Arrow	P28R	1P/S	750	1,000	I
PA-28RT Arrow 4, Turbo Arrow 4	P28T	1P/S	900	1,000	I
PA-32R Cherokee Lance, Lance, Saratoga SP/2 HP/2TC, Turbo Saratoga SP	P32R	1P/S	850	1,000	I
PA-34 Seneca	PA34	2P/S	1,300	1,300	II
PA-38 Tomahawk	PA38	1P/S	750	750	I
PA-44, Seminole, Turbo Seminole	PA44	2P/S	1,100	1,000	II
PA-46 310P/350P Malibu, Malibu Mirage	PA46	1P/S	1,000	1,000	I
PA-31T1–500 Cheyenne 1	PAY1	2T/S	2,200	2,000	II

PITTS AEROBATICS (Manufactured by Christen Industries, Inc.) (USA)

		Description	Performance Information		
Model	Type Designator	Number & Type Engines/Weight Class	Climb Rate (fpm)	Descent Rate (fpm)	SRS Cat.
S-1 Special	PTS1	1P/S	1,500	1,500	I
S-2 Special	PTS2	1P/S	1,500	1,500	I

ROCKWELL INTERNATIONAL CORP. (USA)

		Description	Performance Information		
Model	Type Designator	Number & Type Engines/Weight Class	Climb Rate (fpm)	Descent Rate (fpm)	SRS Cat.
112, 114 Commander 112/114, Alpine Commander, Gran Turismo Commander	AC11	1P/S	1,000	1,200	I
680F, 680FP, Commander 680F/ 680FP	AC68	2P/S	1,375	1,375	II

SAAB (Sweden/USA)

		Description	Performance Information		
Model	Type Designator	Number & Type Engines/Weight Class	Climb Rate (fpm)	Descent Rate (fpm)	SRS Cat.
340	SF34	2T/L	2,000	2,000	III
2000	SB20	2T/L			III

Airport and Navigation Aid Identifiers

Most of the airports worldwide that are served by airline and business aviation aircraft use four-letter airport identifier abbreviations. Similar identifiers have also been created for every airspace fix, flight procedure, navigation aid, weather station, and manned air traffic control facility.

Two airport identification systems are in use. The system used by the International Air Transport Association (IATA) is a three-letter code identifying each major airport in the world. Many civilians who travel by air are familiar with these codes: for example, LAX to identify Los Angeles International, SEA for Seattle-Tacoma International Airport, and PIT for Pittsburgh International Airport.

THREE-LETTER FAA IDENTIFIERS

The FAA developed the three-letter identifier codes that designate each U.S. airport and identify it internationally. Additional three-, four-, and even five-letter name codes are sometimes used for smaller airports in the United States; however, these codes are not internationally recognized.

In the FAA identifier codes, the initial letters N, W, Y, and Z are reserved for other uses. The Department of the Navy assigns three-letter identifiers beginning with the letter N for the facilities that are exclusively used by naval aviation. Transport Canada assigns two-, three-, and four-character identifiers, including three-letter identifiers beginning with letters Y and Z, for its areas of jurisdiction. The Federal Communications Commission (FCC) assigns blocks of identifiers beginning with K and W for its areas of responsibility. Codes beginning with the letter Q are under international telecommunications jurisdiction. The National Weather Service assigns four-letter, one-number identifiers for certain weather requirements. Three-letter identifiers prefixed with the letter "Z" are reserved for air traffic control facilities.

THE ICAO IDENTIFYING SYSTEM

Air traffic controllers use the International Civil Aviation Organization (ICAO) standard identifying system. This system differs from that used by IATA in that identifiers are four letters long, with the first two identifying the airport's geographic area and country. For example, the code for Heathrow

Airport, London, is EGLL: "E" for Europe, "G" for Great Britain, and "LL" for London Heathrow. As you learned in the main text of this book, the first letter of the ICAO identifier for each airport in the continental United States is always "K"; the next three letters identify the specific airport. For example, Los Angeles International becomes KLAX, Seattle-Tacoma International Airport becomes KSEA, and Pittsburgh International Airport becomes KPIT. Airports in the Pacific region (Alaska and Hawaii in particular) are prefixed with the letter "P." Other U.S. territories and protectorates use similar coding schemes depending on their geographic locations.

This appendix includes a list of the more common airport identifiers you'll encounter in air traffic control. Listings for all of the United States and Canada can be obtained in the FAA Order 7350.7, Location Identifiers.

ICAO Identifying Codes: United States Airports

KABI	Abilene Regional Airport	Abilene, Texas
KABQ	Albuquerque International Sunport	Albuquerque, New Mexico
KACT	Waco Regional Airport	Waco, Texas
KACY	Atlantic City International Airport	Atlantic City, New Jersey
KAFF	United States Air Force Academy Airfield	Colorado Springs, Colorado
KAFW	Fort Worth Alliance Airport	Fort Worth, Texas
KALB	Albany International Airport	Albany, New York
KAMA	Rick Husband Amarillo International Airport	Amarillo, Texas
KANE	Anoka County-Blaine Airport (Janes Field)	Minneapolis, Minnesota
KANJ	Sault Ste. Marie Municipal Airport (Sanderson Field)	Sault Ste. Marie, Michigan
KAPA	Centennial Airport	Centennial, Colorado
KARR	Aurora Municipal Airport (Al Potter Field)	Aurora, Illinois
KASH	Boire Field	Nashua, New Hampshire
KATL	Hartsfield-Jackson Atlanta International Airport	Atlanta, Georgia
KAUS	Austin-Bergstrom International Airport	Austin, Texas
KAZO	Kalamazoo-Battle Creek International Airport	Kalamazoo, Michigan
KBDL	Bradley International Airport	Windsor Locks, Connecticut
KBDR	Igor I. Sikorsky Memorial Airport	Bridgeport, Connecticut
KBED	Laurence G. Hanscom Field	Bedford, Massachusetts
KBFI	Boeing Field/King County International Airport	Seattle, Washington
KBHM	Birmingham International Airport	Birmingham, Alabama
KBKL	Cleveland Burke Lakefront Airport	Cleveland, Ohio

ICAO Identifying Codes: United States Airports *(continued)*

KBLV	MidAmerica St. Louis Airport/Scott Air Force Base	Belleville, Illinois
KBNA	Nashville International Airport	Nashville, Tennessee
KBOI	Boise Air Terminal (Gowen Field)	Boise, Idaho
KBOS	Logan International Airport	Boston, Massachusetts
KBTR	Baton Rouge Metropolitan Airport	Baton Rouge, Louisiana
KBUF	Buffalo Niagara International Airport	Buffalo, New York
KBUR	Bob Hope Airport	Burbank, California
KBWG	Bowling Green-Warren County Regional Airport	Bowling Green, Kentucky
KBWI	Baltimore-Washington International Thurgood Marshall Airport	Baltimore, Maryland and Washington, D.C.
KBYH	Arkansas International Airport	Blytheville, Arkansas
KCEA	Cessna Aircraft Field	Wichita, Kansas
KCHA	Chattanooga Metropolitan Airport	Chattanooga, Tennessee
KCHS	Charleston International Airport (Charleston Air Force Base)	Charleston, South Carolina
KCIU	Chippewa County International Airport	Sault Ste. Marie, Michigan
KCLE	Cleveland Hopkins International Airport	Cleveland, Ohio
KCMH	Port Columbus International Airport	Columbus, Ohio
KCMI	University of Illinois Willard Airport	Champaign, Illinois
KCNO	Chino Airport	Chino, California
KCOS	Colorado Springs Airport (City of Colorado Springs Municipal Airport)	Colorado Springs, Colorado
KCOU	Columbia Regional Airport	Columbia, Missouri
KCPR	Natrona County International Airport	Casper, Wyoming
KCRP	Corpus Christi International Airport	Corpus Christi, Texas
KCRW	Yeager Airport	Charleston, West Virginia
KCVG	Cincinnati/Northern Kentucky International Airport	Hebron, Kentucky (near Cincinnati, Ohio and Covington, Kentucky)
KCXY	Capital City Airport	Harrisburg, Pennsylvania
KDAB	Daytona Beach International Airport	Daytona Beach, Florida
KDAL	Dallas Love Field	Dallas, Texas

ICAO Identifying Codes: United States Airports *(continued)*

KDAY	James M. Cox International Airport	Dayton, Ohio
KDCA	Ronald Reagan Washington National Airport	Arlington County, Virginia (near Washington, D.C.)
KDEN	Denver International Airport (replaced Stapleton International)	Denver, Colorado
KDET	Coleman A. Young Municipal Airport	Detroit, Michigan
KDFW	Dallas-Fort Worth International Airport	Dallas and Fort Worth, Texas
KDLH	Duluth International Airport	Duluth, Minnesota
KDPA	Dupage Airport	West Chicago, Illinois
KDTW	Detroit Metropolitan Wayne County Airport	Romulus, Michigan (near Detroit, Michigan)
KEFD	Ellington Field	Houston, Texas
KELP	El Paso International Airport	El Paso, Texas
KEWR	Newark Liberty International Airport	Newark, New Jersey
KEYE	Eagle Creek Airpark	Indianapolis, Indiana
KFAT	Fresno Yosemite International Airport	Fresno, California
KFAY	Fayetteville Regional Airport (Grannis Field)	Fayetteville, North Carolina
KFCM	Flying Cloud Airport	Minneapolis, Minnesota
KFFA	First Flight Airport	Kill Devil Hills, North Carolina
KFFC	Falcon Field	Peachtree City, Georgia
KFFO	Wright-Patterson Air Force Base	Dayton, Ohio
KFFT	Capital City Airport	Frankfort, Kentucky
KFLL	Fort Lauderdale-Hollywood International Airport	Fort Lauderdale and Hollywood, Florida
KFOE	Forbes Field	Topeka, Kansas
KFPR	St. Lucie County International Airport	Fort Pierce, Florida
KFRG	Republic Airport	East Farmingdale, New York
KFTW	Fort Worth Meacham International Airport	Fort Worth, Texas
KFTY	Fulton County Airport (Brown Field)	Atlanta, Georgia
KFWA	Fort Wayne International Airport	Fort Wayne, Indiana

ICAO Identifying Codes: United States Airports *(continued)*

KFXE	Fort Lauderdale Executive Airport	Fort Lauderdale, Florida
KGCN	Grand Canyon National Park Airport	Grand Canyon National Park, Arizona
KGEG	Spokane International Airport	Spokane, Washington
KGFK	Grand Forks International Airport	Grand Forks, North Dakota
KGPT	Gulfport-Biloxi International Airport	Gulfport, Mississippi
KGRB	Austin Straubel International Airport	Green Bay, Wisconsin
KGRR	Gerald R. Ford International Airport	Grand Rapids, Michigan
KGSO	Piedmont Triad International Airport	Greensboro, North Carolina
KGTF	Great Falls International Airport	Great Falls, Montana
KHOT	Hot Springs Memorial Field Airport	Hot Springs, Arkansas
KHPN	Westchester County Airport	White Plains, New York
KHTS	Tri-State Airport	Huntington, West Virginia
KHXD	Hilton Head Airport	Hilton Head Island, South Carolina
KIAB	McConnell Air Force Base	Wichita, Kansas
KIAD	Washington Dulles International Airport	Washington, D.C.
KIAH	George Bush Intercontinental Airport	Houston, Texas
KICT	Wichita Mid-Continent Airport	Wichita, Kansas
KIND	Indianapolis International Airport	Indianapolis, Indiana
KJAC	Jackson Hole Airport	Jackson Hole, Wyoming
KJAN	Jackson International Airport	Jackson, Mississippi
KJAX	Jacksonville International Airport	Jacksonville, Florida
KJFK	John F. Kennedy International Airport	New York, New York
KLAF	Purdue University Airport	West Lafayette, Indiana
KLAS	McCarran International Airport	Las Vegas, Nevada
KLUX	Los Angeles International Airport	Los Angeles, California
KLCK	Rickenbacker International Airport	Columbus, Ohio
KLGA	LaGuardia International Airport	New York, New York
KLGB	Long Beach Airport	Long Beach, California
KLIT	Little Rock National Airport Adams Field	Little Rock, Arkansas
KLNK	Lincoln Municipal Airport	Lincoln, Nebraska

ICAO Identifying Codes: United States Airports *(continued)*

KLOU	Bowman Field Airport	Louisville, Kentucky
KLSV	Nellis Air Force Base	Las Vegas, Nevada
KLUF	Luke Air Force Base	Glendale, Arizona
KMAF	Midland International Airport	Midland, Texas
KMCC	McClellan Airport	Sacramento, California
KMCI	Kansas City International Airport	Kansas City, Missouri
KMCO	Orlando International Airport	Orlando, Florida
KMDW	Chicago Midway International Airport	Chicago, Illinois
KMEM	Memphis International Airport	Memphis, Tennessee
KMGY	Dayton Wright Brothers Airport	Dayton, Ohio
KMHT	Manchester-Boston Regional Airport	Manchester, New Hampshire
KMHV	Mohave Spaceport	Mohave, California
KMIA	Miami International Airport	Miami, Florida
KMKE	General Mitchell International Airport	Milwaukee, Wisconsin
KMOB	Mobile Regional Airport	Mobile, Alabama
KMSN	Dane County Regional Airport	Madison, Wisconsin
KMSP	Minneapolis-Saint Paul International Airport	Bloomington, Minnesota
KMSY	Louis Armstrong International Airport	New Orleans, Louisiana
KMYF	Montgomery Field	San Diego, California
KNEL	Lakehurst NAES	Lakehurst, New Jersey
KNGU	Norfolk Naval Station	Norfolk, Virginia
KNHK	Patuxent River NAS	Patuxent River, Maryland
KNOW	Port Angeles CGAS	Port Angeles, Washington
KNTK	Tustin MCAS	Santa Ana, California
KNTU	Oceana NAS	Virginia Beach, Virginia
KNUQ	Moffett Federal Airfield	Mountain View, California
KOAK	Oakland International Airport	Oakland, California
KOKC	Will Rogers World Airport	Oklahoma City, Oklahoma
KOMA	Eppley Field	Omaha, Nebraska
KORD	O'Hare International Airport	Chicago, Illinois

ICAO Identifying Codes: United States Airports *(continued)*

KORF	Norfolk International Airport	Norfolk, Virginia
KORG	Orange County Airport	Orange, Texas
KORS	Orcas Island Airport	Eastsound, Washington
KOSU	Ohio State University Airport	Columbus, Ohio
KPAE	Snohomish County Airport (Paine Field)	Everett, Washington
KPAN	Payson Municipal Airport	Payson, Arizona
KPAO	Palo Alto Airport of Santa Clara County	Palo Alto, California
KPBF	Grider Field	Pine Bluff, Arkansas
KPDK	DeKalb-Peachtree Airport	Atlanta, Georgia
KPHX	Phoenix Sky Harbor International Airport	Phoenix, Arizona
KPIA	Greater Peoria Regional Airport	Peoria, Illinois
KPIT	Pittsburgh International Airport	Pittsburgh, Pennsylvania
KPMD	Palmdale Regional Airport	Palmdale, California
KPNS	Pensacola Regional Airport	Pensacola, Florida
KPSP	Palm Springs International Airport	Palm Springs, California
KPVD	T.F. Green State Airport	Providence, Rhode Island
KRBD	Dallas Executive Airport	Dallas, Texas
KRDU	Raleigh-Durham International Airport	Raleigh, North Carolina
KRNO	Reno-Tahoe International Airport	Reno, Nevada
KROC	Greater Rochester International Airport	Rochester, New York
KSAN	San Diego International Airport (Lindbergh Field)	San Diego, California
KSAT	San Antonio International Airport	San Antonio, Texas
KSBD	San Bernardino International Airport	San Bernardino, California
KSEA	Seattle-Tacoma International Airport	Seattle, Washington
KSFO	San Francisco International Airport	San Mateo County, California
KSFZ	North Central State Airport	Pawtucket, Rhode Island
KSJC	Norman Y. Mineta San José International Airport	San José, California
KSLC	Salt Lake City International Airport	Salt Lake City, Utah
KSMF	Sacramento International Airport	Sacramento, California

ICAO Identifying Codes: United States Airports *(continued)*

KSPS	Wichita Falls Municipal Airport/Sheppard Air Force Base	Wichita Falls, Texas
KSTL	Lambert Saint Louis International Airport	St. Louis, Missouri
KSTS	Sonoma County Airport	Santa Rosa, California
KSYR	Syracuse Hancock International Airport	Syracuse, New York
KTCM	McChord Air Force Base	Tacoma, Washington
KTEB	Teterboro Airport	Teterboro, New Jersey
KTEX	Telluride Regional Airport	Telluride, Colorado
KTHM	Thompson Falls Airport	Thompson Falls, Montana
KTOL	Toledo Express Airport	Toledo, Ohio
KTPA	Tampa International Airport	Tampa, Florida
KVGT	North Las Vegas Airport	Las Vegas, Nevada
KVNY	Van Nuys Airport	Van Nuys, California
KXMR	Cape Canaveral Air Force Station Skid Strip	Cocoa Beach, Florida
KYIP	Willow Run Airport	Detroit, Michigan
KYNG	Youngstown-Warren Regional Airport	Youngstown and Warren, Ohio
MUGM	NAS Guantánamo Bay	Guantánamo Bay, Cuba
PAAQ	Palmer Municipal Airport	Palmer, Alaska
PACD	Cold Bay Airport	Cold Bay, Alaska
PADQ	Kodiak Airport	Kodiak, Alaska
PAED	Elmendorf Air Force Base	Anchorage, Alaska
PAEI	Eielson Air Force Base	Fairbanks, Alaska
PAFA	Fairbanks International Airport	Fairbanks, Alaska
PAIN	McKinley National Park Airport	McKinley Park, Alaska
PAJN	Juneau International Airport	Juneau, Alaska
PAKT	Ketchikan International Airport	Gravina Island, Alaska (near Ketchikan, Alaska)
PAMR	Merrill Field	Anchorage, Alaska
PANC	Ted Stevens Anchorage International Airport	Anchorage, Alaska
PHHI	Wheeler Army Airfield	Wahiawa, Hawaii
PHIK	Hickam Air Force Base	Honolulu, Hawaii

ICAO Identifying Codes: United States Airports *(continued)*

PHKO	Kona International Airport	Kailua-Kona, Hawaii
PHLI	Lihu'e Airport	Lihu'e, Hawaii
PHNL	Honolulu International Airport	Honolulu, Hawaii
PHOG	Kahului Airport	Kahului, Hawaii
PHTO	Hilo International Airport	Hilo, Hawaii
TIST	Cyril E. King Airport	St. Thomas, U.S. Virgin Islands
TISX	Henry E. Rohlsen International Airport	St. Croix, U.S. Virgin Islands
TJAB	Antonio (Nery) Juarbe Pol Airport	Arecibo, Puerto Rico
TJSJ	Luis Muñoz Marín International Airport	San Juan, Puerto Rico

ICAO Identifying Codes: International Airports

BIRK	Reykjavík Airport	Reykjavík, Iceland
CYAM	Sault Ste. Marie Airport	Ontario, Canada
CYAV	Winnipeg/St. Andrews Airport	Manitoba, Canada
CYAW	Halifax/Shearwater Airport	Nova Scotia, Canada
CYBW	Calgary/Springbank Airport (Springbank Airport)	Alberta, Canada
CYEG	Edmonton International Airport	Alberta, Canada
CYGK	Kingston/Norman Rogers Airport (Kingston Airport)	Ontario, Canada
CYHU	Montréal/St-Hubert Airport	Québec, Canada
CYHZ	Halifax International Airport	Nova Scotia, Canada
CYMX	Montréal-Mirabel International Airport (Montréal International (Mirabel) Airport)	Québec, Canada
CYND	Ottawa/Gatineau Airport	Québec, Canada
CYOW	Ottawa Macdonald-Cartier International Airport	Ontario, Canada
CYPR	Prince Rupert Airport	British Columbia, Canada
CYQB	Québec/Jean Lesage International Airport	Québec, Canada
CYQG	Windsor Airport	Ontario, Canada
CYQM	Greater Moncton International Airport (Moncton/Greater Moncton International Airport)	New Brunswick, Canada

ICAO Identifying Codes: International Airports (continued)

CYQR	Regina International Airport	Saskatchewan, Canada
CYQT	Thunder Bay International Airport (Thunder Bay Airport)	Ontario, Canada
CYQX	Gander International Airport	Newfoundland and Labrador, Canada
CYQY	Sydney Airport (Nova Scotia)	Nova Scotia, Canada
CYSB	Greater Sudbury Airport (Sudbury Airport)	Ontario, Canada
CYSJ	Saint John Airport	New Brunswick, Canada
CYUL	Montréal-Pierre Elliott Trudeau International Airport (Montréal/Pierre Elliott Trudeau International Airport)	Québec, Canada
CYVR	Vancouver International Airport	British Columbia, Canada
CYWG	Winnipeg James Armstrong Richardson International Airport	Manitoba, Canada
CYXE	Saskatoon/John G. Diefenbaker International Airport	Saskatchewan, Canada
CYXU	London International Airport (London Airport)	Ontario, Canada
CYXY	Whitehorse International Airport	Yukon, Canada
CYYC	Calgary International Airport	Alberta, Canada
CYYT	St. John's International Airport	Newfoundland and Labrador, Canada
CYYZ	Toronto Pearson International Airport (Toronto/Lester B. Pearson International Airport)	Ontario, Canada
CYZR	Sarnia (Chris Hadfield) Airport	Ontario, Canada
EDDB	Berlin-Schönefeld International Airport (to be expanded and renamed Berlin Brandenburg International Airport in 2011)	Berlin, Germany
EDDF	Frankfurt International Airport	Frankfurt am Main, Germany
EDDH	Hamburg Airport	Hamburg, Germany
EDDK	Cologne Bonn Airport	Cologne, Germany
EDDM	Munich International Airport (Franz Josef Strauß International Airport)	Munich, Germany
EDDT	Tegel International Airport (closing in 2011)	Berlin, Germany
EGBB	Birmingham International Airport	Birmingham, United Kingdom

ICAO Identifying Codes: International Airports *(continued)*

EGCC	Manchester Airport	Manchester, United Kingdom
EGGW	London Luton Airport	London, United Kingdom
EGKK	London Gatwick Airport	London, United Kingdom
EGLC	London City Airport	London, United Kingdom
EGLF	Farnborough Airfield	Farnborough, United Kingdom
EGLL	London Heathrow Airport	London, United Kingdom
EGPH	Edinburgh Airport	Edinburgh, United Kingdom
EGSS	London Stansted Airport	London, United Kingdom
EGSU	Duxford	Cambridge, United Kingdom
EGUL	RAF Lakenheath	Lakenheath, United Kingdom
EGUN	RAF Mildenhall	Mildenhall, United Kingdom
EHAM	Amsterdam Schiphol Airport	Haarlemmermeer, near Amsterdam, The Netherlands
EICK	Cork International Airport	Cork, Ireland
EIDW	Dublin International Airport	Dublin, Ireland
EINN	Shannon Airport	Shannon, County Clare, Ireland
EKCH	Copenhagen Airport	Kastrup, near Copenhagen, Denmark
LFPB	Paris Le Bourget Airport	Paris, France
LFPG	Paris Charles de Gaulle Airport (Roissy Airport)	Paris, France
LFPO	Paris Orly Airport	Orly, near Paris, France
LIRA	Ciampino Airport (Giovan Battista Pastine Airport)	Rome, Italy
LIRF	Leonardo Da Vinci International Airport (Fiumicino International Airport)	Rome, Italy
MMAA	General Juan N. Álvarez International Airport	Acapulco, Guerrero, Mexico
MMML	General Rodolfo Sánchez Taboada International Airport	Mexicali, Baja California, Mexico

ICAO Identifying Codes: International Airports *(continued)*

MMMX	Benito Juárez International Airport	Mexico City, Distrito Federal, Mexico
MMMY	General Mariano Escobedo International Airport	Monterrey, Nuevo León, Mexico
MMPR	Gustavo Díaz Ordaz International Airport	Puerto Vallarta, Jalisco, Mexico
MMTJ	General Abelardo L. Rodríguez International Airport	Tijuana, Baja California, Mexico
RJAA	Narita International Airport (New Tokyo)	Narita, Chiba, Japan
RJBB	Kansai International Airport	Osaka, Japan
RJBH	Hiroshima-Nishi Airport	Hiroshima, Japan
RJOO	Osaka International Airport (Itami)	Itami, Hyogo, Japan
RJTT	Tokyo International Airport (Haneda)	Ota, Tokyo, Japan
RKSI	Incheon International Airport	Seoul, South Korea
UUDD	Domodedovo International Airport	Moscow, Russia
UUEE	Sheremetyevo International Airport	Moscow, Russia
VABB	Chatrapati Shivaji International Airport	Mumbai (Bombay), India
VIDP	Indira Gandhi International Airport	New Delhi, India
VHHH	Hong Kong International Airport	Chek Lap Kok, China
YSSY	Sydney (Kingsford Smith) International Airport	Mascot, New South Wales, Australia
YMML	Melbourne International Airport	Tullamarine, Victoria, Australia
ZBAA	Beijing Capital International Airport	Beijing, China
ZSPD	Shanghai Pudong International Airport	Shanghai, China

About the Author

Michael S. Nolan (B.S., Industrial Technology, Illinois State University; M.S., Instructional Development and Educational Computing, Purdue University) is a former air traffic controller and holds licenses and certification as a commercial pilot, flight instructor, instrument instructor, control tower operator, airframe and power plant mechanic, and aviation weather observer. He has taught aviation courses at the University of Illinois and Purdue University, where he currently teaches in the Aviation Technology Department and directs the ATC program.

NOTES

NOTES

NOTES

Peterson's
Book Satisfaction Survey

Give Us Your Feedback

Thank you for choosing Peterson's as your source for personalized solutions for your education and career achievement. Please take a few minutes to answer the following questions. Your answers will go a long way in helping us to produce the most user-friendly and comprehensive resources to meet your individual needs.

When completed, please tear out this page and mail it to us at:

> Publishing Department
> Peterson's, a Nelnet company
> 2000 Lenox Drive
> Lawrenceville, NJ 08648

You can also complete this survey online at **www.petersons.com/booksurvey**.

---

1. **What is the ISBN of the book you have purchased? (The ISBN can be found on the book's back cover in the lower right-hand corner.)** _____

2. **Where did you purchase this book?**
   ❑ Retailer, such as Barnes & Noble
   ❑ Online reseller, such as Amazon.com
   ❑ Petersons.com
   ❑ Other (please specify) _____

3. **If you purchased this book on Petersons.com, please rate the following aspects of your online purchasing experience on a scale of 4 to 1 (4 = Excellent and 1 = Poor).**

	4	3	2	1
Comprehensiveness of Peterson's Online Bookstore page	❑	❑	❑	❑
Overall online customer experience	❑	❑	❑	❑

4. **Which category best describes you?**
   ❑ High school student
   ❑ Parent of high school student
   ❑ College student
   ❑ Graduate/professional student
   ❑ Returning adult student
   ❑ Teacher
   ❑ Counselor
   ❑ Working professional/military
   ❑ Other (please specify) _____

5. **Rate your overall satisfaction with this book.**

Extremely Satisfied	Satisfied	Not Satisfied
❑	❑	❑

6. Rate each of the following aspects of this book on a scale of 4 to 1 (4 = Excellent and 1 = Poor).

	4	3	2	1
Comprehensiveness of the information	❑	❑	❑	❑
Accuracy of the information	❑	❑	❑	❑
Usability	❑	❑	❑	❑
Cover design	❑	❑	❑	❑
Book layout	❑	❑	❑	❑
Special features (e.g., CD, flashcards, charts, etc.)	❑	❑	❑	❑
Value for the money	❑	❑	❑	❑

7. This book was recommended by:
- ❑ Guidance counselor
- ❑ Parent/guardian
- ❑ Family member/relative
- ❑ Friend
- ❑ Teacher
- ❑ Not recommended by anyone—I found the book on my own
- ❑ Other (please specify) _____

8. Would you recommend this book to others?

Yes	Not Sure	No
❑	❑	❑

9. Please provide any additional comments.

_____

_____

_____

_____

Remember, you can tear out this page and mail it to us at:

> Publishing Department
> Peterson's, a Nelnet company
> 2000 Lenox Drive
> Lawrenceville, NJ 08648

or you can complete the survey online at **www.petersons.com/booksurvey**.

Your feedback is important to us at Peterson's, and we thank you for your time!

If you would like us to keep in touch with you about new products and services, please include your e-mail address here: _____